Negotiating Development in
Muslim Societies

Negotiating Development in Muslim Societies

Gendered Spaces and Translocal Connections

Edited by Gudrun Lachenmann
and Petra Dannecker

LEXINGTON BOOKS

A DIVISION OF
ROWMAN & LITTLEFIELD PUBLISHERS, INC.
Lanham • Boulder • New York • Toronto • Plymouth, UK

LEXINGTON BOOKS

A division of Rowman & Littlefield Publishers, Inc.
A wholly owned subsidiary of The Rowman & Littlefield Publishing Group, Inc.
4501 Forbes Boulevard, Suite 200
Lanham, MD 20706

Estover Road
Plymouth PL6 7PY
United Kingdom

British Library Cataloguing in Publication Information Available

Library of Congress Cataloging-in-Publication Data

Negotiating development in Muslim societies : gendered spaces and translocal
connections / edited by Gudrun Lachenmann and Petra Dannecker.
    p. cm.
Includes bibliographical references and index.
1. Women in politics—Islamic countries—Case studies. 2. Women—Islamic
countries—Case studies. 3. Women's rights—Islamic countries—Case studies.
4. Women in development—Islamic countries—Case studies. 5. Non-governmental
organizations—Islamic countries—Case studies. I. Lachenmann, Gudrun. II.
Dannecker, Petra. HQ1236.5.I74N44 2008
    305.48'697—dc22   2008011398

ISBN: 978-0-7391-2619-6 (cloth alk. paper)
ISBN: 978-0-7391-2620-2 (pbk. alk. paper)
ISBN: 978-0-7391-4586-9 (electronic)

Printed in the United States of America

~

Contents

v

~

Acknowledgments

This publication is the outcome of a research project conducted at the Faculty of Sociology, Bielefeld University, Germany, at what was formerly known as the Sociology of Development Research Centre, now renamed the Transnationalization and Development Research Centre. It was financed through a two-year research grant by the Volkswagen Foundation. Whereas the editors held staff positions, continuation and finalising of the work of Salma Nageeb and Nadine Sieveking was supported by Lise-Meitner postdoc scholarships granted by the State of North Rhine Westphalia. Anna Spiegel continued to work with us within the framework of her doctoral studies. We are very grateful for these funds which also allowed us to conduct an international workshop in Bielefeld in order to discuss our findings with colleagues from other universities and, perhaps most importantly, with researchers and activists with whom we had contact in the three countries studied. This "translocal space" has been very rewarding and we hope that it will continue.

Gudrun Lachenmann, Petra Dannecker
Bielefeld, 30 September 2007

~

List of Abbreviations

ABIM	Angkatan Belia Islam Malaysia, Malaysian Islamic Youth Movement
AI	Amnesty International
APROFES	Association pour la Promotion de la Femme Sénégalaise
ASC	Association Sportive et Culturelle, Association for Sports and Culture
AWAM	All Women's Action Society
CAEF	Centre Africain de l'Entrepreneuriat Féminin, African Centre of Female Entrepreneurship
CEDAW	Convention on the Elimination of All Forms of Discrimination against Women
CFA franc	Franc de la Communauté Financière d'Afrique
CIRCOFS	Comité Islamique pour la Réforme du Code de la Famille du Sénégal
CNRS	Centre National de la Recherche Scientifique
CNS	Comprehensive National Strategy
COSEF	Conseil Sénégalais des Femmes, Senegalese Council for Women
CPA	Comprehensive Peace Agreement
EU	European Union
FGM/FC	Female Genital Mutilation/Female Circumcision

FNGPF	Féderation Nationale des Groupements de Promotion Féminine, National Federation of Groups for Women's Advancement
GAD	Gender and Development
GIE	Groupement d'Intérêt Économique, Group of Economic Interest
GPF	groupement de promotion féminine, group for women's advancement
GUSW	General Union for Sudanese Women
HAC	Humanitarian Aids Commission
IAD	Institut Africain pour la Démocratie, African Institute for Democracy
IFAN	Institut Fondamental d'Afrique Noire
ILO	International Labour Organisation
ISA	Internal Security Act
IWRAW	International Women's Rights Action Watch Asia Pacific
JAG	Joint Action Group on Violence against Women
JAM	Joint Assessment Mission
JIR	Jama'aatu Ibadu Rahmane
MAC	Malaysian Aids Council
NCP	National Congress Party
NCWO	National Council of Women's Organisations
NEP	New Economic Policy
NEPAD	New Partnership for Africa's Development
NGO	Nongovernmental organisation
NIF	National Islamic Front
ODC	Oslo Donors' Conference
PAS	Parti Islam Se-Malaysia
PCP	Popular Congress Party
PERTIWI	Pertubuhan Tindakan Wanita Islam, Muslim Women's Action Society
PRSP	Poverty Reduction Strategy Paper
RADI	Réseau Africain pour le Développement Intégré, African Network for Integrated Development
RAFET	Réseau Africain pour la promotion de la Femme Travailleuse, African Network for the advancement of Working Women
RIP	Réseau Islam et Population, Islam and Population Network
RND	Rassemblement National Démocratique
RSJ	Réseau Siggil Jigeen, Siggil Jigeen Network

SIS	Sisters in Islam
SNEEG	Strategy for Gender Equality and Equity
SPLM/A	Sudan's People Liberation Movement/Army
SUDO	Sudan Social Development Organisation
UMNO	United Malays National Organisation
UNAMIS	United Nations Advanced Mission in Sudan
UNDP	United Nations Development Programme
UNESCO	United Nations Educational, Scientific and Cultural Organisation
UNICEF	United Nations Children's Fund
UNIFEM	United Nations Development Fund for Women
VAW	Violence Against Women
WAD	Women and Development
WAO	Women's Aid Organisation
WID	Women in Development
WIJADI	Wanita Inovatif Jaya Diri, Women's Innovative Self-Development Movement
WILDAF	Women in Law and Development in Africa
WLUML	Women Living Under Muslim Laws

I

INTRODUCTION

~

Introduction

Gudrun Lachenmann and Petra Dannecker

Embedding the Project

The book is the product of a three-year research project entitled "Negotiating Development: Translocal Gendered Spaces in Muslim Societies" which was conducted under the umbrella of a research project funded by the Volkswagen Foundation and directed by the editors who had been doing fieldwork in Senegal and Malaysia respectively. It began as a response to the Volkswagen Foundation's call for research projects on "How do we perceive or shape 'foreign' and 'native' cultural identities? Research on processes of intercultural dissociation, mediation and identity-shaping" (das Eigene und das Fremde, literally "the self and the other"). In order to carry out this research a group of five sociologists and social anthropologists, based at the Faculty of Sociology, Bielefeld University, Germany, applied both theoretical and empirical approaches to investigate how development is negotiated in Muslim societies.[1] We hope that we have achieved our goal of making a significant contribution to empirically grounding globalisation theories as well as exhaustively discussing and developing translocal methodologies (carrying out global ethnography or multisided ethnography) while at the same time elaborating on comparative approaches in order to understand diversity and commonalities following dimensions or typologies such as "Muslim societies." The research project's basic idea is to take development as one form of knowledge production through negotiation in translocal spaces and to argue that globalisation is constituted through new social forms of organisation and epistemic communities. Indeed, taking female global networks and the development world as a global knowledge framework turned out to be a very fruitful perspective.

The members of the project team each spent six months in the field: Salma Nageeb in (her home country) Sudan. The other two researchers, Nadine Sieveking conducting research in Senegal and Anna Spiegel in Malaysia, split the case studies into two phases. Gudrun Lachenmann spent two months conducting research in Senegal while at the same time supervising a student research project.[2] The splitting of the field trips allowed us to discuss preliminary results amongst the team, develop categories further, write up, and also offered an opportunity to do a re-study and deepen some aspects more specifically.

The research project included local workshops based on work in progress which were held in Senegal, Malaysia, and Sudan, and served for common reflections and discussions with partners and organisations. First findings and interpretations were discussed with researchers and female activists who had been interviewed at the same time. This challenge of cross-cultural discussion as a principle of sharing academic knowledge and of disseminating empirical results was very encouraging and we much appreciated the overwhelming "scientific hospitality" in the sense of both openness for debate and of course support in all respects.

The general findings were discussed in a common workshop held in Bielefeld in October 2005 together with colleagues from other universities and our research partners (Nageeb, Sieveking, Spiegel 2005b). We were able to thoroughly present our framework and empirical results which were then reflected upon and discussed by the participants in a sensitive and constructive manner. We hope that we have been able to capture the broad array of views that we gained through these encounters in the chapters which follow.

Aim, Rationale, and Structure of the Book

We approached development in this project as a field of inquiry in order to study the links and interactions between categories that are often placed in opposition, such as the "Muslim world" versus the "West." In Muslim societies, global development concepts such as human rights, gender equality, or violence against women are subject to multilevel negotiations which ensure the compatibility of development visions with "local cultures" and "Islamic identities" of a given nation or group. In this context, the women and gender questions become instrumental in constructing a culturally specific vision of how to achieve change and development. Thus negotiating development is a process that needs spaces for networking and exchange. These spaces are constituted by social agents who situate their vision of how development should be achieved in a specific context. Among the foremost agents who are involved locally and translocally in negotiating development are women's organisations and activists. Therefore, the main focus of our research was on women's organisations and their activists as well as agency, strategies, local and translocal networks, and networking relations. Through this general framework we were able to follow how different and sometimes competitive discourses and perspectives to development, Islam, gender, and gender relations are negotiated and situated in the social field. Furthermore the perspective chosen also allowed us to highlight how these processes of negotiation lead to social restructuring.

The three countries in which our field studies took place, namely Senegal, Sudan, and Malaysia, are subject to different degrees of Islamisation processes. The purpose of the empirical research was to identify women's organisations and groups through a design of complex qualitative methods, as well as to study their development visions, translocal networking, and their interactions with other actors such as the state, international organisations, or other civil society groups. The comparative design and interpretation evolved and was thoroughly elaborated during the field research processes. Thus we have explicitly formulated dimensions of contextualisation and also worked out typologies that might—at least to some extent—be the same for all three countries. An engendered qualitative interpretative approach was adopted in addition to the concept of social space. The concept of social space is clearly linked to agency, to the production of gender-specific and culturally defined meanings, and to the social construction of reality and the life-world. Gendered social spaces in particular can be seen as constituting a nonhomogeneous public sphere, one that does not come up with one common public interest. We also applied a translocal approach which implied studying networks and networking relations as modes of interrelating "local" and "global" structures and cultural forces.

Our analysis led us to the following major findings: While women activists and NGOs are negotiating global development concepts, translocal gendered spaces are (re)constituted by differentiating and reconstructing the local discourses on Islam. Thereby globalised modes of interaction and communication are popularised. At the same time, othering processes are taking place that reshape or de-legitimise traditional social spaces. On the conceptual level, the negotiation processes have moved from the notion of vulnerability to a globalised discourse on rights. By exploring the relations between everyday life and social structure, the local and the global, private and public spaces, the Muslims and the West, Women and Development and Feminisms, as well as traditional Islam and Islamism, the dichotomised approaches to these issues, which tend to prevail in most of the literature on gender, Islam, and/or Islamism were challenged. Furthermore, such an approach emphasises the link and interrelatedness between various identity discourses, levels, and structures.

We hope that our book will be a significant contribution to the fields of sociology, the sociology of development, social anthropology, and gender studies by providing an empirically grounded study, a comparative multi-level research plan, and a theoretically engendered endeavour.

The book is divided, apart from a methodological first chapter, in two different sections: the first one entitled "Women's Organisations and their Agendas," the second one "Negotiating Development: Networking and Strategies of Women's Organisations." Both contain a chapter about each of the three different case studies presenting the findings in an empirically grounded way. Additional chapters provide a more generalised analysis of the first section respectively in terms of general conclusion.

In the first chapter Lachenmann introduces the important questions of the research endeavour. Do female spaces intersect with a societal public sphere, or does this concept need to be qualified, in the case of the Muslim societies, into a gendered social structure? Does the state discourse continue to dominate, or do the female social spaces and the interfaces they institutionalise become the relevant agents in civil society, such as in Malaysia and Sudan? Or are women in general marginalised and reduced to female vulnerability and rights discourse as it seems to be the case in development discourse in Senegal? And to what extent does the engendering of development take place?

Lachenmann also discusses the highly contrasting case studies which took place within countries and societies where the relevance of Islam is completely different regarding its importance to the state and society in general, the types of development and socioeconomic issues, or international and societal conflicts. The case of Senegal, a secular state, illustrates the making of development with a focus on the local level. There, women's networking and the linking of development and women's rights can be analysed with respect to the relevance of popular Islam, as expressed in public discourses against the concepts of equality. To date, the development discourses and politics of the state have been largely disconnected from local religion and female spaces. But due to the rise of diverse Islamic movements new alliances between the government, civil society, and religious actors are forming. Sudan, a country governed by an Islamist regime since 1989, is representative of a society where Islam is highly politicised and civil wars reflect the strive for democracy and equality by different ethnic groups and regions. In this context, women and women's NGOs engender peace and development and negotiate their room for manoeuvre by defining the meaning of global development as being against the hegemonic discourse and politics of Islamists. Their social spaces have grown enormously in the context of present-day conflicts and peace debates. Supported by the international donor community, these actors have constituted a very interesting arena of societal transformation. The case of Malaysia shows that women's as well as feminist organisations and their networks have problems of positioning themselves within a national context determined by political ethnicity and national Islam. However, there are very important feminist organisations and networks which enter into specific Islamic debates on situated interpretations of Islam concerning, for example, women's rights. Thereby they seriously challenge hegemonic religious and state authorities as well as Islamic institutions.

In this chapter Lachenmann develops how the methodology evolved in order to contribute to the empirically grounding of globalisation theory which might correspond to what has been called "global ethnography" (Burawoy et al. 2000). By focusing on social spaces and knowledge production, the agency and networking of women in the development field is analysed as a structuring force in the constitution of translocal flows and landscapes. She shows that through the case studies references to different Islams and claims to everyday Islam as an argument against global homogenisation and fundamentalisms have been found. In the same way, different feminisms are articulated regarding regional and political diversity. Although there is consensus on the diversity of feminisms in the global arena, this might cause new boundaries to be drawn and othering processes and exclusions to be produced.

She explains how the complex comparative design and interpretation evolved and was thoroughly elaborated during and after the field research process on the basis of a mix of methods and ongoing new questions. Furthermore the formulated dimensions of contextualisation which are directly relevant to the researched problem are introduced. They constitute an instrument of validation, and not, as is often the case, merely background information. The same applies to the typologies, which might, at least to some extent, be the same for all three countries (with potential generalisation). She shows that the researchers came up with distinct concepts of gender and social equality, and types of gender constructs (with regard to occupying public spaces and carrying out economic activities). Also, concepts of poverty and wealth and societal obligations, types of NGOs and their closeness to the state, and types of intensity of inward and outward looking social legitimacy of gender policies were specified.

The first chapter ends with a critical reflection on the ambivalent character of the results of the studies. The gender networks and public debates seem to be very diverse indeed but at the same time relevant for constructing the global arena. Therefore Lachenmann raises the question of the extent to which these debates in the global arena relate to national civil societies or a global public sphere, or whether they are only tolerated and instrumentalised by global governance.

The first section of the book, "Women's Organisations and their Agendas," begins with the chapter on Senegal by Sieveking. She shows that mainstream development discourses in Senegal reflect the commitment of the state to its secular constitution and protecting religious pluralism. Until recently the domain of religion was seldom mentioned in official discourses and policy papers concentrating on the agenda of poverty reduction. However, since spring 2005 a new focus on the global concept of "gender equality" has led to a slightly changed discursive strategy concerning the issue of religion in general and public discourses on Islam in particular. This second chapter analyses these changes as a joint effort of the Senegalese state together with women's NGOs and other civil society agents, including "progressive" Islamic scholars, to push the issue of "Gender and Islam" into the public sphere. The presented case studies focus on organisations which are operating on the level of women's everyday life. It is argued that this effort is motivated by the intention to strengthen the secular basis and broaden the conceptual horizon of the government's gender policies. While the discursive framework of this initiative links up with global concepts, on the national level it can be interpreted as a reaction to the rise of popular Islamic renewal and reform movements.

In the third chapter Spiegel discusses the diverse and even contradictory positions within the process of negotiation of gender relations and the meaning of religion by women's organisations in Malaysia. She argues that on the one hand, social work organisations constitute a space where women can negotiate dominant gender relations and power structures in the family, but without participating in debates in the public sphere about existing laws or challenging hierarchies and unequal entitlements in the process of knowledge production concerning religious issues. On the other hand, secular and multiethnic women's organisations are more disconnected from the concrete local context and seek a transformation of society through public education, law reform, and the monitoring of the state's performance in fulfilling its responsibilities concerning gender equality. Despite the parallel issues addressed by these two types of women's organisations—discrimination, rape, and sexual harassment—the localisation of these issues takes place within different analytical frameworks. Within the translocal Islamic framework these social issues are addressed as "social ills" that endanger women's dignity; within the global feminist framework they are addressed as a result of uneven power relations between men and women in society, which are only endured by the process of Islamisation. Spiegel argues that in a modern, multiethnic state such as Malaysia these negotiations are embedded in reinterpretations of culture, Islam, and democracy.

In the fourth chapter Nageeb analyses an event, a workshop organised by the United Nations Development Programme (UNDP) Khartoum/Sudan to discuss the possibilities of adopting the Convention on the Elimination of All Forms of Discrimination against Women (CEDAW). She shows that today, after signing the 2006 Comprehensive Peace Agreement (CPA) between the North and South of Sudan, events such as workshops and training sessions represent an important space for women activists in Sudan. These events are increasingly recognised within the context of peacebuilding, which means—among other things—an intensification of the flow of global funds and discourses aimed at supporting the implementation of the peace agreement. The chapter thus reflects on the various types of women's organisations and activists in addition to the relations between these organisations, their development agendas, relations to the state, religious, and social structures, and transformative potential.

In the final chapter of the first section Dannecker and Spiegel present a comparative analysis based on the findings from the three different cases, Senegal, Malaysia, and Sudan. They discuss the different modes of constituting spaces by women's organisations and activists in different settings and how the constitution of these spaces restructures the public sphere. The following dimensions are elaborated which—despite the heterogeneity of the different cases—play a significant role in each context but were combined in different and context specific ways as the chapter reveals: local and translocal networking, the popularisation of certain modes of social interaction and communication such as language and dress, alliance building between actors in different fields of knowledge, and the redefinition of places.

The second section, "Negotiating Development: Networking and Strategies of Women's Organisations" again begins with a chapter on Senegal by Sieveking. She shows that in the process of establishing women's rights in contemporary urban Senegal, diverging visions of development are negotiated by different actors, connecting globalised concepts to local discourses and social practices. This chapter describes this process with respect to a case study in the context of a nationwide NGO campaign for the reform of the national family law. The latter has constituted a battlefield since its constitution, confronting the positions of civil society actors and the Senegalese women's movement, Muslim authorities, and the secular state. The different positions concerning the concepts of women's rights and gender equality are analysed with a special focus on women's organisations' relations with representatives of distinct social spheres. The networking between various actors, as well as their differentiating strategies in the process of negotiating and localising global concepts, leads to the constitution of new social spaces and a redefinition of their cultural legitimacy.

In the following seventh chapter Spiegel focuses on the translocal connections of which the Malaysian civil society groups are part. She argues that within a limited democratic space, translocal networking between civil society actors at a global level constitutes a crucial practice to enhance the room for manoeuvre vis-à-vis an authoritarian state and hegemonic ethnicity as well as religion-based identity constructions. For the Malaysian women's movement, translocal networks based on a regionally defined Asian or a religiously defined Muslim identity play an important role for the transfer of critical knowledge and local empowerment. This argument is developed out of the analysis of discourses on the concept of "rights," which have become increasingly important for a wide range of NGOs in Malaysia. It is applied in different social contexts, since a multiplicity of women's, workers', and other civil society organisations in Malaysia work within the framework of relevant UN declarations such as the Universal Declaration of Human Rights, the Convention for the Elimination of All Forms of Discrimination against Women, or the World Habitat Convention. Among the different actors, there is an ongoing debate about which issues are to be considered political and hence should be at the centre of political debate, about the content of these rights, and about the question of the prioritisation of different rights.

In the last empirical chapter Nageeb takes the example of the agenda of Violence Against Women (VAW) and demonstrates how women's NGOs are changing their strategies to approach the local field within the context of peacebuilding in Sudan. The shift of strategies of women's NGOs takes place from de-politicising to politicising women and gender issues. VAW gained special importance within the context of the conflict in Darfur, and various women's NGOs have adopted the global agenda of VAW for tackling local gender issues. To show how it is locally embedded, three social trajectories of activists working with this agenda are discussed. As well, local and translocal networking between women activists and NGOs is analysed in order to discuss how women's NGOs create a space for their agendas. Nageeb argues that by adopting the agenda of VAW and through networking at the local and translocal levels, women's NGOs constitute a space to negotiate the social gendered structure and the process of peacebuilding and democratisation in Sudan. This space is translocally embedded.

In the last chapter based on the empirical studies Nageeb analyses networking and negotiation strategies and processes which women's NGOs adopt in order to work with global concepts like women's rights in Muslim societies or Violence Against Women. It is argued, in this analytical chapter, that the negotiation of these concepts and the networking relations developed by women's NGOs to promote women's rights in Muslim societies are leading to the constitution of translocal gendered spaces and alternative visions of Islam. The constitution of these spaces is to be understood within the framework of women's NGOs advancing, both locally and translocally, the discourse on rights which competes with the old "vulnerability" approach. In addition, translocal gendered spaces are constituted by the very process of negotiating global concepts of rights by women's NGOs. Translocal networking, global discursive order, and the relation between women's NGOs, states, and international development agents are important analytical dimensions of this chapter showing how localisation is constructed through the agency and constitution of gendered translocal spaces. A certain ambiguity, however, remains which is seen to be present in the everyday life embedding of Islam as a frame of reference on the one side, and othering with regard to the West on the other.

Notes

1. For half a year Dr. Christine Mueller, who had worked on a related topic in West Africa, joined the team on behalf of the faculty. Sandrine Gukelberger, one of our doctoral students, supported the team, and Ruth Moradbakhti was responsible for office administration.

2. Furthermore additional insights were gained through a diploma thesis on Islamisation processes and gender by Zeycan Yesilkaya.

CHAPTER ONE

~

Researching Translocal Gendered Spaces: Methodological Challenges

Gudrun Lachenmann

Translocal Gendered Research

When studying processes of globalisation and localisation, in the sense of empirically grounding globalisation theories, questions of methodology and design have to be asked in quite a different way than has been the case in development research, sociology, and social anthropology. The point of departure of this book has been a scepticism regarding the adequacy of doing comparative research between different societies, cultures, or civilisations, and between "first world" and "third world," given the very heterogeneous and context-specific developments, and at the same time the conviction not to abandon the idea of comparison altogether. Following the long tradition of regional studies, of case studies in social anthropology, and the fear of transferring Eurocentric concepts in development research, different voices have highlighted the necessity of a fundamental methodological reconsideration of approaches within a process of globalising social science (Albrow, King 1990).

An important element in this debate is the increasing interest in both strengthening qualitative methodology and empirically grounding certain theoretical fields such as the sociology of Islam, gender, and social movements. Making use of the synergy of social anthropology and a sociology of the life-world, two disciplines, whose theories and concepts are connected to specific cases and regions and at the same time aim at increasingly generalizing debates, there is the need to develop a methodology of transcultural "comparative global" social research.

Three different approaches can be taken: First, research could strive for a qualitative analysis of phenomena considered to be constitutive of globalisation, such as social movements and civil society, within a framework of transcultural sociology, thereby avoiding dualisms, that is, of cultural blocks. Second, globalisation can be studied through its relevant practices, such as interlinking and networking, that constitute global flows and translocal social spaces. Third, globalisation can be approached by the way it builds up from below, making use of knowledge accumulated by regional studies. Then, processes of glocalisation and localisation can be studied according to the paradigm of translocality referring to the interactive "(social) construction of reality" (Berger, Luckmann 1966).

An important aspect which changed the landscape of scientific traditions and epistemic communities adhering strictly to one country, society, community, or ethnic group, is certainly the fact that more and more concepts of intercultural and especially translocal, transnational, and also transcultural relevance have been developed in the social sciences. This is probably an empirical feature of glocalisation. We are actively pushing forward this development with our concepts and thereby contributing to a methodological strand which can be subsumed under the label of "global ethnography"[1] (Burawoy et al. 2000).

In order to do so in our research project entitled "Negotiating Development: Translocal Gendered Spaces in Muslim Societies,"[2] we argue that a distinctive feature of globalisation can be found in new social forms of organisation and epistemic communities, with one, possibly the first one (Lachenmann 1998a; see e.g., Lenz ed. 2002), being female global networks, and with the "development" world as a global knowledge framework. In our research it has been proven to be especially useful to organize the empirical research around networking and discourses on development concepts in the different communities.

Today development is negotiated between a broad variety of global, translocal, and local organisations and institutions (Lachenmann, Dannecker 2002).[3] In this new field the links and interactions between actors and concepts belonging to categories such as the "Muslim world" or the "West"—which are often placed in opposition—can be studied. Through translocal networks of NGOs, international development institutions, and groups, development concepts such as human rights, gender equality, or poverty alleviation are transferred to the local level. Accordingly, the negotiation of these concepts takes place not only on a global scale but also acquires new meanings throughout the translocal and local spheres. In Muslim societies global development concepts are subject to multilevel negotiations to ensure the compatibility of development visions with the so called local culture and Islamic identity of the respective nation or group. Thus negotiating development is a process that requires spaces for networking,[4] exchange, and interaction. These spaces are constituted by social agents who attempt to preserve and constitute a specific identity. The rejection as well as the adoption of a specific vision of development is always justified by reference to the national, cultural, or Islamic identities of a group or nation. Different actors and social agents who represent different orientations at the local level compete for the supremacy of their respective views of how to localise these development concepts and visions. A case in point is the way in which questions pertaining to women and gender are instrumental in constructing a culturally specific vision of how to achieve change and development whilst retaining the so-called Islamic identity. Also on a global level constructs of gender and gender relations seem to draw the boundaries between "Muslim culture" and the non-Muslim "others." Obviously the relationship between gender, development, and Islam became an important issue for identity constructions worldwide.

This research project studies the negotiation of development concepts and visions, for example, human rights or gender equality, in three regions—East Africa, Southeast Asia, and West Africa—which are undergoing a process of Islamisation to differing degrees. The focus is on the social agents and the ways they constitute networks and social spaces and construct identities while negotiating development. The major aims of this study are to broaden the understanding of the diverse notions of "Muslim societies" in terms of their different histories, Islamic traditions, and their relations to global forces and discourses. In addition, the connections, forms of interactions, and relations between cultures or regions which are categorically placed as "opposites" are studied. Thereby we want to contribute to the understanding of the meanings of development and development concepts in different cultures in a globalising world.

Within a framework of theory of agency, relationality, and dynamics of social transformation through globalizing forces, we analyse the constitution of social spaces and how they are structured through gender by looking at othering processes and fundamentalisms as negotiated locally at different interfaces. Social spaces can be seen as elements that constitute a nonhomogeneous public sphere, one that does not come up with one common public interest. We are using the concept of social space in the sense that it is a relatively noninstitutionalised delineation; going beyond community, place, and territorial or physical space (see Massey 1994; McDowell 1999; Dannecker 2004; Lachenmann 2004c; Nageeb 2002; Nageeb 2005a). The concept of social space is

clearly linked to agency, to the production of gender specific and culturally defined meanings, and to the social construction of reality and the life-world (see
Spiegel, rapporteur, 2005).

We claim that with this approach we shall contribute to a sociological and
social-anthropological epistemic community working about Islamism, Islam,
modernity(ies) and globalisation in that it will prove beneficial to deepening
globalisation theory. This should be possible by looking at how knowledge
and its structuration through the agency and networking of women in the development field constitutes translocal spaces, flows, and landscapes. In the
sense of empirically grounding approaches developed by Appadurai (2000),
Robertson (1995), or Hannerz (2000), we point to the fact that structuration
(Giddens ed. 1979) of social fields is being engendered, and that the female
negotiation of development and the constitution of translocal and transnational spaces are very pertinent cases to look at.

At the same time it is our ambition not to follow the North-South divide
regarding the production of knowledge by showing that flows and spaces are
constituted horizontally and follow very complex relations, including networking, and—indeed—development work, which can no longer be qualified as North-South transfer (although qualifying these spaces as cosmopolitan would be to euphemise the hegemonic structure of global aid architecture
and governance). Part and parcel of the research design have therefore been
workshops organised in the three respective countries and in Germany—the
latter bringing together researchers and activists we had worked with locally.[5]

Islam (or Islams) came to our interest not as the main subject of the study,
but only insofar as it is relevant, in the constructivist sense, as a frame of reference for action and meaning, that is, of constituting translocality (see e.g.,
Hess 2001). Through this we link up with concepts of multiple modernities
and globalisation theories focusing on Islamisation and reform processes, and
the restructuring of the (Islamic) public sphere (e.g., Salvatore 1997, 2001;
Al-Azmeh 1993; Featherstone, Lash, Robertson eds. 1995; World Bank
2005). We also take into account the often neglected empirical phenomenon
that women's international movements, institutions (like World Conferences, NGO fora, etc.), and networks are very important for groups and organisations working within explicitly Islamic environments because they allow women's groups to come together in the global sphere, unconstrained by
religious or ethnic belonging. Using the concept of glocalisation as interlinked processes of globalisation and localisation, our research takes up relevant global concepts from the "development" world in order to observe how
they are made sense of locally and how they move or travel back to the global
sphere. At the same time we work out typologies cross-cutting our different

country studies at an institutional, intermediary level, as well as dimensions, discourses, and relevant contexts.

The diversity of constellations is only determined to a certain extent by the highly contrasting case studies of countries and societies. Completely different constellations exist regarding the relevance of Islam, its importance for state and society, the type of development and socioeconomic issues, as well as international and societal conflicts. The theoretical sampling (Strauss 1987) of these countries turned out to be complemented by the results which came out when grounded in empirical findings. In Senegal—a secular state—Islam is hardly relevant at all for development efforts. It is, however, omnipresent, in a localised Brotherhood structure and in some newly Islamising forces which are beginning to compete on a national level with state legitimacy (to be seen with regard to family code debates) (Sieveking 2005). Through the empirical results concerning Senegal we highlight how development works at the local level. We show how women's networking, and the linking of religious issues to women's rights with respect to local discourses takes place which tend not to support notions of equality as these are associated with Western feminism.

In Sudan—as an Islamist state—Islam is the force against which women are permanently forced to negotiate for room to manoeuvre in order to define the meaning of global as against popular Islam (Nageeb 2005b, 2005c). At the same time development issues addressing poverty are omnipresent on the agenda of all women's groups. Their social spaces seem to have grown enormously in the context of present-day conflict and peace debates which are supported by the international and donor community. Thereby a very interesting arena of societal transformation is constituted. With peacebuilding developments, Sudan represents in our comparative design the interface between the state and the civil society, through which the latter is being strengthened and the public sphere restructured.

The case of Malaysia, on the other hand, has shown that women's and feminist organisations and networks are actively struggling in the complex national context based on political ethnicity and national Islam (Spiegel 2005a, 2005b). However, there are very important feminist organisations and networks which opened an inner Islamic debate on interpretations of Islam as to women's rights and thereby seriously challenge hegemonic religious authorities and the state as well as locally established Islamic practices. This question concerning the authority of knowledge is an interesting feature in all three societies. However, in Malaysia it seems to be discussed at a highly scholarly level and is especially crucial at this point in time when Islamic criminal law stands to be institutionalised. At the same time women's and feminist organisations seem to mainly obtain their legitimacy from their important transnational presence and reputation in networking. Here, of course, the exchange among Muslim feminists is one important field, but at least as important is their participation in regional and global debates about globally defined rights (see CEDAW) from which they draw their power for national activism.

Conceptualising Translocal Gendered Spaces

Othering processes which take place in the translocal gendered spaces take a very prominent role but are not uniform, as the research in this book shows. In Malaysia women's activists would not claim to be anti-Western but—as in global feminist discourse—antineoliberal and denouncing the impact of globalisation. Although there is consensus on the diversity of feminisms in a global arena, this might indeed cause certain new boundaries to be drawn and othering processes and exclusions to be produced. However, the Malaysian women's movement claims global solidarity and sisterhood of women, which might be constituted in global female spaces where globalisation and relevant concepts seem indeed to be negotiated. In Senegal the othering processes work through different construction of gender and, thereby, a conception of (universal human) equality, not taking up global feminist discourses on difference. In Sudan cultural and gender identities are defined by boundaries towards the West. Also, those women activists who are becoming more and more visible in doing poverty and peace work supported by international donors are struggling against accusations of Western feminism.

This debate always takes place between feeling othered by the label "Muslim women" and claiming universal negotiation, but at the same time working for the consideration of specific, nationally relevant contexts of culture and tradition.

We have seen that some activists and feminist scholars have started to use designations such as "Islamic feminists" (which would imply an internal debate in global female networking, possibly excluding non-Muslims) (Ahmed 1992; Abaza 1998a, 2002; Mahmood 2005; Mir-Hosseini 1996; Othman 1998, 2005). Here the argument is either to have to defend one's "faith" or to push forward alternative scholarly debate, opposing hegemonic Islamic discourses. On the other side, the concept of "African feminists" is quite present in Senegal (and Africa south of the Sahara in general). The othering is more cultural than religious, refers more to gender concepts with regard to development, and is often still linked to the colonial past and thus defined from outside. In such cases the label of "feminist" would be more contested.

Despite these differences we discuss the constitution of public spheres where universal concepts are negotiated and ask how reflexivity (in the sense of postcolonialism, subaltern studies, Orientalism) is present. This can be linked to definitions of "modernity" or "modernities," including postmodernity, and challenges concepts of (monolinear) progress and development (see Escobar 1995; Hobart 1993; Momsen 2004; Nederveen Pieterse 2001). In Malaysia the importance of the women's movement to enter and restructure the public sphere is shown in the quite remarkable Shadow Report elaborated for the Beijing +10 process. In Senegal the official national Strategy for Gender Equality and Equity (SNEEG) adopted in 2005 is of rather low professional quality and totally lacking societal agency and vision of any gender movement, although supported and even contributed to by a large women's organisation. In Sudan it might be said that women's groups have for quite some time been, and in a less conspicuous way than human rights activists, upholding a public discourse concerning women's issues, poverty, and now peace and democracy.

Focusing at localising global concepts of development implies that there is an international epistemic community of women's activists and researchers who have found their way to (certainly not very open) spaces of negotiation. Different regional movements and individuals were indeed very influential; however, their activities might have partly been appropriated on a cosmopolitan level. In a sense through feedback these concepts are renegotiated on the local level, asking for international legitimacy or struggling between claims of culturalist versus cosmopolitan rights.

So we have found reference to different Islams in claims of everyday Islam as against global homogenisation and fundamentalisms. At the same time we have observed claims of different feminisms in regards to regional and political diversity. Also the question of different modernities in regards to public space, secularism, and economic institutions is very relevant. At the same time, translocality is clearly discernable concerning the constitution of all social spaces, whereby globalisation in the making can be explained.

When arguing with regard to culturalism, methodology of comparison, othering, and fundamentalisms as globalizing forces, we are doing so with a theoretical and methodological intention to do comparison in a nondualistic way. By referring to translocality of social realities, to flows, movements, and concrete interactions we intend to methodologically overcome classical oppositional units of comparison. Nevertheless, new forms of comparison on a middle theoretical level become possible through taking into account different "dimensions" (as against indicators) and applying complex methods.

Our qualitative comparative and ethnographic approach enables us to show that Islam is never the determining factor or the constant factor to explain differences. But its relevance for society and development as well as the gender order and translocal references becomes clear in many situations and in multiple forms. What we are able to show is an immense diversity within and amongst the countries—as against the dualistic West-East confrontation—at all levels, sometimes being confrontational at the different "encounters" (Long 2000).

Like in the current debates about Islamic reforms of civil society and the definition of the common good (Salvatore 2001), the authority of knowledge and its different representatives is methodologically a very important aspect. We have seen that nearly exclusively this authority has been captured in Malaysia at least in certain fields (family, the social) by organisations like Sisters in Islam who have acquired legitimacy within an Islamic scholarly framework. Also in Sudan, there are women who are regarded as very educated in Islamic knowledge, but fieldwork has shown that the legitimisation of female interpretations of society have to refer to male authorities who, however, seem to be involved quite strategically. In Senegal sympathetic speakers of Islamic authority are also brought into the discussion. This means that there is no female epistemic religious community that is gaining ground in the general debate and public sphere. In global Islamisation debates there are, of course, female Islamic scholars, but those taking part in the transnational public sphere of UN conferences and women's fora very often are based in non-Muslim countries in, for example, universities (Lachenmann 1998a).

Our concern was to study how female social spaces were constituted in order to observe very diverse negotiations amongst women on local and intermediary levels regarding gender constructs and relations as well as regarding interfaces with the state and translocal and transnational networking. It is true, however, that as far as links are produced to national public debates, the old Women in Development and Women Status approach does prevail before any societal concept of gender and gender order.

Regarding negotiating development—negotiation understood in an interactionist way—we conceive of development in a very broad sense of social change brought about by political action, civil society efforts, and purposeful policy intervention. We might have liked to have been more specific in certain areas and challenged concrete approaches to "mainstream gender," for example in development models, through confronting them with engendering analysis. This has been the case in some very concrete areas such as typical issues of how to organise local development within decentralisation processes (Lachenmann 2006), regarding typical female fields of responsibility such as water schemes, as well as social and health security (in the case of Senegal). However, the empirical reality shows that development negotiations, as conceived in terms of visions of society and gender order, were often quite fundamental in the sense of the legitimisation of rights and social equality (Elson 2002; Hobuss et al. eds. 2001; Molyneux, Razavi eds. 2002; World Bank 2001). On the other hand negotiations were very conflictual as to confrontations of discourses, issues treated, and struggling for room for manoeuvre and social space against authoritarian or noncommitted states and, at least partly, religious authorities.

Transcultural Methodology

With the concept of translocality we focus on the relationships between localities built up through discourses, cultural practices, flows (Appadurai 2000), and knowledge systems. Thereby, we hope to be able to contribute with our research results to grounded theory building (Strauss 1987). Our comparative approach (Lachenmann, Dannecker 2002; Nageeb 2005a, 4 f.) aims at comparing different groups and organisations, forms of networking, public spaces, and discourses involved in constructing these different translocalities. It also embraces the study of the forms of interaction between Islamism and women's groups in different contexts. The comparative approach is thus significant for locating debates on development and civil rights, which are global and international, in local contexts.

We are not comparing Islam and the West but rather different Islams that shape social spaces. Emphasising diversity, difference, and also typologies across countries, we take account of the situatedness of knowledge and phenomena of social restructuration. Also we take the historical development of the respective countries into account through systematic contextualisation. Our research process is accompanied thus by the question of how we, through comparative research, can contribute in a fruitful way to theory building while at the same time understand our special cases.

When researching development and comparing countries of the global South, especially the ones belonging to Islamic culture, the dilemma is that there are too many implicit assumptions on the one hand and essentialisations on the other. In any case, the transfer of concepts especially in standardised studies carries the risk of becoming blind to the social reality and different contexts. Our qualitative approach tries to counteract this tendency especially since it can be observed that dualism has reappeared worldwide opposing Islamic and Western societies.

We can, through our approach, see more and more diversified processes of Islamisation in very different settings. Given the complex situations in Muslim countries which date from historical and present political constellations we cannot generalise any features regarding all Muslim countries researched beyond continents and regions. However, on the national and societal level we have worked out ideal types of national Islamisation processes which could be applied and compared to other societies, such as:

- Type Malaysia: The nation-building process is based on Malayness implying—as against present efforts of the global Umma—a different Islam connected to (Asian) values and ethnicity and a strong self-reliance of economic development. Women's groups and organisations build up strong gendered public spaces and networking in order to negotiate national forms of Islamisation. Human rights discourses are one example. Their activities and strategies are—nearly exclusively—legitimised by a very high degree through external networking, thereby influencing and contributing strongly to inter-Islamic gender discourses.

- Type Sudan: A strong Islamist state is fighting against the diversity of Islam including local, often female popular Islam (although unadmittedly parts of the country belong to other religious dominations). At the same time there is a strong necessity to open up to Western and global development donors (and clients concerning oil resources) as well as to political conflict resolution. This leads to development discourses on poverty, but combined with peacekeeping and conflict resolution processes and activities. These discourses are inclusive regarding religious and ethnic diversity and sometimes take place in female spaces.

- Type Senegal: As a secular state, it increasingly neglects the Muslim societal background in official development policies in favour of very liberal, Western-oriented concepts such as New Partnership for African Development (NEPAD) and very modernist development programmes oriented towards poverty reduction, democracy, and decentralisation. Islamic forces seem to lose influence for negotiating development concepts in the public sphere with regard to gender issues. In contrast the Women in Development approach (as opposed to Gender and Development) seems to regain credence. Furthermore, the political regime has even stronger contact with Muslim brotherhoods. Although neglected in official development politics, Islamisation processes which are going on within the global discourse thus have clear implications for gender and development.

Comparison Through Multiple Levels, Arrangements, Dimensions, and Typologies

A conventional comparative approach is not able to capture the real processes of interaction and deterritorialisation taking place. In classical comparative studies there is often the very tautological reference to the "other society," based on the principle of variance. But there is neither the possibility to understand the social embeddedness of the phenomena under investigation or their social construction, nor the social spaces where issues are negotiated. This would be the case, for example, in studying women's rights conventions and politics in societies with a completely different history and background of women's movement and political struggle. The local relevance of the comparative question must be clear and this requires contextual knowledge.

Not only in development policy but also in a new standardised discipline called "international comparative research" large data sets are handled in order to look at such issues as poverty, marriage patterns, household incomes, or election behaviour. Some authors distinguish between reconstructive (interpretative) and hypothesis-verifying procedures. This difference is important for our approach in order not to standardise the comparison and thereby completely lose sight of the cultural milieu.

In grounded theory there is the idea of hypothesis generation within the framework of (repetitive) interpretation of empirical data. From there it is a matter of saturation. The extreme case study, that is, advancing in the study by searching for special cases, is of course also a comparative concept. The theoretical outcome of grounded theory, of course, will enter into consecutive comparisons. Elwert (2003) introduced the concept of knowledge for orientation and cross perspective analysis.

Stauth's concept of "kulturübergreifende Sozialforschung"—transcultural social research—is very pertinent for the present compilation. He especially criticizes what he calls "comparative sociology of civilisations" for "assuming a homogenous, universalistic classificatory system of communication absent in multicultural societies." He makes the point that this is not possible without basing research on the long-lasting processes of exchange and mutual perceptions, implying what he calls the "standardisation of culture techniques" (1995, 102; 99). There are reconstructive and reflexive procedures which have universalised different cultures through interaction and othering (Dannecker 2002; Grosz-Ngaté, Kolole eds. 1997). Despite the fact that Stauth talks about "cultures" and "civilisations" tout court, this means that no simple comparison is possible, that is, opposing in a dualistic way one system to the other and explaining differences of the researched subject by taking for granted different cultural systems. Terms such as modernities and orientalisations indeed imply that differences in transformation processes must be looked at. These originate from the internal developments which are based on exchange, reflective reconstructions, and interactions and cannot merely be analysed as deficits from a Western perspective.

Within this framework, our approach consists of looking at different dimensions relevant to our subject of engendering development and how these are situated within an Islamic cultural orientation. Thus the comparative perspective we follow (Nageeb 2005a, 4; Klein-Hessling 1999) does not aim at developing fixed categories or indicators for comparing the various cases under investigation. Rather it is based on "comparing by contextualising" and explaining the ways in which the issues under study, be it the creation of social spaces, or the negotiation of development concepts, are embedded in specific local and translocal contexts. Indeed the nature of the state, Islamisation processes, development institutions and policies, and political and social structures present themselves in very decisive ways and influence our subject matter. Thus we have clearly discovered that the actors and arenas involved in the field of negotiating development as well as the subjects under negotiation are different in the three different regions under study. The comparative perspective is accordingly meant to reflect on the different nature of the actors involved and their modes of interaction in each context. The variation lies in the development concepts which are signified as subjects for negotiation in each case, and the kind of spaces and identities which are being constituted while negotiating development in the different countries under study. Further, the comparative approach also aims at studying the social, political, and cultural context which leads to the existence of variation/similarities in the nature of the actors, agents, development concepts, identities, and spaces. Nevertheless this does not mean that we focus only on individual actors or small groups and the ways in which they handle the meaning of development and negotiate it. Rather we take similar interest in institutional actors like the state (Malaysia and Sudan), relatively big Islamic groups (Brotherhoods in Senegal), or peasant or women's organisations, all of which we treat like an actor among others but not as the centre of analysis.

In the process of our common discussions within the framework of our research project, we worked out typologies which might—at least to some extent—be the same for all three countries (with potential generalization). We came up with concepts often based on emic ones, regarding gender and social equality as well as types of gender constructs with regard to occupying public spaces and doing economic activities. Also we focused on concepts of poverty, wealth, and societal obligations. We compared types of NGOs and their closeness to the state, as well as variations of intensity in terms of the inward- and outward-looking social legitimacy of gender policies. At the same time we elaborated on female ways of representing Islam including local or popular ones and discourses regarding gender and development. We distinguished different degrees and forms of doing transnational networking. It was very useful, apart from looking at the "landscape" of female spaces and organisations, to systematically look at discourses and compare and contextualise them.

Regarding the interrelatedness between development and women's organisations in the Islamic context, we saw that foreign NGOs as well as bilateral and multilateral agencies work in all three countries with civil society movements, and, in Senegal, decentralized communities as well as national poverty-reduction programmes, but under different conditions.

We asked how are Islam, religion, religiosity, and rules addressed by the organisations researched, be it in texts, discourses, as well as in interviews, narratives, and conversations (directly, indirectly; without or with explicit questioning by researcher)? What kind of development or economic model or image is underlying cultural fields of different actors in different situations? What are the ascriptions made by different types of religious women regarding the West and their religiosity and its connection to gender and development, economy, education, and public sphere participation?

What concepts of economic activities for women prevail: formal or informal, production or trade, employment or entrepreneurship? Income-generating activities can be looked at as global concept, how can differences be established? Are there no Islamic critics of interest rates? What are local-level concerns such as family law in respect to family conflicts, land rights and access? When and how are certain issues taken up by the state, such as human rights, following (women's) civil society activities, especially their external visibility? Are there new forms of third sector social services arrangements, such as health funds (mutuelle de santé) in Senegal, livelihoods in Northern Malaysia (as against human rights abuses in the South)? Which types of NGOs are active in development and religious identity discourses? How is internal networking linked to external donors (Sudan), political activity to civil society activity (Malaysia), losing importance respectively becoming more confrontational (women und peasant organisations, Islamic organisations, Senegal)? How are women's groups aligning with donor strategies (as, for example, against government policies)?

In light of these questions and issues, during the process of comparative analysis the reasoning on possible differences and similarities became more analytical. For example, gender discourse is influenced in Malaysia by the high industrial participation of women, in Senegal by poverty, and in Sudan, especially recently, by conflict and peace constituencies. De-politicisation is taking place in Malaysian society due to successful economic development; in Senegal it can be observed in the women's movement but not in other movements such as the peasant movement; in Sudan this is the case through women's instrumentalisation with regard to building the Islamist state. Local moral discourse on gender and religion in Malaysia takes place through clear instrumentalisation of an image of the "good Muslim woman"; in Senegal a conventional "women in development" approach is dominant whereas feminism is regarded as Western or non-African and nonreligious; in Sudan processes of complete othering take place, although more and more local NGOs have been created which are cooperating with external donors. Development discourses are missing in Malaysia mainly because they are taken over by the state, therefore discourses on violence and human rights are led by transnationally networking women's organisations; in Senegal livelihoods are of general importance, but within the framework of the Poverty Reduction Strategy Paper these processes are reinforcing the vulnerability discourse; in Sudan, income-generating activities and conflict transformation become the main focus.

Ethnic and religious differences in Malaysia play an important economic, national, and social role; in Senegal, they are of minor relevance though certain Islamic affiliations are clearly linked to ethnic differences; in Sudan ethnicity and identity discourses are highly political and conflictual as the current political situation shows. Foreign NGOs are cooperating in all three countries with civil society movements but under very different conditions. In Malaysia it is hardly possible; in Senegal some cooption by the state has taken place; in Sudan the social space constituted through this cooperation is the most relevant one for restructuring the public sphere. Foreign donors, including NGOs, to a certain extent avoid cooperation with the state and prefer to cooperate with civil societies in all three countries. However, approaches of international cooperation such as good governance or peacebuilding and constitution writing are hardly gendered.

Empirically Grounding Globalisation: Doing "Global Ethnography"

In general it is astonishing how little explicit debate and writing exists about how to empirically do research that captures translocality. The main outcome of our research might be one of methodology. It became clear that we cannot separate an interactive and translocal approach from a comparative approach. Comparison according to the concept of interface of knowledge systems (Long 1992) does not entail regarding one logic as against the other but rather the construction of meaning (and different meanings) from situatedness. With this in mind one must make comparisons in the sense of deconstructing concepts regarding certain phenomena. The decisive question is that of the explanatory power of a concept of society which must be shown in the research as a methodological procedure. The adequacy of the methods must be discussed by taking into account newly observed processes and problems which are constitutive of globalisation such as local or national confrontations and questions of autonomy, political ethnicity, identity, constitution of a public sphere, of social spaces, and knowledge production (Lachenmann 2004b).

Within our approach comparison is possible on a middle level using middle range theories and trying to explain the differences through contextualisation. In short our methodology is transculturally interactive and diversity oriented. By explaining integration through difference as well as through glocalisation and localisation our comparative approach is able to overcome common dualisms. Theoretical sampling (Strauss, Corbin 1998) takes place following assumptions and ideas which one comes across during fieldwork. These are reflected and systematised in a meaningful design following ideas of similarity or of difference, in our case within the three countries. Taking grounded theory seriously, the outcomes from empirical research can be incorporated and extended to other contexts, though this is not a comparison in the classical sense. Grounded theory generates theses which can be fed into further research.

We very clearly realize that the relevance of our research subject for the context, that is the adequacy regarding the object of research, has to be challenged in each and every case with regard to the relevance structure of the respective community or society. An example would be studying women's rights conventions and politics in our sample societies within the context of completely different history and background of women's movements and political struggle.

Furthermore, this implies the application of a mix of methods and a thoroughly elaborated, complex design evolving during the research process. It might be captured by an approach of "multilevel analysis" (Lang 2005; Berg-Schlosser 2000) linked through interfaces. We explicitly formulate dimensions of contextualisation which are directly relevant to the research problem, thereby constituting an instrument of validation—and not, as is often done—just one of background information. In this respect we did indeed restrict the scope of our empirical studies, looking very specifically at female activities and the gendered structure of development processes. We are able to arrive at more generalising outcomes beyond merely comparing the three cases. Dense methods of empirical research are used for structuring the analysis of data, including contrasting case studies, typologies (even transcultural), interfaces between different actors and knowledge systems, trajectories of activists in networking, and event analyses. When analysing workshops, for example, we ask who organises, invites, participates, excludes? What are the major topics, discussions, conflicts, consequences? When doing organisational analysis we look at leaders, discourses, and networking.

The debate on comparison and its new forms takes place mainly in political science, history, and sociology (Kaelble, Schriewer eds. 2003; Kaschuba 2003). In social anthropology the majority of methodological debates continues to focus on the question of "defining the field" which is important in translocal research but until now hardly goes beyond debates on unit, text, voices, in other words, well justified postmodern and postcolonial queries. Gupta and Ferguson (1997, 25), however, claim that "it is not necessary to choose between an unreconstructed commitment to traditional fieldwork . . . and more macroscopic or textual approaches." Marcus (1998, 10 ff), who introduced the very pertinent and often quoted concept of "multi-sited ethnography," discusses this issue extensively. In his chapter on "ethnography of the world system" (79 ff.) he stresses contextualization. Mobile ethnography according to him constructs "aspects of the system itself through the associations and connections it suggests among sites." He takes an interesting position regarding "the loss of the subaltern" (85), thereby also decentring the resistance and accommodation framework "for the sake of a reconfigured space of multiple sites of cultural production." He claims that "comparison re-enters the very act of ethnographic specification by a research design of juxtapositions in which the global is collapsed into and made an integral part of parallel, related local situations rather than something monolithic or external to them" (Marcus 1998, 80, 85 f.).

Inda and Rosaldo (2002, 26 f.) edited case studies on "the anthropology of globalization." They argue against the "discourse of cultural imperialism . . . of the imposition and dominance of Western culture over the rest of the world." They uphold that people interpret ideologies and other cultural phenomena according to local conditions of reception, pushing forward the "view of the world as a dislocated cultural space" (referring to Laclau), and capturing the "complexities of the globalization process." Thus they argue for an anthropology "exploring the local experiences of people as their everyday lives become increasingly contingent on globally stretched out social relations." This argumentation directly strengthens our efforts to focus on the local processes of negotiating concepts and meanings.

As referred to above, another very challenging and relevant approach is presented in the work of a group of sociologists from Berkeley (Burawoy et al. 2000) which widely corresponds to ours, bringing together everyday life experience with global transformations. This group explicitly aims to link critical ideas of globalisation theories (considered to be of too high abstraction) and political economy with what it calls "ethnography unbound." The approach concentrates on and elaborates further the "extended case method," not without asking whether this method is "flexible enough to link everyday life to transnational flows of population, discourse, commodities and power" (Burawoy et al. 2000, x, ix). This is how we in the present volume open new perspectives and make them explicit regarding the concrete fieldwork aimed at grounding globalisation research, capturing "what is experienced on the ground, the ways globalization attaches itself to everyday life, the way neoliberalism becomes 'common sense.'" This leads to what we call empirically grounding globalisation theory (see above), and Burawoy (2000b, 339, 341, 343) calls constructing "perspectives on globalization from below," in short, "grounded globalizations."

Additionally Burawoy et al. (2000, xii) raise the interesting question "whether exploring the global dimensions of the local changes the very experience of doing ethnography" as they see "the narrow boundaries of the traditional ethnographic 'site' as conceived by the Chicago school . . . permeated by broader power flows in the form of local racial and gender orders, free-flowing public discourses, economic structures." We very much endorse the statement that "ethnography's concern with concrete, lived experience can sharpen the abstractions of globalization theories into more precise and meaningful conceptual tools." For us this also means, for example, that social movements must be studied in relation to one another in "their internal diversity, their interweaving, the dialogues through which they achieve their own trajectories" (Burawoy 2000a, 4 f.).

The important aspect in globalisation theory of space and time is linked to how to conduct fieldwork with the necessary flexibility regarding the everyday world whose totality is also conceptualised: "Within any field, whether it had global reach or was bounded by community or nation, . . . fieldwork had to assemble a picture of the whole by recognizing diverse perspectives from the parts, from singular but connected sites," striving for a "historically grounded, theoretically driven, macro ethnography" (Burawoy 2000a, 24).

Doing "global ethnography" brings in the reflexivity we asked for above by studying processes of othering, based on the assumption that "no longer can we pretend to any clear demarcation between us and them." This implies thorough contextualisation, and necessitates "systematically incorporating historical and geographical context" and to extend "observations over time and space" in order to understand "the succession of situations as a social process" as well as elaborating a "'structured' macro-micro link . . . in which the part is shaped by its relation to the whole" (Burawoy 2000a, 21, 27, 17).

The third methodological dimension when studying "global connections" refers to "multi-sitedness [which] becomes the object of theorization" implying that there is no "disembedding" but rather intensification. We also think that thereby it is important to "demystify . . . globalization as something given" and study "how different images of globalization are produced and disseminated" through for example social movements. "Thereby global imaginations reconfigure what is possible, turning globalization from an inexorable force into a resource that opens up new vistas," in the end forming a "thickening global public sphere" (Burawoy 2000a, 30–32).

In order to overcome generalised criticism of the "impact of globalization" on, for example, the situation of women on the ground, we follow Burawoy challenging "external forces" by seeing them as "product of contingent social processes" to be "examined as the product of flows of people, things, and ideas." Global forces and connections are then regarded as being "constituted imaginatively, inspiring social movements to seize control over their immediate but also their more distant worlds, challenging the mythology of an inexorable, runaway [referring to Giddens, G.L.] world" (Burawoy 2000a, 27, 17, 29).

Although the aim of the above cited authors corresponds very much with the intentions of our own approach, it is evident that more recent Continental developments in hermeneutic and interpretative sociology and the sociology of knowledge, such as presented by Forum Qualitative Sozialforschung (continued), Flick et al. ed. (2004), Knoblauch (2001) (see Lachenmann 1995) including further developments of grounded theory have not come into sight. To these we add the methodologically and empirically very fruitful approach of Long (1998, 2000, 2002) which brings power relations and agency together, advancing classical Manchester school and interpretative sociology.

Following qualitative sociology and social anthropology (Bernard ed. 2000; Denzin, Lincoln eds. 1994), and in particular gender methodology (see Bell, Caplan, Karim eds. 1993; Golde 1986; Whitehead, Conaway 1986; Wolf 1996) it is important to operationalise the dimensions which are missing in classical ethnography, and to complement the new methodological approaches discussed above by using an interface approach that brings in power constellations and takes into account new translocal social constellations. We further develop what can be called complex methods that crosscut communities, places, levels, time, space, and social worlds such as the method of trajectory. In our research domain this applies to individuals whose personal history and career in different knowledge spaces, institutions, and organisations we follow based on the narrative approach, thus going over and beyond biographic research (e.g., Fischer-Rosenthal, Rosenthal 1997). Here we would concretise the approach of agency, knowledge, authority, and meaning.

Thus when preparing field research the respective domains of research, their structuration,[6] and preliminary assumptions have to be discussed, including the relevance of the subject within globalisation processes and theories. Additionally the position of the researcher in the field has to be thoroughly reflected. According to grounded theory ideas about the field, new questions are permanently developed in so-called memos thereby finally leading in a circular research process including key concepts which structure the whole field. Data are materialized in protocols of interviews and conversations, as well as in group discussions. Ex-post protocols are very important, such as field notes, transcripts, protocols of observations, and case descriptions out of which instruments for permanent reflection are developed such as memos, text analysis, participatory reconstructions of models, ranking, and mapping. And of course the researcher must continuously analyse secondary material.

A complex design is subjected to permanent reflection and development by theoretical sampling, graphical presentation, and looking at different levels and sites. Case studies (extended, crucial, or contrasting) including event analysis represent the most important ethnographic approach when treated on the basis of translocality as mentioned above. According to what Schlee (1985) called mobile research, one must follow people, goods, travelling concepts, etc. Triangulation takes place through differentiation of perspectives and methods including different expert positions. The relational approach is able to grasp interactions, connections, and biographies by combining techniques of mapping, schemes, trajectories, event analysis, and discourse analysis in a comparative perspective. Interfaces are conceived to take place in different encounters, social domains, and arenas (Long 2000, 191 ff.).

The data is analysed according to grounded theory through coding and developing categories, (key) indicators, and (working) hypotheses. Interpretation, (multiphase) analysis, and validation take place through actors' perspectives, comprising their logics of action, strategies, and room for manoeuvre. Modes of transformation and production of knowledge are elaborated through the reconstruction of cases and dense description, working out structures of relevance, and structuration of fields of action. Conceptualisations are based on emic terms, theoretical debates, and discourse analysis. Typologies are drawn up; processes, dynamics of social transformation are elaborated. Validation takes place by looking at multiple meanings, perspectives, horizons, and other possible interpretations.

Translocality of Networking and Constitution of Public Sphere

As became clear during our common discussions within the research project, we have been encouraged in our endeavour to pursue in depth our theoretical and methodological interest with regard to the dimensions of networking and of restructuring the public sphere (Spiegel rapp. 2005; Spiegel, Harig rapp. 2002, see Habermas 1989 (1962), 1992). These main concepts in our research project have been empirically grounded by asking common questions.

Does networking indeed take place to such an extent that one can say that this is where glocalisation takes place? Do female spaces indeed intersect with a societal public sphere, or do we need to qualify this concept more for Muslim societies in the sense of their gendered structure? Does the state discourse still dominate, or would indeed the female social spaces and the interfaces they institutionalise be the relevant actors in civil society—such as in Malaysia and Sudan? Are they marginalised and reduced to female vulnerability and rights discourse, restricted to gender-specific difference or Women in Development discourses as it seems to be the case in Senegal? Does this mean that no engendering of development takes place?

The theoretical and political importance of networking, constituting, and restructuring the public sphere is evident. We think that both methodologically as well empirically our decision to focus on interfaces between different female social spaces and cross-cutting national boundaries as well as on diversity and battles within national and transnational spheres has proven very fruitful. On this basis we argue that it is possible to draw conclusions concerning national societies and processes and institutionalisation of globalisation.

In showing a great diversity of "feminisms," "Islams," typologies of women's organisations, contested issues and discourses as well as translocal practices and interactions with the state (see Kandiyoti ed. 1991) we were indeed able to go against crude ideas of a "clash of civilisations" in public debates and culturalist ideas in development circles. The gender perspective turned out to contribute to the understanding of ongoing social processes as a whole. The theoretical concept of constitution of translocal spaces showed its analytical content, whereas the research theme of development turned out to embrace social transformation in a broader sense, especially within a wide framework of discourse on (human, women) rights. The relevance of Islam is very basic in all societies and frameworks studied, but in varying degrees and occasions. However, the often assumed strong homogenizing force of Islamisation leaves much room for manoeuvre for different actors and takes place on very different "battlefields of knowledge" (Long 1992). On the other side, networking and knowledge exchange take place to a large extent, but not always, in an Islamic framework.

The constitution of public spheres where universal concepts are negotiated has been a very interesting dimension of comparison. Various forms of activism (such as that taking place at women's days events) could be discerned and its different types described as very oriented towards global culture (e.g., malls in Malaysia), very conventional (such as in Senegal), or ambivalent such as in Sudan where women's groups enter the peacemaking process but very seldom the constitutional debates.

The term *civil society* was very useful in sociological theorizing regarding the structuring mechanisms that make public debate possible, redefine public issues, and shape creative and innovative changes, as well as power of association and coherence, including integration through difference. However, we do not find the concept very helpful when simply viewed as being one actor within the international development jargon because often this only means nongovernmental organisations and overlooks social movements and, therefore, could easily be conceptualised as third sector organisations. Citizenship is another global concept brought up, next to empowerment, in global gender discourses, but strangely enough it did not become very relevant in our research context.

The concept of an Islamic public sphere (put forward by Stauth in: Spiegel rapp. 1995, 17; Stauth 1998) might be pertinent, since it is very progressive in creating a linkage between institutions and private life—a space within which movements with transformational character can develop. We can confirm having found its reflexivity through debates about the common good, flexibility of boundaries, recognition of the other, and independence from the state. Accordingly, Muslim groups can be seen to have the power to create a vibrant civil society that goes beyond the modes of official governance.

The result of our studies hence seems ambivalent. The gender networks and public debates seem indeed to be very diverse and relevant for constructing the global arena. On the other hand we might question the extent to which the link between national civil society and the global public sphere does indeed take place in regards to relevant issues of hegemonic concern, or whether it is a field tolerated and instrumentalised by global governance.

Notes

1. This term is used by Michael Burawoy et al. (2000). Inda and Rosaldo (ed. 2002) use the term "anthropology of globalization"; Long (2000, 184 ff.) talks about "exploring local/global transformations."

2. Financed by VolkswagenFoundation, directed by Prof. Dr. Gudrun Lachenmann and Dr. Petra Dannecker with case studies in Senegal, Sudan, and Malaysia (Lachenmann, Dannecker 2002; Nageeb, Sieveking, Spiegel 2005a, 2005b). Our main researcher, Dr. Salma Nageeb, who did her doctorate in Bielefeld, spent five months in her home country Sudan; for Anna Spiegel—a sociologist from Bielefeld—and Dr. Nadine Sieveking—a social anthropologist from Berlin—it turned out very fruitful to split up their six months respectively of field research in Malaysia (Petra Dannecker had done fieldwork there before) and Senegal (where at the same time I again did fieldwork), so that we were able to do quite continuous discussions in Bielefeld and participate in project meetings and work.

3. In March 2002, Wendy Harcourt edited a thematic issue of the journal *Development* with the title "Place, Politics and Justice: Women Negotiating Globalization" (see Harcourt 2002). This new conceptual endeavour is more oriented at the "fate of the place," but our frameworks are rather close.

4. Focusing on an explicit network approach with regard to the "Islamic World" see Loimeier ed. (2000) and therein Harders (2000).

5. Local workshops based on works in progress have been held in all countries and served for common reflection and discussion with partners and organizations. First findings and interpretations were discussed with researchers and female activists who had been interviewed. This challenge of cross-cultural discussion as an ethic principle of sharing academic knowledge and of disseminating empirical results has been very encouraging and we are very grateful for the overwhelming "scientific hospitality" in the sense of openness for debate. During the phase of bringing our results together, we organized a final workshop in Bielefeld, bringing together many of our resource persons in the field and a larger community of researchers to discuss with us the outcome of our research (Nageeb, Sieveking, Spiegel 2005b).

6. See Cagatay, Elson, Grown (1995) who are using the concept of "economy as a gendered structure."

11

WOMEN'S ORGANISATIONS AND THEIR AGENDAS

CHAPTER TWO

~

Women's Organisations Creating Social Space in Senegal

Nadine Sieveking

Negotiating Development between Secularism and Islamic Revival

Mainstream development discourses in Senegal reflect the commitment of the state to its secular constitution and its role in protecting religious pluralism. Following this secular orientation religious issues are avoided in official discourses. This rule is in line with both the liberal and Western-oriented development politics of the government that concentrates on the agenda of poverty reduction. Senegal's economy, based on agriculture (mainly groundnut, rice, and cotton), fishing, and phosphate, has experienced a series of unprecedented crises since periods of severe drought in the 1970s, the implementation of structural adjustment programmes in the 1980s, and the devaluation of the CFA franc in 1994. Regarding social structure this has led to rural exodus, massive migration, and a process of urbanisation without industrialisation.[1] While the number of urban poor is growing, the majority of the poor population still lives in rural areas where the crisis of the groundnut economy and environmental degradation is felt most intensely, access to health services most difficult, and the literacy rate the lowest.[2]

The official, strictly secular agenda of the Senegalese state reflects the strong influence of international development agencies and Western donors who dominate national development politics including efforts within the framework of New Partnership for Africa's Development (NEPAD). Recently, however, the particular way in which a new focus on the concept of "gender equality" has been introduced in Senegalese development discourses indicates that the domain of religion can no longer be completely avoided. In spring 2005 the Ministry of Family, Social Development, and National Solidarity[3] published a document concerning the "National Strategy for Gender Equity and Equality" (République du Sénégal 2005) which was accompanied by two leaflets containing an explicit "religious argumentation for gender equity"—one formulated from a Muslim perspective, the other from a Christian perspective. The publications were intended to balance the religious perspectives on the issue in accordance with the principle of the state's neutrality in the domain of religion. However, they marked a subtle change in the position of the government concerning the connection between the domain of development politics and religious issues in general and Islam in particular.

Generally Islam has become an increasingly relevant feature of the public sphere in Senegal. This trend can be observed in the mushrooming religious associations organised in all kinds of different social milieus: within neighbourhoods, workplaces, schools, or on the university campus. The symbolic politics of the government vis-à-vis Islamic authorities and institutions can be seen as an element that contributes to the dynamics of Islamic revival. After the democratic elections in 2000, the new government, formed by the coalition for the "alternation" under the leadership of President Abdoulaye Wade, has repeatedly confirmed the secular basis of the Senegalese constitution. At the same time, however, it has promoted a new liberalism regarding religion. Since it came to power the increasingly autocratic Wade regime has tried to enhance its legitimacy and popularity by publicly staging its alliances with Muslim authorities on the local and national, as well as on the international level. The participation of the president or important government representatives at religious ceremonies are always well covered by national television. Although this kind of public staging of the president's allegiance to Muridism and his frequent visits to his marabout in Touba[4] before taking political decisions have been vividly criticised by civil society organisations. Wade has completely ignored this critique, multiplying at the same time his efforts to establish and maintain the image of the Senegalese state as a model for democracy and defence of human rights on the global scene.[5] In this context, the government is careful not to lose the support of translocally and transnationally connected women's organisations, who are promoting global development concepts, such as women's rights and gender equality (see chapter 6).

This chapter will analyse the efforts of the Senegalese state together with women's NGOs and other civil society agents to promote the notion of gender equality in public discourse as a strategy to cope with the rise of popular Islamic renewal and reform movements all over the country. The analysis will focus on the case of a locally grounded NGO and its networking practices on various societal levels. The argument is that this joint effort is motivated by the intention to strengthen the secular basis of national development policies. Women's organisations, on their part, have developed diverse negotiation and networking strategies to deal with the established Islamic institutions and the growing reform movements. The latter might be very heterogeneous in their outlook and development agenda, but they have in common a more or less radical anti-Western rhetoric and a general rejection of anything identified with (Western) "feminism." Hence, they see their own vision of an Islamic national culture and society (including the vision of an Islamic state) as opposed to secular, Western-oriented visions of development (women's advancement in particular).

This opposition, however, is neither the only, nor the dominant pattern shaping the discourses on development within Senegalese Muslim society. The ambivalence of many women's activists concerning the cultural and religious legitimacy of their claims for the implementation of gender equality indicates the complex dynamics of these negotiation processes. The ambiguity and multiplicity of negotiation strategies are a particular feature of women's rights discourses in Senegal. In contrast to the position of an increasingly globally connected Muslim feminism that can be found in other contexts (see other contributions in this volume), in Senegal it is difficult to discern an articulated female perspective arguing for gender equality and women's rights from within Islamic discourse (Sow 2003, République du Sénégal 1993).

As empirical research has shown, a major challenge for the implementation of gender policies in Senegal is the fact that while the government's official development discourse and politics links up with global concepts it tends to be disconnected from local Muslim society. In contrast to state-related development agencies, women's organisations have taken up this challenge by negotiating development from below, localising global discourses, and carving out new social spaces to bridge the established divide between Western-oriented and Islamic visions of development. In the following, the case of a conference organised by a women's NGO for the occasion of International Women's Day 2005 under the motto of "Gender and Islam" will be described to exemplify these processes. During this event the concepts of gender equality and women's rights were explicitly linked to Islamic principles. Therefore it can serve as a starting point to analyse the position of women's organisations vis-à-vis the secular state on the one hand and Islamic authorities on the other. In the course of this chapter the interactions between development agents related to these different domains of knowledge and power will be analysed. The analysis will focus on various types of women's organisations ranging from state-related institutions, to secular NGOs and local women's groups, to religious associations.

Promoting "Gender and Islam" at the Grassroots Level

"You ask me about women's situation in Senegal? This is not one question, this is a hundred questions!" (Fatou Sow, 16 April 2004). This is a comment by the Senegalese sociologist Fatou Sow, a researcher at the Institut Fondamental d'Afrique Noire (IFAN) who teaches half of the year at the Cheikh Anta Diop University of Dakar and the other half at the Centre National de la Recherche Scientifique (CNRS) in Paris. Speaking from a cosmopolitan point of view (she is a member of the UNESCO Global Scientific Committee) she points to the differences characterising women's particular situations according to their social, educational, and family background, their professional or economic activities, and the specific rural or urban milieu shaping their living and working conditions. Women's development visions, as well as the potential and modes of articulating them, are thus no less diverse.

"I have a feminist approach to the Senegalese society. When I discuss with my students I realise that because of my age I can pronounce myself on issues concerning violence against women or sexuality in a way that is not possible for many women living in the regions. . . .[6] But me, I am a teacher at university, I am a married woman with a family. Even as a feminist I can consider myself as a normal woman because I have a husband and children. Thus I am not a white, lesbian feminist. This is a condition to bring us further to discuss things" (Fatou Sow, 16 April 2004).

Fatou Sow's statement indicates that women's ways of articulating and negotiating their visions of development are not just determined by a set of given social norms, moral restrictions, and discursive stereotypes (reflected in the counterimage of the morally deviant and sexually "abnormal" white, lesbian feminist). Women's negotiation potential is also characterised by their particular social position, their place in the age- and gender-determined hierarchies, and their often ambiguous relations to the sphere of the (male-dominated) religious and secular political establishment. This ambiguity corresponds to women's diverse social locations, but also to their strategies in creating multiple social relations and new social spaces in order to enlarge their room for manoeuvre.

The question how women develop agency through their relations with other social actors, within women's organisations and their networks, as well as in relation to other development agencies and the institutions of political and religious power has therefore been a central question for the present empirical research. A multilevel perspective was adopted here to be able to follow the diverging logics characterising the interactions with development agents from different social spheres. During the research it became clear that not only the social position but also the geographical location and regional aspects are quite relevant when it comes to relations with the centralised state administration. Organisations which are mainly working on the local level tend to occupy a position at the periphery and are easily marginalised if they do not have strong networks within the Dakar-centred national and international development community.

In the following the case of a locally oriented NGO acting within a multitude of translocal and transnational networks is presented. How these interactions are related to different social spheres and discourses is illustrated by the celebration of 8 March 2005 in Kaolack. This event can be seen as an interface where the negotiation of global development concepts in the context of local Muslim society takes place. At the same time it can be analysed as part of a process in which religious discourses and practices are being reshaped and a new kind of translocal Islam is articulated in the public sphere.

Preparing for International Women's Day in Kaolack
Kaolack is a turbulent city situated in the groundnut basin of Sine Saloum at the major crossroad connecting the northern and the southern part of Senegal, as well as the west-coast and the eastern regions. It is three hours drive from Dakar (if the highway is not blocked) and is Senegal's fourth biggest city.[7] It is the capital and economic centre of the region of Kaolack, a place all travellers to Gambia or the southern region of Casamance have to pass through. Kaolack is one of the central regions that is most affected by poverty and environmental degradation. The city itself has the bad reputation of being a dirty place, particularly during the rainy season, because of poor infrastructure, with difficult climatic conditions and a high incidence of malaria. However, the city is also well known for its economic and social dynamism which is related to its huge market and its strong associative movements.[8] It is a particularly interesting site to study gender policies because it represents important elements of the Senegalese women's movement which, through its struggle to enhance women's social and political negotiation power has been transgressing the boundaries of the academic elite in Dakar and reaching out in the spheres of rural society.[9] Kaolack is the only region in Senegal where a women has successfully and continuously occupied the post of president of the regional council.[10] This is due to the strong support she gets from the local communities and her capacity to mobilise women across different societal levels.

Just as in other Senegalese cities the International Women's Day on 8 March 2005 was celebrated in Kaolack with various public events, organised by civil society organisations, including the participation of representatives of the state administration. A well established local women's NGO, the Association for the Advancement of the Senegalese Woman (Association pour la Promotion de la Femme Sénégalaise, APROFES), celebrated the day with a conference on the subject of "Gender and Islam." In the preparatory process there had been intensive discussions among the staff of the NGO concerning the topic of the event and the way it was to be formulated. The background of these discussions was provided by the "national theme" for the celebration of International Women's Day, determined like every year by the Ministry of Family. This year's theme was formulated in a somewhat long-winded and indistinct way: "Equality according to gender beyond 2005: constructing a more certain future."[11] APROFES had been informed about this formulation by the umbrella organisation Siggil Jigeen Network (Réseau Siggil Jigeen, RSJ).[12]

Women's NGOs Networking on the Ground

The RSJ, established as an NGO with its head office in Dakar, has been one of the most active women's organisations operating at a national level.[13] Since it was founded in 1995 the RSJ has become the most important women's NGO network in Senegal, regrouping eighteen organisations, APROFES among them. Besides its networking activities, its focus is on developing women's agency at the interface between the state and civil society through lobbying and campaigning. The RSJ has assumed a strong presence in the public sphere by organising training, meetings, and demonstrations, and using the media (particularly the radio, the press, the Internet, and its own newsletter which is accessible in a printed and an online format). It maintains intensive working relations with the Ministry of Family and has contributed to the evaluation of the National Action Plan for Women as well as to the official report concerning the Convention for the Elimination of All Forms of Discrimination against Women (CEDAW).[14] More importantly in this context, the RSJ has also substantively participated in the elaboration of the above-mentioned paper concerning the new National Strategy for Gender Equity and Equality. And it has launched a nationwide campaign for a reform of family law which would enhance women's rights and gender equality within the framework of national legislation. While the RSJ has strong networking relations on the national and international level it cannot assume the direct interaction with the women at the grassroots level—a task that is left to its member organisations.

APROFES is one of the most dynamic members of the RSJ, linked to various networks and organisations on the national as well as on the international or global level.[15] Its most characteristic feature, however, is its social engagement and intensive networking on the local level. The latter is due to its particular social embeddedness in Kaolack and its history that goes back to a popular neighbourhood-based youth organisation, the *Magg Daan*,[16] founded in the late 1970s in the quarter of Kasnack. The *Magg Daan* was formally established as an Association for Sports and Culture (Association Sportive et Culturelle, ASC) and in the beginning its main activities consisted of organising soccer competitions during the holidays—just like any other ASC which exist all over the country. Then a group of female members started to challenge the limits of their own position in charge of "social animation." They started to engage in further activities aimed at changing the difficult living conditions of local women. A "process of reflection" began, leading to the creation of the NGO. When APROFES was formally constituted in 1987 its members had already gained notoriety as being the "Amazons" and "revolutionaries" of the quarter (Binta Sarr, president, 06.05.04). In contrast to the majority of formalised local women's groups, the association was not only concerned with fighting poverty by way of economic activities, but also wanted to promote women's rights and access to positions of decision making.

Most of the NGO's members come from community organisations. Even among the permanent staff members, only very few have a higher education—the president, who is a hydraulic engineer and former state official in the domain of rural development, is an exception.[17] To realise its diverse projects on the ground APROFES works together with local agents from the different fields of policy intervention, including rural as well as urban and suburban communities, with women's and youth organisations, state services, and local administration. The domains of the organisation's activities are diverse: running a centre for women victims of violence, organising training courses and awareness raising (ranging from agricultural production techniques, economic management skills, adult literacy, to family planning, HIV prevention, and diffusion of texts concerning women's rights), building up infrastructure for urban and rural development (including reforestation, water supply systems, horticulture), and establishing schemes of microcredit and local health insurance.

In all these fields of intervention APROFES collaborates with stakeholders of various social institutions, including religious authorities. Public meetings or events, such as the celebration of International Women's Day, are carefully planned and often include the participation of a theatre company.

The latter develops pieces around the main issues of the organisation's development agenda, expressing them in the vernacular and in a body language based on popular imagination and satirical illustrations of current discursive stereotypes. The theatre company is affiliated with the NGO and participates in many of its activities, particularly in the context of social milieus whose members have a low level of formal school education (the majority of the local population, particularly women).[18] The origin of the company goes back to the activities of the same local youth organisation, the ASC *Magg Daan*, which had been at the root of APROFES.

Its embeddedness and long-standing presence in local society on the one hand and the experience of going through a tedious process of formalisation and professionalisation, thereby building up organisational capacities and management skills on the other, has been of particular importance for the NGO's success. Its members have a concrete and personal knowledge of the difficulties at the interface between local women's groups, the regional council, state administration, and other national as well as international development agencies. This knowledge is essential in order to understand the needs and expectations of those women's groups which still mainly function at an informal level of organisation.

Preparing the event of the 8th of March in Kaolack, the staff members of APROFES concluded that the formulation of the national theme had to be modified because "with respect to our reality it was a little bit complicated" (Ndeye Diagne, 11.04.05). They thought that in the official formulation the national theme could not easily be understood by the population: "If they say gender, people understand women, but it is men, women, and the whole family."[19] During their discussions the women activists in Kaolack tried to figure out how the notion of gender equality could be explained to the local population. The background for their discussions was furnished by their experiences in promoting the concept of gender equality with respect to women's rights and giving training on "gender and leadership" to local women's groups and representatives of other social groups. They knew that for many women from the local communities the concept of gender equality is too contested and thus not useful to enhance women's social position because it will not lead to a consensus but "only causes more problems" (see chapter 6). As a result of these discussions it was decided to focus on Islam, because in this way questions concerning the religious foundation of the concept of gender equality, or rather the objections against it, could be directly addressed. Hence, to organise a public conference on "Gender and Islam" was seen as a good strategy to adapt the national theme proposed by the ministry to the way social reality is reflected and articulated by the local population. The conference was organised by APROFES in coordination with diverse representatives of civil society, such as a local teachers' network, and other NGOs with whom they used to frequently collaborate.

Among the most important partners of APROFES in Kaolack is the regional section of the African Network for Integrated Development (Réseau Africain pour le Développement Intégré, RADI). RADI is constituted as a pan-African NGO, with its head office in Dakar.[20] It is well established in different regions of Senegal and works intensively on the local level. Although the NGO is not explicitly constituted as a women's organisation, the Senegalese section focuses very much on women's rights, relating them to the domains of poverty alleviation, sustainable development, decentralisation, and civic education. The regional office in Kaolack maintains a centre for juridical information and frequently organises discussions concerning issues of women's and civic rights.[21] On the national level, however, the regional section of RADI in Thiès is most active.

To celebrate International Women's Day 2005 in Thiès, RADI organised a discussion concerning the notion of "parental authority." This topic was related to the campaign for a reform of family law launched by the RSJ and RADI's own ongoing activities in promoting the concept of an equality of rights within national legislation. The panel for the celebration of the 8th of March included a jurist, a sociologist, and a religious scholar. The latter held a speech on the topic of "women's place in the Muslim religion," where he pointed to the problem that most women in Senegal had never really learned anything about their religion. He underlined that if it was not for the men, who interpreted the Quran in their own way, "the woman would be queen." The same Islamic scholar had already collaborated with RADI during another campaign, ongoing since 2003, where he had elaborated a religious argumentation against the "wastefulness" (gaspillage) which characterised the extensive ritualised donations of traditional family ceremonies.[22] In the course of this campaign RADI had strongly collaborated with the local rural communities and encouraged them to establish "commissions on wastefulness" in charge of elaborating a set of rules restricting or substituting the culturally legitimised but often excessive donations. In public discourse these are generally considered in an economic sense as an unnecessary waste, and even as a major cultural obstacle for the country's economic development. In these commissions not only the local women's groups and youth associations, but also the elders and religious authorities, were represented. Representatives of the commissions were also invited to participate in the celebration of International Women's Day.

Another partner of APROFES is the Senegalese Council for Women (Conseil Sénégalais des Femmes, COSEF), focusing mainly on female leadership, women's political participation, and access to positions of decision making. This NGO was created in 1995 in the aftermath of a congress on the topic of women and politics, organised by the African Institute for Democracy (Institut Africain pour la Démocratie, IAD). The congress had taken place within the framework of the meetings of African women's organisations in Dakar in preparation for the 1995 World Conference on Women in Beijing. According to Aminata Kassé (29.04.04), then director of COSEF, the organisation was the first to unify women of different social strata and political orientations, including professional women engaged in political parties, labour organisations or jurist associations, the academic and educational sector, as well as women working "at the ground" in the rural communities. COSEF also networks intensively with other NGOs engaged in the domain of human and civil rights.

The regional section of COSEF in Kaolack is presided over by Aminata Sarr (20.02.06), a former teacher and the first female school inspector in Senegal. She is another important figure among the Senegalese women's movement, with a very long career of political and civic activism. She belongs to the first generation of women activists who had started to militate in the opposition against the French colonial regime. After independence she continued in the opposition against the Senghor-regime as a leading member of the Pan-Africanist party Rassemblement National Démocratique (RND), founded by Cheikh Anta Diop. She was among those women who created in 1955 the Union of Senegalese Women which fought for Senegal's independence and voted against the community with France at the time of the famous referendum in 1958. Until recently she directed the women's movement of the RND but because of her age she has resigned and now occupies the post of *présidente d'honneur*. She is also a founding member of a long list of civic institutions and political or social welfare organisations such as the first national teachers' labour union, the African Cultural Centre, as well as the above-mentioned IAD.[23]

Aminata Sarr was invited to be the second speaker in the conference. As the main speaker APROFES had invited an Islamic scholar, Taha Amadou Sougou, who has frequently acted as a resource person for the RSJ and other NGOs in the context of their activities concerning women's rights and family law.[24] Among the other "usual" invited guests were the members of APROFES and the collaborating NGOs (women's groups from the urban surroundings as well as from neighbouring rural communities, including representatives from peasant organisations), as well as local authorities, including state officials and the local imam. The event took place on the street in front of the office of APROFES in Kasnack.

Celebrating the Event:
Performance and the Creation of a Public Sphere

Only a few paved streets cross the rather quiet quarter of Kasnack which is located near the city centre. The broad sandy paths between the houses leave enough space for soccer competitions that take place almost every afternoon among the children of the neighbourhood or the organised groups of local youth associations. The streets are also the place for the frequent celebration of family ceremonies such as weddings, naming ceremonies, or funerals. While the public part of these ceremonies normally happens during daytime, other kinds of public events take place in the streets until late at night. The latter include the frequent religious ceremonies which are characterised by the amplified sound of ritual chanting, as well as secular events, such as the popular sabar performances,[25] dance competitions organised by young women's age groups or neighbourhood associations. Promotions and campaigns organised by local politicians constitute another kind of public event in which the same physical space and similar modes of cultural expression, particularly popular music and dance, are used (Heath 1994). Although the latter are de facto part of various kinds of local religious practices (particularly in the Sufi context), Islamic authorities have repeatedly attempted to ban or restrict music and dance performances in public, particularly the female sabar dance styles, famous for their very provocative sexual character.[26]

To see some tents, a lot of chairs, and a huge loudspeaker put up in the street in front of the office of APROFES was nothing unusual in this neighbourhood. The music (latest hits of local stars, very rhythmical and danceable) that entertained the public until the ceremony finally started might have been interpreted by an outsider as the usual preparations for a family ceremony. The NGO, however, often organises public events in the court of its office or on the street, if more space is needed or a larger public is to be addressed. Neither did the setting of the celebration of 8 March 2005 differ much from other occasions, such as the annual assembly of the mutual savings groups or the mutual health insurance groups that are part of APROFES, nor was the public essentially a different one—except for the invited speaker. The setting of the celebration of the 8th of March was clearly marked as a secular event, drawing on the resources of local popular culture.

In this framework the meaning of "Gender and Islam" was to be discussed from a scholarly perspective, represented by Taha Amadou Sougou. But before he started, the terrain had already been prepared by a theatrical play. The performance had been executed in a very popular satirical way, making use of local musical and theatrical traditions, including various short sabar improvisations. With a lot of humour the actors had displayed the contradictions and inconsistencies of established gender relations and hierarchies. Pointing to the difference between the behaviour of husband and wife in the public and in the private sphere, they suggested that men might eventually change stereotypes of gendered labour division and decision making but would not recognise this in public.

As it is custom in the context of local performance traditions, the musicians had already been playing to create a festive atmosphere among the audience until the preparations were completed. When all the invited guests were present and the official speaker had finally taken a seat at the podium, the actual beginning of the ceremony was indicated by the intensification of the sabar drums. This provoked spontaneous reactions amongst the female audience—while the men remained in their seats, some women jumped off theirs to interact with the drummers in short sabar dance improvisations. These were conceived as individual articulations of pleasure and highly appreciated.

The audience's active participation in a musical or theatrical performance is an integral part of Senegalese cultural traditions, constituting a visual link between the aesthetic and the social (ethical) dimensions of the event (Chernoff 1979). APROFES consciously makes use of elements of popular culture and performative techniques in order to integrate actors from different social milieus and enhance the visibility of women's participation in the public sphere.

Islam and Development: A Religious Perspective

In the introduction to his speech Taha Sougou referred extensively to the performance that had opened the event. He contextualised the issue of "Gender and Islam" with respect to the actual general situation of social crisis and conflict which had provoked the very "human" and "natural" reactions that had been displayed by the actors. He related the comical aspects of the play to the existing contradictions between male privileges (in the public) and female power (in the private) sphere. He criticised men's anxious concern of maintaining the established gender order and hierarchies as a hindrance to development. Referring to the 1980s and the "climate of conflict" that had been provoked at that time by women's "struggle for liberation" he made a strong point by explicitly recognising the achievements of "the feminists in Senegal" of having questioned the traditional system of gender relations. He pointed out that because of this critical attitude towards the traditional gender order, feminists used to be treated as "atheists" being the "cause of all evils on earth." Criticising the way "traditions" used to be legitimised by men with reference to religion, he called for a new reflection on processes of social change as a necessary step for the common project of nation building and human development.

Then he identified four different parts of society which would be necessarily involved in these processes: the holders of power, who take decisions; the intellectuals, who develop the concepts to transmit the messages; the traditionalists, who preserve customs; and the religious experts, who define the sacred foundations of the laws. While criticising the traditionalist bias of legitimising local customs as deploying "too easy" and reductionist interpretations of the Quran, Sougou asserted the role of intellectuals and religious scholars in giving the holders of power all the "necessary elements" to take the right decisions. The latter had to correspond to a consensus in order not to divide society. Therefore he underlined the importance of public debate and consciousness-raising. Emphasising that he did not consider himself an "advocate of women" he pointed to several examples mentioned in the Quran illustrating women's abilities and competence that proved their spiritual equality compared to men, as well as their specific "wisdom" and moral power. Therefore, he concluded, men and women had to accept each other as partners in the construction of society and "the nation."

When Taha Sogou had finished the floor was given to Aminata Sarr, who mainly focused on the aspect of (secular as well as religious) education. To illustrate women's ability to acquire religious knowledge she referred to the example of the prophet's wife Aisha. She insisted that it was "imperative" for women "to know our religion" in order not to be abused by the "obscurantism" of the traditionalists who interpret Islam in their own way and according to their own interests.

"Islam Is the Solution":
Women's Advancement and the New Turn towards Religion

Aminata Sarr conceives of Islam as an important resource for women's agency in the process of development. This becomes even more clear in the context of her personal trajectory that she described in an interview conducted in February 2006. Her main motivations as an activist are rooted in anticolonialism and the struggle for a rehabilitated African national culture "enlightened" through education on the one side, and her commitment to do social work (faire du social) on the other. Concerning the latter, she underlines her own very privileged social and economic position which enabled her to become engaged in charitable and social welfare activities. As an example she mentioned her membership in the Sonta Club, a "very elitist" and rather "closed" organisation based in Chicago, not open to "other women" who could not afford the required monthly assessments or the high travel costs for the meetings that take place all over the world. In any case the branch of the Sonta Club in Kaolack has ceased to exist. Moreover, the over-all conditions for doing social or humanitarian work have radically changed. According to Sarr there are few people in Senegal now who have the social position and the means to finance social welfare activities like the members of her club did in the past. Furthermore she points to another factor that con-tributed to the "eclipse" of the kind of organisations in which she herself used to be engaged: the evolution of a new kind of NGO (such as APROFES or RADI) that are less elitist, more embedded in local society, and oriented to-wards the masses of the population.

After almost fifty years of intensive involvement in political struggles and social activities, Aminata Sarr continues to be an activist. Yet, facing the on-going social and economic crisis, she has revised the ideological foundations of her political convictions: "All these ideologies have gone bankrupt: com-munism, socialism, all these words with '-ism'; capitalism . . . don't even men-tion it!" From her point of view the reason for the new turn towards religion, particularly salient among the "disoriented youth," is the fact that "within the younger generation people start to become conscious." This conscious-ness goes along with a rejection of Western influence and domination: "It's the failure of the ideologies that have always been brought to us." The grow-ing Islamic revival movements can thus be seen as a search for an alternative development vision, and at the same time as a kind of retreat towards the "last refuge": "Islam solves all the problems of social life. Everything, every-thing, everything—politics, health, legislation, everything is inside!" (Ami-nata Sarr, 20.02.06).

According to Aminata Sarr, the organisation best representing this kind of "consciousness" is the Islamic association Jama'aatu Ibadu Rahmane (JIR), based in Thiès. JIR is currently the most developed and organised reformist organisation in Senegal, with an extended membership and branches all over the country (Loimeier 2006; Loimeier 2000a; Renders 2002, 64 f.). Sarr de-scribes the members of JIR as "very cultivated people" who are well in-structed concerning their own religion and do not adhere to Islam only as a matter of "mimetism." Many among them have known different Islamic doc-trines and some have even "tangled with Western culture." This background, however, does not prevent a male *Ibadu* Rahmane from following his own in-terests and even trying to cheat women by his interpretations of Islam, espe-cially when it comes to questions concerning gender relations. To illustrate this, Sarr recalls an incident that happened at the occasion of a conference organised by JIR in Thiès to which she had been invited:

The lecturer was talking and talking. He talked about a woman he had seen in a journal who was not happy to have a co-wife: 'Look at this kind of ego-ism!' he said. When he finished I asked to have the floor. I said: 'But, dear re-ligious compatriot, this woman is right! She has the right! She is not better than all the other women who are given co-wives. If God has saved her, she can rejoice with this and congratulate herself. If she wants, she can even or-ganise a party!' Then, the whole auditorium was laughing. 'And I will tell you why: polygamy is not an Islamic option, polygamy is something Islam has found here, it was an option of those societies which existed here before. Is-lam, on the contrary, has regulated this tradition because before one could marry many women. God, who has created men, knows that men are polyga-mous by nature! Even the Westerners do it, but in another way, having their mistresses. Therefore God did not make it vanish, but regulated it.' And I said: 'The Islamic option is monogamy! Because to be polygamous, there are conditions. Too many conditions, no man could fulfil them. Thus, this means interdiction.' And I said: 'Don't stuff these women, you are about to sow the seed of obscurantism!' I asked the women: 'Who is the woman who wants a co-wife? Who is for polygamy?' No finger went up. Hence, I said: 'Don't mess around with us. They don't want to tell you, because of delicacy, but I am a woman, I questioned them. Nobody, no woman wants it. And this woman does not have the right to be delighted?' Since then we became friends. He [the lecturer] always brought me their journal, addressing me *sokhna si*.[27] I told him I know very well my rights within Islam, you cannot cheat me. . . . 'Since this day between these *Ibadus* and me there was peace, we have become friends.' (Aminata Sarr, 20 Feb 2006)

From Aminata Sarr's point of view, the lesson to be learned from Islam is that women have rights, including the right to articulate themselves and the right to be instructed. The latter is a necessary condition for development, particularly for women, as she underlines:

You have to know, I always tell women to get instructed and learn about their religion, because if you really look at it, there is no contradiction between women's advancement and religion, Muslim religion in particular. On the con-trary, Muslim religion gives women more rights than any other religion, any other juridical system! Because in Islam the woman can dispose of her material goods like she wants. It's her husband who is in charge of financing the woman. She can participate if she wants, but this is no obligation. (Aminata Sarr, 20 Feb 2006)

Thus, Aminata Sarr sees women's subordinated position in Senegal as a feature of local traditions and "obscurantism," related to the problem of miss-ing instruction and women's lack of religious knowledge, but not related to

Islam itself: "Here, people mix religion and tradition . . . they want to bring Islam back to the tradition."

Negotiating Diversity: Muslim Society and Development in Senegal

Muslim society in Senegal has always been far from homogeneous. The dominant forms of local Islam, the Sufi brotherhoods (most important, in terms of numbers, are the *Tijaniyya*, *Muridiyya*, and *Qadiriyya*), are internally differentiated and mutually competing (Villalón 1995, 60 ff.).[28] This competition contributes to a sense of religious pluralism that is part of the Senegalese national identity which is characterised by a diversity of ethnic and linguistic groups. The symbolic systems of the various religious groups are overlapping with complex social stratifications including regional belonging, clan systems, family origin, the still significant distinctions between so-called casted and noncasted people, as well as educational and economic background (Villalón 1995, 56 f.). Which features of identity actually dominate depends on the concrete context. The "entrenched system of trilateral relations between the state, the religious elite, and a well-organised religious society" (Villalón 1999, 129) can be considered so far as a guarantee for the remarkable political stability in Senegal compared to other cases in the region as well as in the broader Muslim context.

However, with the breakdown of the groundnut economy and the pauperisation and growing dissatisfaction of the population (Diop 2004, Lachenmann 1993; 1997a, Oya 2006), the economic basis of the long-standing arrangements between the state and the Sufi orders has increasingly eroded. This has opened the door for alternative development concepts and discourses brought forward by Islamic reform movements. Their importance grows with the declining power of the marabouts in terms of spiritual authority and internal conflicts among the increasingly diversified Sufi organisations. While the first Muslim reformers in Senegal mainly criticised the "un-Islamic" practices of local marabouts, the new Islamic reform groups which have emerged in the 1980s and 1990s turn themselves increasingly against the secular state and the hegemony of Western culture (Loimeier 2000a, 183). Calling for a transformation of society corresponding to Islamic principles, the Muslim reformers are questioning the secular constitution and openly confronting the state-promoted project of modernisation. This confrontation is particularly articulated in the debate on the family law that has been ongoing since the establishment of the law in 1973 (see chapter 6).

The conflict concerning family law and its secular foundation points to the importance of gender issues for contemporary Islamic movements on a global scale. To understand the national context, however, it needs to be stressed that although the Sufi brotherhoods are clearly dominating the religious landscape, there is no single institution representing an "official" national Islamic discourse or a homogeneous "Muslim perspective" on issues like the implementation of women's rights and gender equality. The different Muslim organisations and branches of the Sufi orders have evolved into a rather competitive interrelationship, emphasising the unity of their faith at times, but maintaining their differentiating strategies and insisting on divergent positions at others.[29] The relations between secular, rights-oriented women's organisations and Islamic groups and authorities are thus highly ambivalent. Aminata Sarr's statement concerning the "obscurantism" of Muslim traditionalists, however, does not reflect this ambiguity, but rather projects the vision of a global modern Islam that corresponds to the development concepts promoted by women's NGOs like APROFES. Thereby she is downplaying the ongoing conflicts provoked precisely by those modernising Islamic reformers who not only criticise the government and Western-oriented secular development agents but also the institutions of traditional Islam.

There is a tendency among the diverse currents of Islamic revival or renewal movements to reject the Western influence in national development politics in general and the repercussions of globalised feminism in particular. The significance of the "women question" is reflected in the common traits of various Muslim organisations expanding on the national and local level. Its most visible manifestation is the rapidly growing number of young Senegalese women adopting styles of Islamic veiling which were unusual amongst the previous generation, conveying the image of a new Muslim identity and habitus (Augis 2003, Cantone 2005, Schulz 2007).[30] The popular expression to denote any woman carrying an Islamic veil in this new style is to call her an *Ibadu*. The expression refers to the above-mentioned, formally recognized and highly structured association Jama'aatu Ibadu Rahmane (JIR). But in everyday language the term *Ibadu* stands for a very broad and heterogeneous reform movement which seems particularly appealing for the young generation with access to modern French or Franco-Arabic education.

Young *Ibadus* adopt their new identity as a way to distinguish themselves from other Muslims, who are considered to be "ignorant" or still "unconscious" of the right way to be a Muslim. To opt for the veil is a way for them to express the superiority of their own interpretation of Islamic doctrine and practice based on what they consider to be a proper understanding of the Quran (and which ideally includes knowledge of Arabic). Many of them criticise their parents' ritual practices and particularly object against the many culturally established social obligations in the context of traditional family ceremonies. Almost every young woman veiled in an *Ibadu* style interviewed during this research referred to education as the key element for her personal advancement if not for development per se (as exposed by Aminata Sarr). Analysing the individual development visions of these women, it becomes very clear that most of them do not really intend to restrict themselves to the position of the housewife that appears nonetheless to be the common ideal of the diverse reformist Islamic discourses (Janson 2005). Getting a job in terms of a formal employment, typically as some kind of state official, teacher, nurse, or certified midwife was the main aim for many of them. Therefore marriage, which remains a very important issue for the majority of Senegalese women (Adjamagbo, Antoine, Dial 2004), was often postponed, something to do after having finished school, studies, or professional training. This means that irrespective of the position they would defend on the level of Islamic discourse, these young Muslim women increasingly claim access to and affirm their presence in secular domains of the public sphere.

The Politics of Women's Advancement: Potentials and Challenges

In Senegal, officially recognised development organisations in general and women's NGOs in particular are, as a majority, secular organisations. Attempts to integrate Islamic principles in development programmes on a national scale, such as developed within the tradition of the peasant movement (Lachenmann 1993), have not been taken up by the state. National and international development politics and discourses distance themselves from the domain of religion, let alone popular Islam as lived by the majority of the population. The use of different languages (French for state administration and the representatives of the international development community, Wolof or other local languages for popular Islam) is an important symbolic marker to separate these spaces.[31] Furthermore there are legal constraints for the formal constitution of religious organisations. Islamic political parties are constitutionally forbidden in Senegal. Some formalised Islamic organisations and NGOs exist, but are under severe control by the secular state and largely excluded from the mainstream development community (Renders 2002, 62 f.).

The position of women's organisations with respect to the symbolic confrontation between the secular state and the diverse Islamic movements is ambivalent. This reflects the tensions between the different positions women occupy within local Islam, the new Muslim reform movements, and the state-promoted process of secular modernisation. At the same time it indicates that the different kinds of women's organisations develop quite divergent strategies with respect to their relations with the state as well as with the institutions and authorities of local Muslim society. Within national development models women were conceived as agents of cultural transformation, emancipating themselves from those traditional cultural patterns that were held responsible for their suppressed and "alienated" status. In this sense the development programmes conceived by the state and foreign donors to promote women's advancement challenged the social structures and hierarchies embodied in local Sufi Islam. But at the same time the brotherhoods and the women's organisations could both be considered allies in the state's fight against reform Islamic movements.

In this political constellation Muslim women often find themselves in a rather ambivalent position. Particularly intellectual women with an explicit feminist orientation might experience the "contradictions of professed theories . . . and opposing socioreligious daily realities" (République du Sénégal 1993, 65). The trajectory of Aminata Sarr, starting from political activism in the framework of Marxist and Pan-Africanist visions and ending up embracing a vision of globalised Islam,[32] can be interpreted as a reflection of these contradictions. However, the indicated gap between the theoretical and practical dimensions of Senegalese women's development visions is not a uniform phenomenon—in this case it is shaped by Aminata Sarr's specific position as a representative of a particular generation and a privileged social milieu.[33] In a general way one can say that the contradictions between different development visions are reflecting social cleavages and that women have to deal with these in their daily practices and negotiation strategies.

The National Women's Movement and
Formalised Development Organisations

Ever since its constitution the Senegalese state has promoted women's advancement as an integral part of its nation-building project and development programme. In fact a huge number of officially recognised women's organisations exists, constituting a female associative movement that is very heterogeneous, comprising different visions and beliefs, reflecting women's diverse political and social positions, as well as geographical locations. This pluralism reflects the complex stratification of contemporary Senegalese society and its hierarchical structures ever present in its social and political, as well as in regional, ethnic, or religious diversity. More specifically it is a reflection of the history of the Senegalese women's movement. The origins of the latter can be traced back to colonialism and French administrative politics, and political mobilisation since the preindependence era, as well as to the introduction of women's right to vote in 1944 (Wone 2000). Later it was strongly influenced by the international feminist movements of the 1960s.

The rise of the Senegalese feminist women's movement since the 1970s constituted a counterforce, challenging the established gender order and calling for the transformation of society. The international context of the first World Conference on Women in Mexico in 1975 and the following UN women's decade deeply influenced its formation. At a later stage the 1995 World Conference on Women in Beijing and its preparatory process leading to the formation of the African platform in Dakar in 1994 gave important impulses to its dynamics, organisational structures, and networks. A lot of NGOs were founded during this period such as the above-mentioned RSJ or COSEF, as well as other organisations focusing more on the aspects of economic and social rights such as the African Network for the Advancement of Working Women (Réseau Africain pour la promotion de la Femme Travailleuse, RAFET).

However, the most important aspects in the context of the historical evolution of women's organisations in Senegal probably have to be related to the social repercussions of the economic crisis because it was in this context "that men were obliged to let women go out and earn money" (Fatou Sow in Nageeb, Sieveking, Spiegel 2005b, 17). In this situation women appropriated the globalised discourses on women's social and economic empowerment spread by the agencies of the UN system and multilateral cooperation which were ready to finance female income-generating activities (Lachenmann 1996). The state-guided project of "women's advancement," its programmes for the promotion of female entrepreneurship (mainly through microfinance), and its liberal practice of recognising the official status of women's NGOs can thus be seen as an attempt to channel the funds from foreign donors.

Nevertheless the joint effort of the state and foreign aid institutions to reduce poverty and improve women's situation in order to achieve this goal (or vice versa) have not been successful so far. On the contrary, the permanently conjured up vision of women's advancement obscures the fact that national (and international) development policies have contributed to women's political and economic marginalisation. The shortcomings of the politics of women's advancement are particularly striking in the rural areas, where the state's development programmes concerning women have mainly focused on constituting formalised Groups for Women's Advancement (groupements de promotion feminine, GPFs). These groups are organised in a centralised hierarchical structure, headed by a national umbrella organisation, the National Federation of Groups for Women's Advancement (Fédération Nationale des Groupements de Promotion Féminine, FNGPF).[34]

According to its coordinator, Mouslymatou Ndiaye, the FNGPF aims at promoting citizenship and strengthening civil society. Its development vision is based on the idea of women's self-help (auto-promotion). The FNGPF has served as an organisational basis for the implementation of major externally funded development programmes mainly aimed at strengthening women's economic capacity (through the above-mentioned microcredit schemes), alleviating their daily work tasks, building up a sustainable infrastructure, and raising women's low level of education. While its effectiveness in achieving these objectives can be questioned, the organisation has contributed considerably to the Senegalese nation-building project, legitimising the government in power through mobilising women and the masses of the rural population (Lachenmann 2001, 85; Wone 2002, 2). The FNGPF has been characterised (not only by state representatives but also by feminist scholars and activists) as an organisation which has given Senegalese women—rural women in particular—a means to articulate their voice.

However, the space opened up through the creation of formalised women's groups is restricted and one could question the extent to which it has enabled women to articulate themselves without being instrumentalised. The centralised structure of the organisation is not suited to establishing a dialogue between the members at the ground and at the top. The voice of women at the grassroots level can hardly be recognised in the affirmative rhetoric of the organisation's official representatives. As far as no critical attitude towards the state is allowed, one can ask how far the organisation has gone in creating a space for women to contribute to the constitution of civil society. GPFs are considered as belonging to the social rather than to the economic sphere—in contrast to a formalised Group of Economic Interest (groupement d'intérêt économique, GIE) which is the usual form of economic organisation among men (Lachenmann 2001). GPFs are de facto excluded from large-scale national projects and restricted to small projects in commercial horticulture, animal rearing, cattle fattening, or handicrafts (République du Sénégal 1993, 14). Thus official women's projects have not only become disconnected from the "informal" local women's groups and female spaces but also systematically marginalised with respect to the state's own development projects.[35]

"Informal" Women's Organisations and Local Female Spaces
To understand the importance of local women's organisations, one must consider that the vast majority of Senegalese women is actively participating in the popular or 'informal' economy while only a tiny minority is connected to

the formal sector. Women thus generally do not rely on state-provided social security, but build up their own multilayered social and economic networks to cope with insecurity (Laaser 2005). Often they are active in various forms of female associations such as the traditional age groups, neighbourhood or village associations, and mutual savings or self-help groups. Most of the informal local organisations are based on kinship, ethnicity, religious belonging, or economic activity. While on the one side these associations perpetuate and reenact the existing systems of social, economic, and cultural differentiation, on the other side they constitute a dynamic force in actually shaping economic development and social change. So-called traditional organisations which have evolved in rural contexts are transposed to urban settings where they become part of new social practices. This can be exemplified with the widespread Wolof notion of *mbotaye*,[36] designating local forms of female associations. These associations often function as the basis for the formation of various kinds of organisations and frequently overlap. A *mbotaye* might, for example, be the starting point for some kind of tontine,[37] which is characterised by slightly different modalities for the contributions and the use of the capital accumulated. Often it is still functioning informally at the heart of a formalised organisation, like a GPF, a GIE, or larger organisations such as mutual savings banks or translocally connected NGOs.

The transformational aspect of traditional forms of organisation and their significance in the reconfiguration of social boundaries can also be shown through the example of religious associations called *dahira*.[38] With rural out-migration, *dahiras* were established in the urban context as important meeting centres and networks (Fall 1994), satisfying the social needs of the (originally) mostly young male migrants, helping them to build up economic relationships while at the same time guaranteeing a strong relation with the religious authorities (Loimeier 1994, 103 ff.). *Dahiras* have incorporated some modern administrative structures such as the function of a president and a treasurer—structures that can be traced back to the French colonial experience (Villalón 1995, 154). They parallel the structures of the state-promoted associations, GPFs, and GIEs, but are also characteristic of self-help organisations within social movements such as the Senegalese peasant movement. Having proved to be a very effective form of organisation, *dahiras* have in the meantime re-migrated to the countryside. With the feminisation of migration and due to the increasing popularity of *dahiras* among women their gendered structure changed (Rosander 1998, 159 ff.). Nowadays most *dahiras* are mixed, though more and more female-dominated *dahiras* exist. They are embedded in everyday social practices and constitute a form of organisation in which social, economic, and religious dimensions are inextricably interwoven. This allows women to develop agency, enlarge their room for manoeuvre, and redefine the boundaries of traditional social structures without explicitly putting them into question (Mbow 1997; Rosander 1997).

The characterisation of an association as traditional thus does not mean that its form and structures of organisation are opposed to the modernisation of society. On the contrary, they have to be considered an important element in the process of social transformation. This can also be observed in new "creative 'informal' coping practices" (Lachenmann 1998a: 9ff.). Following Lachenmann's argument, the notion of 'traditions' refers to specific logics of action linked to an ideal of solidarity, reciprocity, and trust which are embodied and frequently reenacted during the important family ceremonies (like weddings, baptisms, and burials) and in the framework of religious networks (Fall, Guèye 2002). The most popular forms of organising solidarity among those women whose life-world is still centred on kinship networks and the local neighbourhood are certainly the above-mentioned *mbotayes*. Recently *dahira* organisations have been spreading out as a more translocally or even transnationally connected form of setting up and maintaining social relations and, moreover, as a liable moral code by way of religious belonging.

Women who can rely on social relations based on these kinds of organisations are more likely to be successful in linking up to formalised associative structures that are recognised by the state such as the above-mentioned GPFs or GIEs (Sarr 1998, 26). Referring to the outcome of an action research project on Muslim Women and Development, Khadija Doucouré, the director of the women's NGO African Centre of Female Entrepreneurship (Centre Africain de l'Entrepreneuriat Féminin, CAEF), also points to "the development potential of brotherhoods' forms of association."[39] Thereby she refers to her experiences of collaborating with *dahira* organisations within the framework of the activities of the CAEF. This NGO is one of the few officially recognised development institutions focusing on women that is working with "informal" religious female associations.[40]

Khadija Doucouré emphasises women's agency in organisations where they "can act independently" and highlights that in this sense female spaces based on gender segregation are important because in mixed organisations men tend to control the important posts and "women do not have a chance" (Centre Africain de l'Entrepreneuriat Féminin 2001, 15) unless they build up parallel structures of representation beside the men's (Lachenmann 2004a, Rosander 1998, 160). That the latter is rather the norm was confirmed by the president of APROFES, the above-mentioned NGO in Kaolack: "Here in Senegal you will hardly find a woman who is not organised, be it in a traditional association, a formalised women's group, an NGO, or an age group. Even within a mixed *dahira* you will find a woman's organisation" (Binta Sarr, 8 May 2004). However, according to the classical model of state promotion, women's groups have to get formalised and registered first before being able to relate to the programmes of the government or other development institutions. There is still a reluctance to recognise traditional sociocultural patterns and local forms of organisation as having significant potential for development.

Conclusion: Connecting Global Development Discourses and Local Muslim Society

State institutions and related organisations like the FNGPF represent the official national politics of women's advancement and its inherent contradictions. In contrast to these structures, the above-mentioned women's NGOs stand for a type of organisation that is much more embedded in local society and the life-world of women at the community level. This type of organisation is exemplified by APROFES, as a locally based (although translocally and transnationally connected) NGO having emerged from a neighbourhood community organisation (ASC). There is also RADI, as a Pan-African NGO with strong local basis and networking structures on the level of rural communities, or the just-mentioned Dakar-based CAEF, which intensively interacts with formalised as well as "informal" local women's groups in the domain of female entrepreneurship.

The example of APROFES makes the difference with regard to the FNGPF particularly clear. The NGO is connected to global development discourses and joins in the official national politics in bringing forward the notion of women's rights and gender equality. Its focus, however, is clearly directed towards networking on the ground. Translocal relationships are essential for APROFES' negotiation strategies, but its members are very reluctant to identify with other national NGOs located in Dakar and express a nonpolitical attitude which is clearly articulated against the so-called *politique politicienne* (in contrast to other women's NGOs, like for example the above-mentioned COSEF, or even the network RSJ, which is intensively collaborating with the government). While APROFES always tries to include local representatives of the state administration in the negotiation processes and never forgets to invite the official authorities, neither from the secular nor from the religious spheres, it keeps the distance from the centre of political power.

Comparing the discourses and practices of APROFES and the FNGPF, some characteristic aspects of the negotiation of development by women organisations in Senegal come to the fore. The latter represents the position of the government and functions very much according to the hierarchies and centralised administrative structures that are established by the state. The former, in contrast, illustrates the position of civil society organisations playing their part in national policies by connecting global discourses to local practice. Both organisations link their agenda to the concepts of poverty reduction and women's rights, but do not give them the same relevance and meaning. In this respect the structures of communication and the means to establish a real dialogue, instead of just trying to "pass on the information," are very central (see chapter 6).

As has been indicated, the aspect of language was very important for the organisation of the above described event on the occasion of the International Women's Day. Aminata Sarr made this also clear when she described her quarrel with the JIR representative in Thiès and concretised the way she had intervened in the discussion: "I said it in Wolof, I addressed the women, I am like them, and I might speak Wolof even better than them. So the message was transmitted." Another important element of women's negotiation strategies is the kind of alliances that Sarr referred to when she resumed the outcome of the encounter with the JIR: "we became friends." Such kind of (potential) relations are not only structuring communication but eventually enabling consensus despite social and political disparities. To relate to an important person as a "friend" does not necessarily imply an intimate personal relationship, but rather indicates a strategic alliance. In this sense, the members of an organisation like APROFES have a lot of "friends" in different social spheres (most important tend to be the relations of the president, Aminata Sarr, who is related for example as a "friend" to the president of the regional council).

The particularity of an organisation like APROFES is the systematic use of popular modes of expression and nondiscursive cultural practices with strong integrative performative dynamics. The networking practices of RADI, as described in the context of the campaign against the "wastefulness" of traditional family ceremonies, have a similar effect. However, even NGOs like APROFES or RADI, which are very active in connecting the different (secular and religious) domains that constitute local society, hardly interact with the spheres of traditional female religious associations like the *dahiras* or the new Islamic currents, such as the *Ibadu* movement. The hostility of the relations between APROFES and JIR is outspoken, mainly due to JIR's vehement critique of the promotion of women's rights on the basis of secularism.

Rights-oriented women's NGOs rather collaborate with individual religious authorities and progressive Islamic scholars such as the above-mentioned Taha Sogou. The latter stand for a rather cosmopolitan, moderate, and liberal-oriented Islamic discourse. They are much more connected to a globalised academic and NGO community than to the different local Muslim organisations which have in common the rejection of Western influence on national development politics.

The discursive stereotypes on both sides (like the images of the "Western feminist" or the "Muslim traditionalist") are interrelated and the example of the alliances between women activists and male Islamic scholars illustrates the efforts to create a shared discursive space, where such stereotypes can be deconstructed. However, the relations between secular development agendas and religious visions of development remain uneasy and the disillusion concerning the politics of the secular state tends to provoke a generalised attitude of "Islam is the solution." This attitude is enforced by the systematic neglect within official development politics of the economic potential of informal women's associations which constitute an important element for the success story and the ever-increasing social and economic dynamics of the brotherhoods organisations. Thus the constructed opposition of "Western" and "Islamic" development projects is perpetuated and conjured up whenever the state politics fail. At the same time the considerable achievements of the Senegalese women's movement and the diverse secular women's groups and organisations are rendered completely invisible.

The blaming of culture or tradition instead of religion furthermore contributes to the de facto marginalisation of women because in the field of cultural practices women do assume a recognised authority (as "guardians of traditions"), while in the field of religion Senegalese women to date do not exercise authority in any publicly recognised way. The separation of mainstream development discourses and practices from the domain of religion and the failure to analyse lived religion as a social reality is a major factor in the described dynamics. It is disconnecting the Western-oriented development project and the globalised concepts of women's rights and gender equality, promoted by the secular state, from the strong dynamics of popular religious movements and Islamisation processes on the ground.

Notes

1. The last census from 2002 has shown that half of the Senegalese population lives in urban areas. Migration towards Touba, the "biggest village in Senegal," has been particularly strong (le Soleil, 31.07.2004, p.12).

2. Literacy among persons of 15 years or more is estimated to be around 24 percent in rural areas compared to an estimated 57 percent in urban milieus (République du Sénégal 2002, p.10).

3. The ministry in charge of the family is also in charge of women's promotion. It will be referred to in the following as Ministry of Family.

4. Muridism stands for the specific forms of organisation and practice of the *Muridiya*, which is one of the most important Sufi orders in Senegal. Its spiritual centre is the city of Touba, where the General Khalif of the order resides. For a detailed account of the intermingling of religious and mythical symbolism with complex sociopolitical and economic patterns structuring the urban space in Touba see Guèye (2002).

5. Wade's efforts to enhance his popularity by allying with established religious authorities could even be interpreted as a strategy to counter the power of the secular institutions of civil society because their critique of the government's lack of democracy can be more dangerous for his position than the antistate discourses of local Islamic authorities.

6. Senegal is divided into eleven regions. From a Dakar-based perspective "the regions" symbolise the rural and traditional, less urbanised and modernised parts of Senegalese society, located at the periphery of the metropolis.

7. Dakar, Thiès, and Saint Louis are the biggest cities. Touba, the second largest urban agglomeration and most rapidly expanding economic centre of Senegal, representing at the same time the spiritual centre of the *Muride* brotherhood, is not counted because it is officially ascribed the status of a "village."

8. Concerning local development and decentralisation policies see Lachenmann (2004a, 2006); and Lachenmann et al. (2005).

9. The peasant movement, on the other side, representing an important social movement with its own vision of alternative development, has contributed to the broad social and political foundation of the women's movement in Senegal (Lachenmann 1993).

10. Mata Sy Diallo took over this post after being deputy and vice president of the national assembly during the legislative period 1993–1998. She continues to occupy this post and is one of the very rare female personalities in Senegal with a long political career, dominating the sociopolitical landscape in Kaolack until today (Diaw 2004, 234).

11. "L'égalité selon le genre au delà de 2005: construire un avenir plus sûr."

12. The Wolof term *siggil* means "straighten, lift up, raise your head"; *jigeen* means "woman."

13. The RSJ was set up by former leaders of the prominent feminist and much more radical women's group Yewwu Yewwi (Creevey 2006, 165). Since 2005 the RSJ is struggling with a crisis on the level of leadership and financing. The RSJ is mainly supported by Canadian, Belgian and UN development agencies.

14. The Convention for the Elimination of All Forms of Discrimination against Women (CEDAW) was ratified by the Senegalese government without reservations in 1985. The official CEDAW report was published in 2004.

15. APROFES is a member of various international organisations, such as the Conseil des Organisations Non Gouvernementales d'Appui au Développement (CONGAD), the network Women in Law and Development in Africa (WILDAF), or the African Women in Economic Policies Network (AWEPON).

16. Wolof: to be big, victorious.

17. The singled out position of the president, a very charismatic person who cannot easily be replaced, indicates a prevalent problem of leadership among women's organisations in Senegal.

18. The company works in the tradition of the so-called community theatre or theatre for development, well established in the African context.

19. The association of the term *gender* with the notion of the family might be due to APROFES' participation in the campaign for a reform of the family law, launched by the RSJ during the same period (see chapter 6).

20. RADI was founded in 1985 and includes members from Gambia, Mali, Guinea-Bissau, Guinea-Conakry, and the Central-African-Republic (http://courantsdefemmes.free.fr/Assoces/Senegal/RADI/RADI.html).

21. Like APROFES, RADI has been part of the national campaign for a reform of the family law (see chapter 6).

22. The "wastefulness" of Senegalese family ceremonies is vividly criticised by the Islamic reform movements (for a similar critique by Islamic groups in the Gambia see Janson 2005).

23. The IAD and the COSEF are not only personally linked but also share the same office in the centre of Dakar.

24. Taha Sougou published a study on the interpretation of the notion of parental authority from the perspective of the Islamic legal doctrines (http://www.famafrique.org/parenteconjointe/documentsecrits/docbase.html, download 26.05.06; enda / Dior Fall 2001).

25. The term *sabar* designates the event of such a dance competition as well as the instrument used for it (Heath 1994, Sieveking 2006).

26. The reappropriation and transformation of the "dangerous and profane" if not "satanic" power ascribed to the rhythms of the sabar drums in the frame of local Sufi traditions has been described by Heath (1994, 94).

27. A Wolof term expressing respect for a woman with a high(er) social status.

28. Although the adherents of the *Tijaniyya* outnumber the other brotherhoods, the literature on Senegalese Islam mainly concentrates on the particularities of the indigenous *Muride* order, its economic organisation, and political role (for a recent overview see Loimeier 2006, Cruise O'Brien 2003).

29. The different Muslim organisations (*Tidjaniya*, *Muridiya*, and Islamic reform groups in particular), for example, have repeatedly fixed diverging dates for important Muslim ceremonies, like the end of the Ramadan, *tabaski*, or *korite*. Given the high degree of public participation in Muslim ceremonies and rituals, these incidences are vividly discussed in popular discourses and the media and have a strong effect in the sense of raising public awareness concerning religious particularisms.

30. Research has mainly focused on the academic milieu, although reformist trends and new veiling styles, which are also manifest within the Sufi organisations (Villalón 1999, 138), are increasingly spreading out in suburban and rural environments (a similar reform movement in the Gambia is described by Janson 2005).

31. The use of Wolof in the negotiation of women's rights is described in chapter 6. For the strategic meaning of the use of language see also Nageeb, chapter 4.

32. Aminata Sarr's trajectory is strikingly similar to the political career of Babacar Niang, president of the Comité Islamique pour la Réforme du Code de la Famille du Sénégal (CIR-COFS), an Islamic reform organisation that calls for the introduction of the Sharia in the domain of the national family law (see chapter 6). Like Aminata Sarr, Babacar Niang has been a member of the RND and fighting at the sides of Cheikh Anta Diop against Senghor's politics of "cultural assimilation." While his ideological reference has changed from Marx's Capital to the Quran, he has not changed the basic orientation in terms of his cultural identity politics, maintaining his radical critique of "Westernisation" and "Christianisation."

33. The professional career of her daughter, Marie Pierre Sarr Traoré, who was nominated in 2006 as minister for the domain of small and medium enterprises, female entrepreneurship

and microcredit (Petites et Moyennes Entreprises, de l'Entrepreneuriat Féminin et de la Micro-finance) may be seen as an illustration that certain ideological positions have vanished in the following generation.

34. The FNGPF was founded in 1987 by the Ministry of Family and formally transformed in an NGO in 1992.

35. "On a fait des projets féminins qui étaient marginaux face aux projets de développement eux-mêmes." (Fatou Sow, interview 16.04.04; République du Sénégal 1993, 14; Lachenmann 1997a)

36. Mbotaye is a Wolof term, often used in everyday language to designate female associations in a very general way. In a more strict sense, the term refers to a traditional form of self-help organisation based on age groups, providing women with collective material and financial assistance to perform important family ceremonies like weddings, baptisms, or burials (Sarr 1998: 41 FN4).

37. The term tontine is well established in the francophone context, designating a Rotating Saving and Credit Association (ROSCA) (see Ardener 1964, Ardener and Burman 1995). These associations collect, at fixed periods, sums that the members use in turn. Tontines play an important role in controlling women's working capital. Since the 1980s the emergence of this kind of informal financial institution in Africa, Asia, and Latin America has received increasing attention (concerning the situation in Africa see Lelart 2002).

38. The term (derived from Arabic: da'ira, meaning circle) and the specific institutional form, based on meetings with the role of the host circulating among the members, are original to Senegal (Villalón 1995, 149 ff.).

39. This comparative study of Muslim women in different countries was financed by the Netherlands cooperation (http://www.kit.nl/frameset.asp?/specials/html/mw_muslim_women .asp&frnr=1&, download 25.08.06) and carried out 1998–2000. The research in Senegal was coordinated by Khadija Doucouré (Centre Africain de l'Entrepreneuriat Féminin 2001).

40. Another example is the Mouvement Citoyen, directed by the renowned historian and feminist Islamic scholar Penda Mbow (Thiam in: Nageeb, Sieveking, Spiegel 2005b, 13).

CHAPTER THREE

~

Women's Organisations and Social Transformation in Malaysia: Between Social Work and Legal Reforms

Anna Spiegel

In February 2006 the *New York Times* (Perlez 2006) reported about two incidents which led to controversial public debates in Malaysia. The first incident was the expressed intent of the government to pass amendments to the Islamic family law and the successful protest of women's organisations, one of them the internationally well known Sisters in Islam, against these amendments. These organisations criticised not only the fact that the amendments would have made it easier for men to practice polygyny and to divorce, but also the undemocratic procedures of the enactment. According to the article the amendments had been passed only because those female delegates, senators, and ministers who personally were against the amendments had been forced to vote according to party lines. What followed was a process of consultation between women's groups, Islamic scholars, and clerics which finally led to the withdrawal of the amendments. The second incident that the article referred to was a debate that arose around the fact that the Islamic religious authorities rejected to defer the Islamic burial rituals of a Malaysian celebrity of Indian descent who had officially converted to Islam. Although his family insisted that he continued to be a practising Hindu until he passed away, his body was taken away by the respective religious authorities. This event also led to loud protests of women's groups such as Sisters in Islam.

Both incidents are evidence of the frictions and negotiations that the ongoing process of Islamisation produces in a multiethnic country such as

Malaysia. Only little more than 50 percent of Malaysia's citizens are ethnic ("indigenous") Malay, 34 percent are of Chinese and about 10 percent of Indian origin. Nevertheless the Malaysian nation state is based on Malay political and cultural dominance: Malay language is the official language; Islam is the state religion. Furthermore the constitution states that the Prime Minister and the chief ministers of the individual states had to be Malay (Nagata 1997, 134). Although *jus soli* was introduced to convert the migrant population into Malaysian citizens, Malay primacy is secured in a series of provisions and policies such as the New Economic Policy (Nagata 1994, 69). Nevertheless, precisely because of Malaysia's multiethnic composition Malay-Muslim identity has always been confronted with its boundaries. It is constructed to a significant extent by the direct confrontation with ethnic and religious others: With the West and the non-Muslim others embodied by the British colonisers, but also with the Asian others through the presence of millions of migrants from China and India. Malaysia is a country where several particular cultural identities coexist and shape each other respectively.

Since its independence in 1957 Malaysia has experienced an unprecedented process of social and economic transformation. From a mainly rural society and a colonial economy that concentrated on the export of natural resources, it developed into a mainly urban society (over 60 percent) with a diversified industry (Jomo K.S., Edwards 1993).[1] Economic development went hand in hand with deep social transformations: urbanisation, the reshaping of ethnic spaces through the formation of a Malay middle class, the reshaping of gendered spaces through an increasing rate of participation of Malaysian women in formal economy (Othman 1998, 172), and the emergence of Islamic revivalism and the politicisation of Islam (Camroux 1996; Nagata 1994), which became partially incorporated into state policies. This state-led project of Islamisation resulted mainly in an increased institutionalisation of Islam, with more rigid interpretations and direct translation of Quranic principles making their way into established legal texts. This institutionalisation led to a homogenisation of local Islamic practices and a reduction of personal freedom concerning everyday practices, interpretations, and visions for Muslims. At the same time it also led to the establishment of more pronounced boundaries between the different ethnic groups by accentuating and codifying the differences between Muslim and non-Muslim including eating habits, dress codes, burial rituals, and family laws, among other things.

But the two incidents mentioned above also show the sites of resistance and opposition to such developments. Women's organisations, whose involvement in public debate about politics, women, and gender issues date back before independence, play a significant part in this resistance. And ever since, the issues of ethnicity and religion have led to constant tensions within the women's movements as well (Stivens 2003).

The aim of this chapter is to present two distinct types of women's organisations which are quite differently located within such discourses on gender, religion, and cultural identity: advocacy groups, mainly based in Kuala Lumpur, and social work organisations, mainly based in peripheral areas of the country.[2] Starting with a typical event of each of the networks the analysis will focus on the agendas and programmes of the organisations, their relation to the state, and their approaches towards the process of Islamisation. In a second step the negotiation process among these organisations on the issue of gender equality, which led to the constitution of a public sphere, will be analysed.

Women's Organisations and Advocacy

On the first weekend of March 2004 I attended the celebration of International Women's Day which was represented with the motto "A Girl's Day Out" in Kuala Lumpur's biggest shopping centre, the Mega Mall. For the first time in the history of International Women's Day in Malaysia it was organised not only by some of the most prominent women's organisations—Sisters in Islam (SIS), Women's Aid Organisation (WAO), All Women's Action Society (AWAM)—but also by human rights organisations such as Amnesty International (AI) and the Malaysian Aids Council (MAC). Also the cooperation with the television programme 3R, a programme which is especially popular among young women in Malaysia, for this event was something new. On the official website of 3R, which stands for "Relax, Respect, Respond," the programme presents itself as taking up "women's issues" and as employing staff members who are socially engaged in different NGOs.

The event takes place in one of the exhibition halls of the gigantic Mega Mall where normally commercial exhibitions take place, a typical example being an "Indian Wedding Exhibition." The information booths of the women's organisation, situated in the centre of the hall, are surrounded by commercial promotion and advertising booths of companies such as the Body Shop, Kotex, Johnson & Johnson, Nestlé, and Maggi. Having a break from their shopping tour, hundreds of teenagers—mostly girls but also boys—and young families squeeze themselves between the information and commercial booths.

At the booth of the Women's Aid Organisation (WAO) one of the volunteers explains to interested visitors the cycle of violence in which women are caught if they suffer from domestic violence and how this cycle could be broken. At the booth of the All Women's Action Society (AWAM) visitors of the "Girl's Day Out" are invited to participate in a game of skill. Most participants find it extremely difficult to master the game, which consists of drawing a geometric figure while looking into a mirror. This feeling of being stuck, of being lost and that everything is turned upside down is a common experience that women have in their everyday life, especially when they are survivors of sexualised violence, explains the volunteer. At the booth of Sisters in Islam young women are asked to participate in a poll. They are asked to answer the following questions: Should there be a law that regulates women's dress code? Should a man, despite his precarious economic situation, be allowed to take a second wife? Could it be justified under any circumstances that a man beats his wife? And finally: Should a Muslim woman be able to get a divorce without the consent of the husband? At the booth of Amnesty International, Asha Gill, a prominent figure in the Southeast Asian media landscape, is selling *ban-Ashas*, small bananas which she dips into chocolate or strawberry sauce, and asking visitors to put their coloured handprints on a big poster as a sign against violence against women. This is part of the global campaign "Stop Violence Against Women" which Amnesty International started in March 2004. Asha Gill is one of the most prominent spokespersons of Amnesty International in Malaysia.

The WAO, AWAM, and SIS are at the core of what in most of the literature is referred to as the new women's movement in contemporary Malaysia. Women's movements and women's involvement in politics in Malaysia have a long history. Already before independence women were actively participating in the anticolonial struggles against British and later Japanese occupation. These early women's movements, however, were highly integrated into the ethnonationalist identity constructions of that time. Women were organised within their respective ethnic communities, that is, within the women's wings of the ethnically defined parties, and there was no intent to build up a multiethnic women's movement (Mohamad 2002a, 219; Othman 1998, 171). Shortly after independence the first women's organisation with a multiethnic self-understanding and clear references to the topics of the global women's movement, namely equal pay for women in the public sector, was formed: the National Council of Women's Organisations (NCWO). The women leaders of this umbrella organisation were elected among all three ethnic groups in equal proportions (Mohamad 2002b, 353). Still, this practised multiethnicity in the National Council of Women's Organisations was closely connected to the politics of ethnic elite accommodation, which the ruling Malay party, the United Malay National Organisation, propagated, and did not challenge cultural and political dominance of the Malays. The NCWO was not in the position to oppose the state's paternalistic multieth-nic project with a new, alternative vision of the social organisation of a mul-tiethnic society. The new women's movement consists of several organisa-tions which emerged in the early 1980s under the influence of the UN's Women's Decade, declared themselves as feminists, and took up the issue of violence against women or VAW, as it is abbreviated in the international women's movement language, as an entry point into the public debate about gender equality. In contrast to the earlier women's movements this new movement constructed itself as cosmopolitan, multiethnic, and multireli-gious with a clearly defined critical attitude towards the state.

In the late 1980s the debate about a unified Domestic Violence Act for all ethnic and religious communities in Malaysia changed the landscape for the women's organisations. The WAO in particular broadened its service orienta-tion and was one of the leading actors in the negotiation process with the Malaysian state about the formulation and introduction of a new Domestic Vi-olence Act which would cover all women, irrespective of their ethnic or reli-gious belonging. Such an act that would cross ethnic and religious boundaries was strongly opposed by several Muslim groups with reference to the Quran, ar-guing that it would allow corporal punishment of women by their husbands, but also with the argument that domestic violence would fall into the private realm and had hence to be treated within Sharia law (Anwar 2004). In this debate that was dominated by culturalist arguments it was extremely difficult for a mul-tiethnic women's movement to enter into a fruitful dialogue with religious and state authorities, and to some extent the multiethnic self-understanding of these new women's organisations was challenged. This was the moment when Sisters in Islam came into being as an organisation of Muslim women dealing with VAW from a Muslim perspective. Seven Muslim professional women— lawyers, journalists, academic scholars—who were already active in other women's organisations formed the group and developed a historically sensitive and contextualised approach for the reinterpretation of the Quran to show that the oppression of women in Islamic countries is not based on Islam, but on centuries of male authority over the interpretation of the text (Nagata 1994, 80). The questions in the polling that Sisters in Islam carried out at the International Women's Day provide a good overview over the main issues ad-dressed by the organisation today, namely the increasing pressure on Muslim women to dress according to Islamic attire, polygyny, domestic violence against women, and Islamic family law.

All of these organisations are currently very active in the promotion of law reforms concerning the issue of violence against women. The WAO presented the first Malaysian study about domestic violence, and since the enactment of the new Domestic Violence Act it is constantly monitoring its implementation. The WAO has continued its efforts to push for a law reform concerning women's rights, publishing reports on Sharia and non-Muslim civil laws. Since the 1990s the WAO is the organisation at the national level that works most actively on and with the Convention on the Elimination of All Forms of Discrimination against Women (CEDAW). On behalf of the Ministry of Human Resources AWAM has developed a "Code of Practice on the Prevention and Eradication of Sexual Harassment in the Workplace" for private companies. One of the Sisters in Islam activists summarises her motivation: "What I want to do is to push for a law reform and put forward equality."

In Malaysia the issue of VAW has served as an entry point to negotiation processes on gender equality, a phenomenon that needs some more consideration. Although being an important issue on the international level through the interconnectedness to the "Women's rights are human rights" campaign the discourse on VAW has generally not been very prominent in women's movements in the South who had rather concentrated on socioeconomic rights of women instead of on domestic violence (Holthaus, Klingebiel 2000, 45). The high significance of that issue in Malaysia is also untypical compared with women's movements especially in other Muslim countries where the issue of violence against women has been avoided for being too controversial and is only recently included into the strategies of women's organisations (see Nageeb on Sudan, chapter 4). In relation to these contrasting cases the broad discursive space that is generated around the issue of VAW in Malaysia is an interesting phenomenon that is based on the specific Malaysian constellation in two senses. First, in the interviews several activists pointed out that VAW was a "good issue" to get "normal people" into conversations because it was not immediately associated with being "anti-government." Thus the room for manoeuvre concerning the discourse on VAW is relatively large compared with issues related to socioeconomic or civil rights, topics which the state has coopted and dominated. Organisations and activist who concentrate on such "dangerous" topics have to fear severe consequences such as detention. For example, in 1987 one hundred human and worker's rights activists were arrested under the Internal Security Act with the charge of organising a communist insurgence and threatening ethnic harmony.[3] Second, the issue of VAW, which actually aims at the politicisation of the private sphere is of a high societal relevance in Malaysia where through industrialisation, urbanisation, Islamisation, and the integration of women into the formal sector the relation between private and public spaces has been restructured and reproblematised (Dannecker, Spiegel 2006). This societal relevance of VAW is also reflected in the high connectivity to other issues such as democratisation and political culture, women's participation in public space, freedom of religion, and questions of how a multiethnic society should be arranged. The recent debates about the undemocratic procedures in amending Islamic family law and about the imposition of Islamic burial rituals for a converted Hindu, to which the *New York Times* article referred, illustrate this connectivity.

The use of shopping centres as a location for events relating to the advocacy of women's organisations is a very interesting phenomenon in the context of a country with limited options for civil society actors in the public space. On the one hand, according to many civil society activists it is nearly impossible to organise events in public spaces such as streets or squares.[4] On the other hand, to stroll around and window shop in one of the mainstays of consumer culture in Kuala Lumpur—going to the Mega Mall, or the KLCC (Kuala Lumpur City Centre) is one of the favourite leisure time activities of the urban Malaysian middle classes (Chua 2000) which have emerged through the process of successful industrialisation and urbanisation. It unites the two main features of middle-class lifestyle, namely consumption and leisure time, thereby converting them into a social practice able to display social distinction and to celebrate symbolic consumption[5] like no other practice. These "empires of consumption," as Mona Abaza (2004) calls the malls, are modern temples which glorify unlimited consumption but at the same time also serve the nationalist projects of the political leaders who supported their construction.[6]

Alliances and networks with popular media are another important opportunity for these women's organisations to bring their issues into the public sphere and to create a broad societal basis for the public negotiation of gender relations. Some of the women's organisations regularly publish letters to the editor or other columns in well known Malaysian newspapers: Sisters in Islam in the biggest newspaper in the national language Bahasa Malaysia and the Women's Aid Organisation in the English *Sunday Mail*. Also the radio is used intensively as a medium through which to debate gender relations. The social workers of the WAO are regularly on air: In 2003 with a series about women's issues in general, and in 2004 with a thirteen-part series solely about domestic violence.

The connection between a culture of consumption and political activism is also reflected in the funding strategies of advocacy groups. For most of the NGOs in Malaysia it is very difficult to receive funds from the traditional Western and global donor organisations because officially Malaysia is no longer considered a developing country. Nor do the advocacy groups receive funding from the state because of their critical position towards government politics. In this situation the private sector is turning into the major source of funding, which in turn leads to the commercialisation of some of the women's groups events such as the International Women's Day in the shopping centre which was financed by several corporate sponsors. Of the women's groups represented there, the WAO is the most creative and successful one in the search for alternative sources of funding beyond international donor organisations and the state. In March 2004 the WAO started the campaign "Change for the Better" in cooperation with Burger King.

Such events are laboratories for the development of new ways of doing politics in a highly consumerist and at the same time politically highly restricted society: the politicisation of consumption. In the case of Malaysia, Crouch (1993; 2005) and Kahn (1995) have highlighted the de-politicising dynamics of the global culture of consumption. Kahn argues that the middle classes did not contain the potential for political transformation such as democratisation because it was their first priority to satisfy their consumption needs. The presented case, however, sheds a quite different light on the relationship between consumption and political engagement. The activities of the women's organisations such as the celebration of International Women's Day in a shopping centre show how in a consumer culture where material goods are no longer mere utilities but "communicators" (Featherstone 1991, 84), consumption itself can be politicised. A commercial space is turned into a space for negotiating gender relations and social transformation. To buy a ban-Asha from Asha Gill is not merely consumption but a political statement to support the cause of the women's NGOs. To watch the popular television programme 3R is not merely a diversion but a symbol of engagement with women issues. Women's groups strategically use the lifestyles of the consumption-oriented middle classes and politicise consumption in order to politicise the public space. The meaning of the campaigns analysed in this chapter is ambivalent in the sense that unpolitical consumption and commercial spaces are politicised while at the same time politics is turned into commodities which can be easily consumed like any other global consumption good.

In the following section of the chapter a second type of women's organisations with a totally different strategy towards consumption and political participation shall be presented and analysed according to its agenda and discourses. As with the former case an event is used to locate the presentation and analysis of the organisation within its frame of reference.

Women's Organisations and Social Work

In September 2004 I was invited to join one of the regular meetings of the Women's Innovative Self-Development Movement (WIJADI), a women's organisation which is located in Kota Bharu, the capital of the northern Malaysian state of Kelantan. Six women between 25 and 45 years old have gathered in the small office of WIJADI. All of them are Malay and dressed in colourful *baju kurung*, a loose, knee-length blouse and a long skirt which is considered the Malay national dress, and wear a headscarf known as the *tudung* in the local language. In one corner of the room there is a small table where some of the items are displayed that were produced by the women to generate a higher income: handbags, little baskets, soap, and candles. Referring to the income-generating programmes that the organisation carries out, Saleha, the president of the organisation, states: "Our business is empowerment." In the other part of the room is the office with a desk and a computer. While they sit there, the women discuss the disadvantages of polygyny and the significance of *taqliq*, a contract that Muslims can make with their spouse before getting married. By some of the women's organisations *taqliq* is promoted as a strategy which enables women to prevent polygyny within the framework of Islamic family law. They also talk about the system of dowry. Nazia says: "For Indians, the women must pay the men. But we in Islam, the man must pay for the women. Twenty years ago it was 2,000 Malaysian ringgit, now it is 4,000 to 5,000 ringgit. And in contrast to the Indian system, where the money goes to the parents, the dowry goes to wife. The dowry, this is a property that you get with the marriage and that you can claim. You are allowed to take it."

And they share their stories and experiences with the Sharia courts. Nazia, who is forty-five years old, starts telling her typical story to the others. Before getting married Nazia had worked in a small factory. When she got married she quit her work to dedicate herself fully to family life and became a housewife. After fifteen years of marriage her husband took a second wife, left the joint household and did not contribute anymore to the maintenance of Nazia and their six children. This was a very hard time for Nazia, as she quickly had to find a way to earn money. She opened a small food stall and started to work as a traditional massage woman. Through a friend she got to know about WIJADI. She came to WIJADI because she was keen to meet other women who had experienced similar problems. Now she works as a councillor in WIJADI. Concluding her story she says: "I was very naïve, but with WIJADI I learned how to go through my life with or without my husband."

Besides the advocacy women's organisations which are mostly engaged in the realm of law reform and practice a "critical engagement" with state institutions, WIJADI represents another type of women's organisation which carries out income-generating programmes and vocational training for poor Muslim women, including counselling in legal issues on Islamic family law, and cooperates more closely with the state. Other organisations which belong to this type are the Women's Development Foundation of Kelantan (Yayasan Murni) and the Muslim Women's Action Association (PERTIWI) which operates in Kuala Lumpur.

What these three organisations have in common is the idea of assisting poor women or of "helping unfortunate women," as Rahima, the president of Yayasan Murni, describes her work in an interview. In most of the cases these "unfortunate women" are single mothers: women whose husbands left them because of a second marriage, women who decided to divorce and who are now struggling for maintenance for them and their children, widows or divorcees who want to claim property rights.

WIJADI is located in the state of Kelantan. This state is a mainly Malay area and has been governed since 1990 by the Pan Malaysian Islamic Party PAS, the Islamic opposition party, who subsequently introduced new forms of gender segregation. WIJADI is a relatively young organisation. It was founded in 1999 and currently has forty members. The primary aim of WIJADI when it was set up was to give legal counselling to women who experienced difficulties with Islamic family law in the Sharia court system. Nowadays WIJADI carries out a quite complex range of activities, all of which aim at "empowering" and "making women stronger," as Saleha, the executive officer and chair of WIJADI, explained during an interview. WIJADI provides psychological support and legal aid for women who have cases going on in the Sharia court. Women meet regularly at the organisation's office to discuss their situation and share their experiences with others. Some of the first-generation clients now work at WIJADI and take over the role of counsellors. This self-help approach is of fundamental importance for the organisation's self understanding. "We all know these issues through experience, through our own experience with Sharia laws," said Saleha. Furthermore, WIJADI gives shelter to women who suffered from domestic and sexual violence. They are referred to them by the hospitals in Kota Bharu.

Today the main focus of the organisation is on economic activities. These include an herbal and biodiversity garden with over one hundred indigenous plants and herbs and a 0.8 hectare farm where citronella, basil, and kaffir lime are cultivated. The plants are processed into essential oils which are used to give aroma to herbal soaps and candles. Women are both employed as wage labourers at collective plots and can cultivate vegetables for their own subsistence on individual plots. The combination of supporting women's economic independence and sustainable development through the maintenance of biodiversity is one of the "innovative" aspects of the Women's Innovative Self Development Centre.

Only one year after WIJADI was founded another organisation dealing with women and poverty came into existence and had a trajectory similar to WIJADI: Yayasan Murni. It was formed in the year 2000 and started as a counselling centre for single mothers "to show them that this is not the end of the world," as Rahima, Yayasan Murni's president, explains. In its early phase the foundation gave seminars that focused more on motivation and "giving hope." Beside this psychological aspect it soon became clear that one of the main problems that these women had to face was their difficult economic situation and the responsibility of maintaining a numerous family, often consisting of three generations, with no or only little income. A great deal of them had stopped earning money when they got married, or could not access the money they had earned during their marriage because the shared assets were controlled by the husbands and they did not posses a separate bank account on their own. The focus then shifted from motivational to vocational training and classes on economic issues and entrepreneurship. In 2002 the foundation opened up a Centre for Skills Training for Economic Development where mainly tailoring classes were held. Later on IT and ITC literacy courses were integrated into the programme for the younger women, but the tailoring classes remain the most important part of the work. In 2003 the centre carried out a course on vocational training for domestic workers which had been designed by the Ministry of Women, Family and Community Development.

Through its activities the organisation intends to bring "unfortunate women" back into society, as the following poem by the patron of the foundation shows.

"That which is entangled is simplified, that which is impure is purified.
That which is bumpy is levelled out, that which is bent is straightened.
That which is apart is moved closer, that which is lost is brought back.
That which is unwell is made well."

The organisation makes explicit reference to an Islamic framework, offering, for example, courses in the "Basics of Islamic Faith." Women's rights are grounded within Islam and are always seen in relation to a balanced and morally stable society. Roslina, who works as a legal counsellor in the organisation, said: "Because if women have been abandoned and neglected the impact is not only for women, the impact is to the whole country because it is emphasised in the Islamic teaching that women have to be dignified" (Yayasan Murni's Legal Councillor, 24.10.04).

Also Masrina, the president of PERTIWI, founded in 1967 and based in Kuala Lumpur, defines her work as "helping poor women." She clearly contrasts her work to that of organisations such as Sisters in Islam who engage in public debates about Islamic Law which require profound knowledge of Islamic jurisdiction: "Actually there are two types of Islamic women's NGO's. One deals with charity and social work, the other one, Sisters in Islam, will look into the legal aspects and rights. But a lot of people go into voluntary work because they simply want to help. Not understanding very much of the legal thing, we don't dabble with it. We just want to help." Interestingly, the president of PERTIWI is a patron of Yayasan Murni.

Working in the domain of female poverty, these organisations move within a space that since independence had been nearly monopolised by the developmentalist Malaysian state. Several authors point to the fact that the Malaysian state itself dominates rural development and the provisions of social services, and that only few nongovernmental organisations can be found in the areas of agricultural extension activities, skills development, or credit provisions (Weiss, Hassan 2003a). The few NGOs that do work in that area typically do not challenge or question the state's development project in any radical manner, and the organisations presented here maintain a very close relationship with the state apparatus. Many of the leading women in these organisations are part of government service or of the different bodies of the National Women in Development (WID) Machinery. For instance Rahima, the above-mentioned president of Yayasan Murni, had been the district education officer of Kota Bharu, the capital of Kelantan, for several years. An even more telling example for the interface between NGOs and the state apparatus is Masrina, the president of PERTIWI who had been the chair of the National Advisory Council for the Integration of Women in Development, a body which had been formed in the aftermath of the first women's conference in Mexico 1975. She was part of the government delegation to a number of world conferences and personally knows the Minister of Women, Family and Community Development. Masrina is also a member of one of the subcommittees of the National Council of Women's Organisations (NCWO), the official umbrella organisation for women's organisations in Malaysia. Yayasan Murni is among the ten women's organisations that the government designated as having the best practices. This list is going to be presented at the United Nations, as Rahima, Yayasan Murni's president, told me. The organisation has also won an award from the government department which is in charge of registering NGOs as the most effective NGO.

This close relationship to state institutions of the organisations presented above is also reflected by their funding situation. In contrast to the advocacy organisations presented in the first section of the chapter, the social work organisations carry out programmes designed by different ministries and receive funding for their projects from the federal government, as is the case for Yayasan Murni. The courses in IT and domestic help are carried out in cooperation with the Ministry for Women and Family Development and Welfare. Also the capital for buying the sewing machines was provided by the government.

Hassan and Weiss (2003b) have argued that there is a lack of critical civil society actors in the field of development. This might be partially true for the organisations discussed here because of their strong networks with state institutions. But positively speaking, this strong tie with the state constitutes a hinge between the different spaces of knowledge production on women and gender relations, the state, the UN institutions, and NGOs. PERTIWI is a particularly strong role model for the two relatively young women's organisations in Kelantan who talk about PERTIWI's global contacts, networks, and approaches with considerable admiration. Women's activists in Kelantan perceive a gender approach that could unite women beyond specific professional interests on the basis of a sense of solidarity as something new which they learned from globally connected organisations such as PERTIWI. This knowledge chain does challenge the state's monopoly on defining and executing development to a certain extent. Rahima, the president of Yayasan Murni, criticises the approach on poverty reduction that is adopted by the federal government for not being sustainable: "The government wouldn't be able to help much because once a year during the Ramadan, the government will give each of these poor families 200 ringgit. That should be for their *hari raya*. But what about the day to day basis? The children need to go to school" (23.10.04). The ultimate aim of these organisations is to go beyond mere charity and to provide women with the knowledge and skills necessary so that they themselves can build up economically sustainable livelihoods.

As it could be shown so far, there is a diversity of women's organisations and approaches towards gender issues within the Malaysian women's movement. The approaches oscillate between the fear of the cooption and instrumentalisation of women's and gender issues on the one hand, and the chance to provide women with the possibilities to improve their livelihood significantly on the other; between the aim of reforming the law and the push for societal transformation on a rather abstract level on the one hand, and the urge to improve the economic situation of women on a very concrete level of everyday life on the other; between different modes of negotiating women's issues with the state: a critical engagement in order to foster political, legal, and social transformation on the one hand, and a close cooperation in order to integrate "unfortunate women" into society on the other.

The definitely simplifying, but nevertheless very useful distinction between advocacy groups and social work organisations was chosen in this chapter in order to systematise this diversity. The diversity is the result of a constant process of negotiation among women's organisations about how gender relations should be rearranged and what should be the means of change. But it is not less the result of the very distinct social spaces into which these organisations are embedded: the space of the internationally oriented urban middle classes on the one hand and the space of locally and at the same time very state-oriented milieus on the other hand.

The relationship between these two types of women's organisations presented in this chapter is highly ambivalent. They belong to—also in the spatial sense—differently located networks that in some cases cooperate with each other but are also enrolled in the complex dynamics of othering processes. The discourse on the Islamisation project of both the state government of Kelantan and the federal Malaysian government in particular is one site where the above-mentioned diversity and the processes of othering and distancing become visible. An extract from an interview with Nurhuda, the only Sisters in Islam activist who is located in Kelantan, illustrates this point:

> NGOs here in Kota Bharu are not transformative NGOs. There was no reaction on the proposal to implement Islamic criminal law. Their work does not lead to structural change. They don't have the tradition and experience of fighting as do the Kuala Lumpur NGOs. Also the legal literacy programmes that these NGO carry out do not reach very far. It is a question of whether they only teach the women about the law or if they also encourage critical reading. (Nurhuda, 25 Oct 2004)

Nurhuda strongly criticises the organisations in her town as being not critical enough and of using the concept of rights in a nontransformative way. These ambivalent and even contradictory negotiations shall be treated in the following section. It shall be argued that the gendered structure of space and the question of knowledge and different constructions of Malay identity are the underlying topics of these negotiations.

Creating a Kaleidoscope of New Female Islams: Between Knowledge and Practice

The specific process of Islamisation as it takes place in Malaysia is increasingly limiting the space for alternative visions of Islam and for the organisation of a multiethnic society. Having started in the 1970s as a movement among Malay students and factory workers containing a harsh anticapitalist critique on uneven social development and industrialisation (Camroux 1996, 855), Islamisation soon got incorporated into state policies. These state policies aimed at constructing a new assertive, globally connected 'Islamised' Malay identity in order to oppose the interethnic stereotype of the backwardness and laziness of Malay culture (Mohamad 2002b, 355). Doing so, the state's Islamisation and modernisation projects were ideologically and discursively linked to an "economically induced cultural program" (Mohamad 2002b, 358). In the 1980s this turned more and more into an institutionalisation of Islam (Abaza 2002). Since then the state has been promoting the Islamisation of the public space through mosque building programmes, through the strengthening of the role of religious bureaucracy and Islamic courts at the state and federal level, through the teaching of Islam in schools, through the financing of Islamic schools, and through the creation of an Islamic teachers' college, an Islamic bank and insurance system, and an international Islamic university (Camroux 1996, 857–858).

Today the process of Islamisation is characterised by mutual accusations between government and opposition—that is, between the United Malays National Organisation, UMNO, the main Malay party, and the Pan Malaysian Islamic Party, PAS, the Islamic opposition party—of heresy or lacking faith, and the mutual intents to "out-Islamise" each other. "If necessary, UMNO is ready to fight PAS' Islam with more Islam of its own" (Nagata 1997, 144). This competition has led to the introduction of new Islamic laws or the amendment of existing ones "as part of the government's efforts to upgrade the status of Islam in Malaysia" (Anwar 2004). New Sharia criminal laws were passed and new offences were created such as *khalwat* (close proximity). This process of the increased institutionalisation of Islam leads to a normative standardisation and homogenisation of the religious space, with less room for nonconformist practices, interpretations, and visions for Muslims, especially for Muslim women.

Until 2004 two states in the north of Malaysia with a mainly Malay population, Terengganu and Kelantan, were governed by the Islamist opposition party PAS. Whereas in Terengganu the Islamists lost the 2004 elections, Kelantan still has an Islamist state government. In 1993 the PAS state government of Kelantan managed to pass the Kelantan Sharia Criminal Bill (the so-called *Hudud* Bill) through the Kelantan State Legislative Assembly. The introduction of Islamic criminal law was something new in Malaysia, where until this point only family law had been divided by religion into Islamic family law for Muslims and secular family law for non-Muslims, whereas criminal law was secular and was hence applied equally for all religious groups. Furthermore, there were attempts to ban women factory workers from night shifts and to impose Islamic attire on them. Gender segregation was introduced in queues in supermarkets, movie theatres, and bus stops. Popular forms of art such as the *wayang kulit* (shadow puppets) were banned, and Muslim women workers were fined for not respecting the dress code that demands that the body be completely covered except for the hands and face both in the private and in the public sphere. These amendments also influence the life of non-Muslims in Kelantan, as also non-Muslim women are forbidden to wear, for example, short skirts at their work place. In Terengganu similar measures were taken and an Islamic criminal code was introduced in 2002.

The advocacy women's groups, among them Sisters in Islam, the WAO, AWAM, and others, strongly opposed these measures of the Kelantan and Terengganu state governments as a drive of Islamisation and reacted with a number of press statements, letters to the editor, and memorandums which were sent to the Prime Minister Mohamad Mahathir suggesting their interpretations and visions on Islam. These groups are actively engaged in the creation of an alternative body of knowledge about women and Islam on the level of interpretation, Islamic jurisprudence, and *hudud* laws. Gender segregation of the public space and polygyny are at the centre of the campaigns of Sisters in Islam and other women's organisations in Kuala Lumpur. "The Islamic Family Law was amended to make divorce and polygyny easier for men and reduce men's financial responsibilities towards women" (Anwar 2004). Concerning the Islamic criminal law in Kelantan (enacted in 1993) and in Terengganu (enacted in 2002), the discriminatory effects that these laws have upon women were highlighted (Coalition on Women's Rights in Islam 2002; Sisters in Islam 1993) and the Terengganu law was even more harshly criticised as a "law to protect rapists." In 2002 when the *hudud* enactment in Terengganu was passed, a coalition of women's organisations protested in a public memorandum against the introduction of the *hudud* law, arguing that it "constitutes a gross violation of principles of justice and equality in Islam" and a "total distortion and perversion of God's Law" (Coalition on Women's Rights in Islam 2002, last checked 04.01.06). Both codes deny women the status of being an eyewitness and thus in both codes a woman who has been raped is required to bring four male witnesses to testify to the crime. If not the woman herself can be charged for having committed *zina* (illicit sexual relations). The Terengganu enactment even goes so far as to say that women who cannot prove the rape in the above-mentioned way will be charged for *qazaf* (slanderous accusation) and flogged eighty lashes. It also opens up the possibility for the death penalty for apostasy. Furthermore, the women's organisations criticise that both codes do not take into account the multiethnic composition of Malaysian society and the question of how non-Muslims should be treated under this Islamic criminal law.

As far as the fieldwork has shown, the locally embedded social work organisations in Kelantan but also social work organisations based in Kuala Lumpur such as PERTIWI took a different position within this debate. First, the representatives of the local social work organisations who were interviewed did not perceive this law as discriminatory against women but on the contrary cited the implementation of religious criminal laws as a way to improve the situation of women. Consequently, women who are active in these local social work organisations do not see the need to participate in the protest of the advocacy groups when the Islamic opposition party proposed the implementation of the Islamic criminal law in 1993. Nor was there a local coalition of women's organisations in Kelantan who showed signs of protest or disagreement in public. In the approach adopted by local social work organisations the concept of "dignity" is of fundamental importance. This position is based on the ambivalent combination of a strong regional identity with a global Islamic identity, as becomes clear in the following explanation that Roslina, one of Yayasan Murni's legal councillors, gave me about the *hudud* law:

> From our point of view there is nothing harmful about *hudud* law for women. On the contrary it has safeguarded women in terms of their dignity and their role. But in public the law has been publicised as if it would disregard women as human beings. But here in Kelantan I don't think we are going to get any response from NGOs, maybe because of our culture. In our culture we will accept anything that is related to religious affairs fully and heartily. If you really research yourself, you can see the benefits of *hudud*. You can see Saudi Arabia, they have implemented *hudud* and the number of rape cases there is very low. In general, the number of crimes against women is very low compared to other countries, which have never implemented *hudud* laws. I think that after the implementation of *hudud* laws we could see that it is able to cure some flaws in society. We in Kelantan are Muslims and we accept *hudud* as something that is part of Islam (Roslina, Yayasan Murni's legal councillor, (24 Oct 2004).

In this passage the perceived distinctiveness of her local space, "here in Kelantan," and the space that she describes as "the public"—probably the women's organisations and media in Kuala Lumpur—is very strong. This shows that Roslina was definitely aware of the debate that arose around the issue on a national level as well as the different positions. From her perspective, however, the law is not a law that "protects rapists" or "disregards women as human beings," but on the contrary is a law that is very beneficial for women, reducing the number of rapes and other crimes against women. While strongly arguing from a local identity Roslina is also aware of the global framework, bringing the example of Saudi Arabia as evidence for the positive effects of Islamic criminal law for women. In doing so she refers to a translocal discourse on Islam which tends to idealise the gender effect of Islamisation. The comparison with Saudi Arabia is a clear incidence of such an imagined Islamic community.

The same argument about the positive effects that Islamisation has for women comes up in the context of the gender segregation of the public space that has been enforced by the Islamist Party in Kelantan, and is a second point of debate with different positions among the women's organisations. Saleha, chair of WIJADI, comments on the gender segregation by means of separated queues for men and women in supermarkets and at bus stops: "In my eyes gender segregation is about protecting women. Because there are so many social ills, and you have to do something about it. For instance in the supermarket the separated queues are meant to protect women from being sexually harassed, from being pinched and touched" (Saleha, 24.10.04).

Both women share a similar discourse on the existence of social problems that are depicted as "social flaws" or "social ills," and about the specific gendered aspects of such problems. And they also share a discourse on the need of social transformation in order to tackle such social problems. In talking about discrimination ("disregard women as human beings"), rape, and sexual harassment, the concept of women's "dignity" is central. Women's dignity has to be "safeguarded" as Roslina said, and women should be "protected" as Saleha demanded. The introduction of Islamic criminal law and the gender segregation of public space are for these women two strategies to protect women from mistreatment, to improve the situation for women, and to secure their "dignity."

In contrast to this position the advocacy groups presented in this chapter harshly oppose gender segregation of the public space which in their eyes leads to a "steady erosion of [women's] freedom and rights in the areas of law and [. . .] justice in the Sharia system, social rights in the family, dress, public participation" (Murat 2004, 141). In many publications of Sisters in Islam and of other women's organisations from Kuala Lumpur the fact that women and men have to form different queues in supermarkets and at bus stops and that men and women cannot use swimming pools together is taken as two signs that "we are on the way to a restrictive society that uses religion to control women's lives" (Women's Aid Organisation 2002).

Also on a nondiscursive level of activism and of everyday life the question of space is debated and sometimes very provocatively negotiated by Sisters in Islam activists. During a dinner with Sisters in Islam activists that I attended, Maiza, one of the locally and translocally most active and well known members of Sisters in Islam, told the others very enthusiastically about a group of Muslim women in the United States who every Friday went to the mosque and wanted to pray in the male space, together with the men. Being denied the access to the male space with the argument of tradition these women had answered: 'OK, so what? If we are not allowed because of tradition, then we'll make something new.' After telling the story, Maiza suggested repeating this action in Malaysia: "We should go there on Friday and just reclaim the male space. What can they do? They can't do anything." During the same dinner, Airmy, another Sisters in Islam activist, tells the others about a meeting of oppositional Islamic groups such as the Islamic Party PAS, and the Islamic Youth Movement ABIM at the house of the former deputy Prime Minister Anwar Ibrahim who was still in prison at that time and who had become the icon of an oppositional movement. The organisers had put up a stage for the speaker and told the women to move to the back of the room. Full of indignation about this demand Airmy said: "But there you don't hear anything, you can't even see the speakers. So, I refused to go there. I just stayed in the front. And they got upset, some of the men even left the space around me. But I just did not understand why I should go to the back."

A third point which is controversially debated among the different types of women's organisations presented in this chapter are the different translocal orientations and the different means of reconstructing Malay cultural identity that lie behind these orientations. The positive orientation towards Arabic countries as a role model for Malaysian society which was highlighted by Roslina is particularly opposed by most of the female activists of Sisters in Islam or the other advocacy groups. In the context of the increasing standardisation of women's dress according to Islamic attire which is perceived to be based on Arabic models, Sisters in Islam officially supported a fashion show organised by the Malaysian government with 'traditional' Malay dress for women. Azila, a Malay activist from AWAM, expressed this rejection of an Arabic-oriented Islam very clearly:

I don't want to become Arabic in order to be a Muslim, I want to be able to keep my own culture and be Muslim at the same time. A lot of Malaysians are forgetting that we are Malays, some are forgetting that culture and religion are separate. I really do not want to become naïvely Arabic to prove that I am a good Muslim woman. (Azila, 10 Oct 2004)

What to Roslina in Kelantan appeared to be rooted in her "Muslim" culture, appears to be Arab and hence alien to the way Azila describes her "Malay" culture. Both women use a very strong culturalist language to describe their positions. In everyday life this opposition to an 'Arabic' Islam includes the rejection of Arabic-inspired attire, especially of the headscarf, in favour of a more 'Malay' style which is considered to be more colourful and feminine. A second way to oppose the dominance of an 'Arabic' Islam is the demonstrative performance of a transethnic habitus concerning food, dress, music, and social networks. Maiza, one of Sisters in Islam activists, explains this transethnic habitus in terms of "Malay fluidity":

> I am very secure in my Malay identity. It's my dressing, my culture of this softness of Malay women, this fluidity of it, this softness of it. [. . .] To me I could be wearing skirts one day and tomorrow I will be wearing Pakistani dress and next time I will be wearing *baju kurung*. [. . .] Another thing what I love about my culture is that Malays have always been very fluid regarding religion. We came from mysticism, Hinduism, and Islam. We have always been fluid. (Maiza, 20 April 2004)

These quotations illustrate the ongoing processes of reinventing and reconstructing Malay cultural identity (Pfaff-Czarnecka 2007). For the majority of the women activists in the middle class–oriented advocacy groups the 'Malay way' to practice Islam and to arrange gender relations stands for more space for personal choice, for being less rigid and asymmetric, and more open for the dialogue with other ethnic or religious groups. Doing so, gender equality is traditionalised and historicised in local culture while other types of gender relations which are perceived as being more rigid are alienated by labelling them 'Arab'. However, these cases show that of course giving the discourse on Islamisation a culturalist turn is not unproblematic at all. In Malaysia one risks being instrumentalised in the ethnonationalist politics of the government, as the example of the 'traditional' fashion show suggested. Unlike women from the advocacy groups most women in the local social work organisations, especially in Kelantan, draw on a very much religiously defined local 'Muslim' identity which is not associated with fluidity but instead with clear boundaries between different ethnic and religious groups and with a strong sense of religious authority.

On the level of the programmatic work of the organisation this opposition means challenging the monopoly of knowledge production of established centres of Islamic thought in Arab countries, such as the al-Azhar University in Cairo (Abaza 2002). The following quotations from Maiza from Sisters in Islam reveals the criticism of the Arab monopoly on interpretation and on the question of how Islam should be practised and lived. She pleads for an Islam that can be independent from Arab culture, and clearly supports the point of view that their own 'local' ways of interpretation are as valid and legitimate as any other Arab interpretation.

> We want to beat conservatism in religion. Some kind of people, let's say Arabs, they feel that they know the right Islam. Because the Prophet came from their origin, the Quran is revealed in their language, in Arab language. So, if you are not Arab, you have no qualification to interpret the Quran. We try to beat their argument, to challenge their argument. When you are a Muslim, whether you are Arab or non-Arab, your ability to understand the Quran and to interpret it is equivalent to all other believers. (Maiza, 24 Aug 2004)

What is developed in these quotations is a new type of legitimate everyday knowledge, a knowledge that takes into account diversity and that goes beyond the formal criteria of "traditional" Islamic jurisprudence. This type of knowledge that gives legitimation and authority (Salvatore 1997) to groups such as Sisters in Islam to participate in the public discourse and to challenge dominant interpretations and practices is based on the one hand on their own everyday life experiences of injustice and inequality as women and their own engagement in the cause of social transformation. On the other hand it is to a significant extent based on their translocally shared knowledge and experience with women's organisations in other Muslim countries (for translocal networking see chapter 7). From this socially embedded standpoint the validity of religious knowledge is evaluated.

Remembering what Roslina said about her perspective on religious criminal law another interesting point comes up which sheds light on the constitution of the public discourse concerning religious matters in Kelantan but also in Malaysia in general. Explaining the reaction of Kelantanese NGOs in contrast to other NGOs from outside, she said: "In our culture we will accept anything that is related to religious affairs fully and heartily." This quotation sheds light on the strong notion of authority and hierarchy concerning the production of religious knowledge. What the religious and state authorities have decided should and could not be questioned by other actors. In the interview with Masrina, the president of PERTIWI, this notion of a limited public discourse on religious matters becomes even clearer:

> Certain issues you don't talk about because sometimes it is not easy to talk. Like polygamy, there is nothing to talk about, because it is allowed. So what we do is just to ask for education. You educate the women and the men: The men not to have two wives and the women, not to be willing to accept another

woman's husband. That is the only way. You can't go against what is written in the Quran, including the head of Islamic law, the Sultans. You can't even talk about it. (Masrina, 16 Oct 2004)

That even Masrina, who is located at the centre of state institutions and of the National Women in Development Machinery (see above) does not see herself and the women's organisations as powerful enough to talk about religious matters such as polygyny is indicative of the communicative taboos related to this issue and the little authority that women have to participate in this discourse. Although combined with a strong sense of resignation she perceives herself and the other women in her organisation as not entitled to challenge established knowledge in the field of Islamic family law. To engage in a debate on the contents of law appears to her as "dabbling" in it, as illegitimately interfering in a field without entitlement. These incidents show the fragility of the public space in which such negotiations take place and the highly limited access to such space for actors—women, for example—who are not seen as being entitled to participate in the debate (Nageeb, Sieveking, Spiegel 2005a). For the women in Kelantan the access to the public space appears to be even more restricted. In the case of the introduction of the Kelantan Criminal Code the opponents of the code were accused of apostasy which made a local inner-Islamic discourse very difficult. The fact that the local Kelantanese women's organisation, WIJADI, was one of twelve women's organisations that signed a statement against the enactment of the *hudud* laws in Terengganu, the neighbouring state, while the organisation did not make a public statement concerning the religious criminal law in their own state gives an idea of how restricted the local space for women's organisations in Kelantan is. Only in a space in which they were not embedded through their everyday life was it possible for them to participate in a public debate.

Masrina, who perceived it as impossible to participate at that level of public discourse, adopts an educational approach that is more oriented towards agency and everyday social practices at the ground with the aim to educate women and men not to choose the possibility of a polygynic marriage, but without changing the legal foundations. She stands for an approach that privileges alternative and transformative everyday practices over alternative public discourses concerning religious issues.

One telling example of the transformative power of this everyday life–oriented approach are the trajectories of the women on the ground who are organised in social work organisations such as WIJADI. The case of Nazia showed how power relations in the family could be changed and how completely new models of female agency can actually emerge. Nazia, a divorced woman, describes this new type of female agency: "We have to trust ourselves first, and then we can trust our husbands. I don't think about a second husband any more, I just think about earning money for me and my children. Now I know that my husband is not important." And laughing she added: "I think if I would marry again I could not be a good wife anymore." In this context the question of the control over assets and property, but also of the limitations to women's agency were central for the women. Saleha, the executive officer and chairperson of WIJADI, criticises these power structures openly: "Our Malay women, when they marry, everything goes to the husband. When they marry they don't have their own identity any more. The wife cannot go out anymore. She has to ask for permission from her husband." To break with this financial and social dependence from the husbands was the most significant experience for the women who have organised themselves in the women's groups. As Nazia's statement above indicates, the women stressed the fact that through their activities in WIJADI they had learned to be economically independent from their husbands and to live independent lives on their own.

The women build a space where established norms for gender relations can be challenged, as Nazia's joke about the fact that now, having realised her own strength, she would not be able to be a "good wife" anymore shows. In her opinion being a good wife means to accept anything the husband says without protest and to devote her life to her husband. Also the idea of polygyny can be debated and challenged within this space. Asked about polygyny, Nazia, whose husband had taken a second wife and then left her, answered: "I would agree, if it would be fair. But the husband cannot be fair, this is impossible, the first wife is abandoned by the husband and he only looks for the second wife. The first woman does not have her husband anymore, she loses her husband. And she only depends on her own" (21.10.04). This argumentation is embedded in her personal experiences and contradicts the position that Muslim men have the right to marry up to four women, which is very strongly propagated by Islamist opposition party PAS.

Both cases are an example of the constitution of a female space where common constructs of gender, namely women as dependent and obedient wives, are silently challenged and new models of female agency that are related to economic independence and social and moral strength are constructed. Within this space issues which women in Kelantan cannot negotiate in public such as polygyny are also critically debated on an everyday life level. Within this approach specific socially embedded modes of social transformation are developed. These modes of social transformation, however, are not recognised by parts of the urban, middle class–oriented women's organisations, as the strong criticism of the social work–oriented women's organisation in Kelantan by members of the advocacy groups showed.

Conclusion

Women's organisations in Malaysia take up very diverse and ambivalent positions within the process of negotiating gender relations and the meaning of religion. On the one hand the social work–oriented organisations provide women with space where they negotiate dominant gender relations and power structures in the family. On this everyday life level dominant discourses and models of how a "good wife" should behave and also polygyny are challenged. The aim of these locally embedded women's groups is the empowerment of individual women and the concrete change in the lives of women by giving them skills and providing knowledge about legal matters. However, it seems that this does not lead to the participation in debates in the public sphere about existing laws and to the challenge of hierarchies and unequal entitlements in the process of knowledge production concerning religious issues.

On the other hand women's organisations from the capital are more disconnected from the concrete local context and seek a transformation of society through public education and law reform. Working on a much more abstract level, organisations like the WAO and Sisters in Islam are actively promoting law reform, both of the civil and the Sharia family law. These organisations constantly monitor the performance of the state to fulfil its responsibilities concerning gender equality. CEDAW plays an essential role in this process (see chapter 7). Within these organisations women claim their right to engage in a process of social transformation that categorically includes the transformation of laws. These women's organisations strategically use symbolic means, such as consumer culture and media, as a potential means to constitute a new public space for debates about gender relations.

Women in both Kuala Lumpur and in Kelantan negotiate corresponding issues: discrimination, rape, and sexual harassment. Advocacy organisations in Kuala Lumpur address these issues in the language of the global women's movement as "violence against women"; women in the social work–oriented organisations address them as questions of "female dignity." While there is a parallel of issues addressed within this translocal religious discourse and the discourse of a global women's movement with a more or less secular self-understanding, the localisation of these issues takes different forms. In the case of the women's organisations in Kelantan, the criticised phenomena are conceptualised as "social ills," or "flaws in society" that can be remedied by the implementation of Islamic criminal laws, such as *hudud*, or by segregating gender in public spaces. In the discourse of the middle class–oriented organisations in Kuala Lumpur, violence against women is explained in the framework of feminist theory as a result of uneven power relations between men and women in society and is seen to be endured because of the very process of Islamisation and the implementation of Islamic criminal laws.

The diversity in the approaches towards Islamisation is internally debated within the women's movement and is embedded in a complex set of othering processes among the women's organisations. These contradictions and debates show an ongoing process of negotiation of gender relations and the meaning of religion, but also on different types of activism within different frames of space and time. Both types of organisations contribute to the negotiation of gender relations and the meaning and range of Islam in a modern society like Malaysia.

Notes

1. This development is of course embedded in the changes of the global economic system, the new global division of labour, but it is also the result of forty years of development policies of a developmentalist state with ever-increasing authoritarian features.

2. I conducted my research in Malaysia as a research assistant of the VW research project "Negotiating development: translocal gendered spaces in Muslim societies" at the Sociology of Development Research Centre, Bielefeld University.

3. The operation Lalang, as it is known in the public, was based on the Internal Security Act (ISA) which is one of the most repressive laws that is implemented against civil society actors in Malaysia. It allows the detention without trial up to two years if the government perceives internal security to be threatened. Recently the act has played an important role in the government's antiterrorism policies.

4. This is only one of the restrictive regulations that limit democratic space in Malaysia. The Sedition Act, which penalises statements that might lead to conflicts between the different ethnic groups in Malaysia, the University and College Act, which penalises political activities of students, and the Union Act, which penalises the constitution of national unions, are other examples of the restriction of democratic space in Malaysia. Furthermore, the state's practices of registration for nongovernmental organisations are another example of the limitation of the democratic space. Malaysian government is that restrictive, that some of the most vocal national NGOs as well as branches of internationally established NGOs have not succeeded in getting registered as "societies." Amnesty International, for example, has been applying for registration as "society" under the Society Act for ten years now and has been rejected four times. Still, in order to achieve a legal basis for their activities, these organisations opted to register themselves as companies. The denial of the status as society has to be interpreted as the denial to acknowledge critical civil society actors as equal partners in a public debate about important societal issues (Weiss, Hassan 2003a, 7). NGOs are not acknowledged to participate in the redefinition of important social issues. Although it gives legal certainty to some extent, being registered as a 'company' is a very fragile and ambiguous legal basis for NGOs, as of course their work goes be-

yond the activities of a normal company. That means that they are pushed to the margins of legality and can be objects of state arbitrariness. In the case that an organisation is considered too critical this registration can be withdrawn very easily (Lim Teck Ghee 1995, 167).

5. The symbolism of consumption in the malls is twofold: consumption is symbolic because it is not a mere act of purchasing a good, but is deeply related to the performance and consumption of identities (Gerke 1999), in that case the performance of a global middle-class identity. But for a considerable part of the population, who is not part of this middle-class, it is also symbolic in the sense that the consumption in most cases . . . goes not further than window shopping" (Abaza 2004). One could speak about a symbolic participation in symbolic consumption.

6. In Malaysia especially the KLCC (Kuala Lumpur City Centre) Shopping Centre is intimately linked with the modernistic and developmentalist economic and social visions of the former Prime Minister Dr. Mahathir. Construction of the Twin Towers was completed in 1998 and at that time they were the highest buildings in the world. They symbolise economic competition and the successful cooperation of the government and the private sector "Malaysia Inc." Two companies from Japan and Korea were competing in the construction, each of then building one tower. The national petrol company PETRONAS occupies the main part of the building (Evers, Gerke 1999).

CHAPTER FOUR

~

Women's Organisations and Their Agendas in Sudan: Interfaces in Different Arenas

Salma A. Nageeb

Peace, Development, and Political Transformation: An Introduction

A joke circulating in Sudan at the time that this research was conducted was as follows: "The Muslim brothers came to power in Sudan and started shouting, 'Go to the mosque or you will go to hell'. When they made sure that all the people went to the mosque they ran out of it and shouted sarcastically from the window, 'Ha, ha; now you are all kept here no one can compete with us in the market.'" The joke refers to both the Islamisation project, which was adopted by the Islamist regime in Sudan in 1989 as well as the recent changes in the regime's politics. These recent changes are associated with the peace negotiation and the signing in January 2004 of the Comprehensive Peace Agreement (CPA) between the government of Khartoum represented by the National Congress Party (NCP)[1] and Sudan's People Liberation Movement/Army (SPLM/A), officially ending the longest war in Africa between the North and South of Sudan.[2]

For the two signing parties—the Islamist regime governing Sudan since 1989, and the SPLM/A—the CPA is a political compromise that ends a war which both parties failed to win through military means. For them the peace agreement is a process of partial political transformation that aims at resituating the signing parties in the political map of Sudan without fundamentally questioning the political legitimacy of the current regime (Elbatahani 2004).

On the basis of this partial political transformation Islamists renounced some of their political power over the SPLM/A and the latter accepted the sharing of power with a movement against which they had been fighting for a long time. According to this political compromise, and as expressed in the above joke by reference to the market, the priorities of the peace agreement pertain to questions of the distribution of wealth and power. Indeed this means that the state will not be entirely monopolised by the totalitarian Islamist regime. Nevertheless to make peace in Sudan a fundamental political transformation that would go hand in hand with questioning the legitimacy of the current regime and its political orientation is not a central issue for the two signing parties. Thus, the NCP remains the biggest party in power.

"There is no peace without development and no development without peace." This statement is often repeated in different occasions by state officials, NGO activists, donor organisations, journalists, and social actors who are involved in the fields of politics and development. Though peacebuilding seems to be the concern of the various social actors, there exist considerable differences between the perspectives of the government and that of civil society activists. The partial political transformation mentioned above makes many actors, such as some oppositional parties and NGOs, sceptical about whether the peace agreement will lead to real democratisation in Sudan. Nevertheless the CPA creates a new political reality that allows room for the participation of other actors in peacebuilding. Within this space many political actors seek to situate their perspectives on peacebuilding as a process of addressing the fundamental questions of democratisation in Sudan.

Indeed it is still early to attempt to evaluate how the CPA is implemented; how the implementation process is negotiated by the various stakeholders and which political, sociocultural, and economic transformations have resulted from the implementation of the agreement. However, to understand how development is negotiated it can be viewed as a process whereby different actors are resituating themselves and their development perspectives in the development scenery. These actors include NGOs and especially women's organisations—as one of the most relevant actors, political parties, and international development agencies whose role in local politics of development was systematically marginalised by the Islamist regime before the beginning of peace negotiations in 1997.[3]

Typical at this stage, where different actors are trying to utilise the available political space and negotiate peace and development, is the increase in organised NGO events, particularly in the capital Khartoum where the government and most of the international development organisations are located. The intensification of NGO activities—such as workshops, training programmes, conferences, roundtables, and the like—reflects the attempt of the various social and political actors to place their agency in the field of peace and development.

An example of these events will be considered in this chapter in order to identify, study, and analyse the following issues: who are the main actors in the field of women NGOs? What are their main agendas? And how are their agency and agendas situated within the local peace and development context? Here it is significant to stress that by focusing on discourses and representations of women's NGOs, who are mostly urban based and dominated by educated middle-class women, the agency of this development actor articulates an elite or privileged political and class perspective. However, discourses surrounding issues of gender, peace, and politics in Sudan are still dependant on a specific (privileged) position (Bilal 2004), and on where local development policies and politics are basically shaped, that is, the urban centres and particularly the capital. In addition the one-year-old peacebuilding process is still predominantly negotiated at the national level in urban areas.

To elaborate on these issues this chapter will be organised into five sections. Section one presents a workshop on the Convention for the Elimination of all Forms of Discrimination against Women (CEDAW) as a typical example of an organised event of women's NGOs.[4] Thereby this section aims at introducing the main actors, discourses, and agendas of women's NGOs. The second section presents an overview on the interfaces between the state and women's NGOs and the way these interfaces shape the agendas of women's organisations. The third section focuses on analysing how the current agendas of women's NGOs are situated in the political and public levels. To take the discussion further, the fourth section of this chapter shows how the othering relation between women NGOs is shaping the constitution of social space by women's NGOs. In the fifth section the different types of women's activists and the way they position themselves will be presented. A concluding section will then bring the main arguments of the chapter into focus.

Zooming In: An Event of Women's NGOs

Time: a very hot October morning. It was announced on the radio and TV that people should not leave their houses and offices between 12 and 3 in the afternoon in order to avoid sun stroke.

Place: a meeting room at one of the UNDP offices in Khartoum. The room is darkened with a shaded glass at the windows, furnished with an imported meeting-set, and cooled with a huge split unit. When I entered the room with my companion, who felt very exhausted from the heat outside, she said "Al-hamdoliallah the workshop is organised here, no heat anymore. And this atmosphere is also good for the discussion; one forgets that one is in Khartoum." Laughingly she added, "We can talk freely." This comment referred to a local debate on a government plan to issue an act to organise the work of non-governmental organisations after the signing of the CPA. The possibility of adopting this proposed act created a wide debate among NGOs who criticised this plan as intending to limit the freedom of NGOs and the possibilities of (positive) partnership between the state and nongovernmental organisations. The proposed bill is perceived as a hindrance to the work of NGOs.[5] Different local newspapers each devoted a space to present the position of the NGOs concerning this act. In general it is viewed as running against the main principles that the state should follow to achieve peace. Many NGO activists point out that the proposed bill reflects the contradiction between the discourse and practice of the government.

Event[6]: A workshop financed by the UNDP to discuss women's rights and CEDAW, which was open for the interested public to participate. I attended the workshop with one of the participants with whose organisation I was doing participatory observation at the time. The workshop was part of the activities which the UNDP sponsors and organises to support the process of democratisation and peacebuilding in Sudan. The peacebuilding agenda, according to the discussion during this workshop, could be divided into two main issues: the implementation of the peace agreement and the issue of regional conflict particularly in Darfur.

There was a group of around thirty participants who were already taking their seats when we arrived. The majority of them I recognised as NGO members. There were also some journalists, a representative of the ministry of social planning, and two or three persons coming from European-based organisations. About one-third of the participants were men. Most of them were from human rights organisations in addition to some religious figures.

The meeting started with a small opening speech from a representative of the UNDP, who is a local staff member. She greeted the participants and in particular welcomed some of the religious figures, the director of the Women and Development Desk at the Royal Netherlands Embassy, and the speakers. She then explained how the workshop would be organised and gave the floor to the first speaker.

The first speaker was a female activist who works closely, on a consultancy basis, with the UNDP. She was wearing a traditional Sudanese dress. She delivered her presentation entirely in Arabic. One of my acquaintances who works for a local women's NGO and was sitting next to me could not stop herself from commenting about the presentation of the first speaker. She said: "This presentation is a recycled paper. I assure you this presentation is going to be a recycled paper. But she captures the UNDP and gets all their consultancies; poor [activists] like me have no chance." Such kind of comments one hears very often nowadays in Sudan and it reflects the level of competition among women's NGOs and activists. The competition among women NGOs is particularly growing because of the amount of funds directed to Sudan by the international development agencies in order to support the peacebuilding process. But more importantly this comment shows the differential nature and types of actors who are involved in women's issues. One of the ways used by NGO activists to draw difference between women activists and to characterise them is to describe their relation to international development agencies. In this sense the first speaker is categorised by NGO activists as a translocal actor who networks closely with international development agencies. Activists like the first speaker represent the local epistemic community whose knowledge and expertise in women's issues is significant for linking the international development agents with the local NGOs and communities, and relating gender as an international discourse and analytical tool to the different realities of Sudanese women. This (gender) epistemic community is dominated by a small number of female academics and researchers. The research and consultancies which they conduct for international development agencies are one of the major information sources on women, gender, and the local context. Due to the lack of this type of information the expertise of these women is in high demand, resulting in strong networking relations between this epistemic community and international development agencies.

The first speaker's presentation focused on a discussion of the sociocultural position of Sudanese women and related it to the importance of ratifying CEDAW. Her twenty-minute presentation was based on a rather generalised gender perspective which considered rural/urban classification without integrating other forms of gendered social differentiations such as ethnicity, religion, class, or region. The floor was then given to the second speaker.

The second speaker was a religious sheikh in his mid-sixties who was introduced as an Islamic scholar. The sheikh was involved in the campaign for the eradication of Female Genital Mutilation/Circumcision (FGM/C). He also participates in HIV/AIDS and reproductive health activities. In a different workshop, where the sheikh was also presenting, one of the female activists commented about him saying (laughingly): "Now comes the presentation of the Imam of the women's NGOs." Women's NGOs often cooperate with this sheikh to give an Islamic legitimacy to their programmes and agendas. He is known to be an Islamic and not an Islamist activist, meaning he does not belong to the National Islamic Front (NIF)—the organisation which led the Islamist coup in the early 1990s.

The sheikh focused his speech on the different rights that Islam granted for women. He emphasised that there are no contradictions between Islam and other sources of human and women's rights. This, according to the sheikh, is due to the fact that the main purpose of Islam is to dignify human beings and in particular women (for a similar approach in Malaysia see chapter 3). He then, in his (positively) simplified manner stressed that he did not understand "all the fuss about CEDAW. It is a human, not a God-made law, it can be changed but only by working on it and making sure that there is nothing in it that contradicts the basic principles of Islam."

The third speaker was a female activist in her late thirties. During her university time she was known as a left-wing political activist, with strong ties to the communist party. She represents a type of women's activism that is locally—among NGOs and intellectual communities—known as progressive, meaning those who are very critical about the state's Islamisation project. She was dressed in a Western style, and it seemed as though she could not manage to keep English phrases and terms from her planned Arabic presentation. She focused on highlighting the contradictions between the different Sudanese legal sources and CEDAW. She also stressed that CEDAW does not contradict the basic principles of Islam, otherwise an Islamic government like that of the Kingdom of Saudi Arabia would not have—albeit with some reservations—ratified the convention. She ended her presentation by recommending that women activists should not focus only on the adoption of CEDAW by the government. Rather they should pay equal attention to the process of writing the new constitution, which is part of the peacebuilding process, and they should make sure that women's interests are included there. Such a conclusion is indicative of a typical activist who takes an active role in the various current debates such as engendering democracy, the constitution, and the peace process.

After the three presentations there was a break. I was greeting some of my acquaintances when there was a slight outburst. A woman in her sixties wearing a traditional dress accompanied with a veil, in a style which is typical for members of NIF, was complaining to the organiser of the workshop. In an agitated manner she stated that the UNDP excludes "them" (meaning women who belong to NIF) from speaking at such events and that they were left with no chance to contribute except during the discussion.

When the workshop was resumed and the floor was opened for the comments of the participants this woman was the first to ask for a chance to speak, and she was the first to be given the floor. She was loud and agitated. She attacked all the speakers arguing that "they talk about CEDAW as if it is innocent" and that CEDAW contains "very dangerous articles for the Islamic identity." She referred to issues of sexual and reproductive rights to elaborate her point. And she stated that "CEDAW is one of the conspiracies of the West to limit the number of Muslims in the world by supporting abortion and contraceptives use."

Despite the fact that many participants became agitated to have the chance to comment, the floor was given to a young woman. She was veiled by combining a Western style with a big head scarf. I expected that her intervention would be along the same lines of the previous commenter, as from her veiling style I immediately associated her with members of the NIF.[7] But to my surprise the speaker had a different position.

The speaker, whom I later learnt had studied in the United States and belongs, as I expected, to the NIF where she works in a leading position in the youth administration of the party, was very articulate and eloquent. Her English, which she sometimes used to make her point clear, was of a strong American accent. She directed her comment to the previous speaker attacking her position as representing a closed Islam which is damaging for the status of Muslims around the globe. She then argued that "if Islam is not opening up it will be left behind, it will be dead. And we [referring to her organisation] are not against any international conventions. We are *Isslamy-een*[8] but progressive ones. We are calling for the opening up of Islam to all global changes." This position represents a growing discourse and movement among Islamists in Sudan. It became particularly strong after the events of 11 September 2001. And to a large extent it represents the current discursive position of the government.

The fourth speaker was a man in his late sixties who is known by many to be a sympathiser with the NIF, and he works for one of the Islamic charity organisations. He (in a pedagogical manner directed mainly to the previous speakers) tried to distance himself from the conspiracy discourse of the first commenter with whom the discussion session started. Nevertheless he emphasised that Islam is a religion which is valid for all times and places and that Muslims should seek solutions to their problems within this frame. Later when I had the chance to talk to the young Islamist woman, who represents progressive Islamists, she classified the position of this speaker as "conservative Islamists, who keep a low profile in politics, they don't politicise things too much, but they have the same ideas like the closed Islamists."

The discussion went on for quite a time in this direction until a speaker from the Nuba Mountains changed its direction. The middle-aged woman is an activist in the Peace Network, a network of women's organisations working in the area of peace and supported by the Women and Development Desk of the Royal Netherlands Embassy. Many organisations from the regions of conflict like the south and the Nuba Mountains are active in this network. The speaker said (in Arabic): "Please let us not forget that this Sudan is not only inhabited by Muslims. Now the peace agreement is provisionally signed and all of us Sudanese with different religions and different colours and languages have to give each other the chance to live in peace in this country." She then argued that what is important for her is not whether CEDAW contradicts Islam and Christianity or not. What is important is whether the signing of the convention will bring any changes to the lives of poor women in the Nuba Mountains and in other marginalised parts of Sudan. She went on, inviting all those participating to focus on what she called "real issues and problems," which she specified as "how to make the peace agreement a reality? How to stop the conflict in Darfur and save the women who are being raped every day? How to feed the hungry people? And how to fight poverty? These are issues that we should focus on as long as the government is not paying much attention."

At this point in the discussion a representative of the General Union for Sudanese Women (GUSW) became restless and insistently asked for the floor. The GUSW is a state-affiliated organisation. It is the official representative of women and women's interests. Thus it is led by activists known as *kozat*, a local term used publicly to refer to the female members of the NIF. The organisation has an official position of power and works closely with various state institutions. The speaker directed her intervention to answer some of the issues raised by the Nuba Mountain activist. She started by stressing that the GUSW is directing its programmes to fill the gaps of the government. Thus the various departments of the Union, be it the health, economic, education, legal, and social departments, are working intensively to improve the status of Sudanese women and to address their special needs. She then elaborated that the twenty-seven regional offices of the union enable it to reach women all over the country without any discrimination. And that the Union is working closely with local administration and social leaders, a fact which makes it an acceptable umbrella to address women's problems. She then shifted her focus to the issue of Darfur, saying:

> As concerning the problems in Darfur and the issue of rape, these are scattered cases that we should not make very big. The Union is following the issue closely, and our reports confirm that rape in Darfur is not an organised crime. We are surely calling for the punishment of whoever commits such a crime.

But we should also be careful and not play the game of the Western media. Rape is a bad thing and it might happen in any conflict situation, but let us not exaggerate it and give the West a hand in our local affairs.

One of the participants could not help herself from speaking without been given the floor. She was then asked by the moderator to introduce herself and speak. She is an activist working for a local NGO specialised in the area of training and advocacy. She is one of the activists who identifies herself as feminist. She received much training abroad in Asia and Europe; in addition she is involved in various translocal networks. Accordingly she is often travelling, a fact which makes some women activists characterise her and similar women as "the activists of the airplanes." This labelling is referring to the women activism which is focusing more on translocal networking than on working with the so-called grassroots.

The feminist activist, who had been subjected many times to security investigation during the 1990s when the government was severely restricting civil activism, focused her intervention on the issues raised by the representative of the GUSW. She attacked her, saying, "you represent the position of the government and not the position of Sudanese women." She then went on to elaborate on the issue of rape in Darfur and that it is an organised war crime and women NGOs should unite and concentrate their efforts to address this problem no matter what it costs them.

The discussion went on raising similar issues such as Darfur conflict, regional inequality, and poverty. At the end of the workshop the participants clustered in groups, networking together and discussing various issues. One important invitation was then distributed by a local NGO working mainly on the area of legal aid. The invitation was to a one-day workshop on women and the new constitution. The workshop was funded by the Friedrich Ebert Foundation[9] and various civil activists were participating. It is another event of women NGOs that is organised in collaboration with an international development agent, and reflects the frequency of such events in the context of peacebuilding. I took my invitation, packed my things and left the place to be met again by the heat of Khartoum.

Women's NGOs and the State

How are the current development discourses structured? And what are their gender implications? To answer these questions one needs to refer to the state's Islamisation project. For more than a decade (1989–2001) the Islamist regime in Sudan had tried to implement an Islamisation project. This project can best be described as an acculturation project which aimed at changing all spheres of life according to the Islam discourse of the state. The homogenisation process that was intended to draw in the different cultural orientations and ways of life in Sudan under the frame of the Islamic way of life as envisaged by the Islamist state was based on a demarcation between what is Islamic and what is foreign to Islam according to the view of the Islamists. Various global development concepts such as human rights or gender equality were classified as non-Islamic, non-Sudanese, and as ways to channel foreign interest to the country. Hence civil society organisations, and in particular women's organisations who are working with global development agendas, were mostly banned, and those which were able to function were severely monitored and often harassed by the state security. The implementation of the Islamisation project was thus a process that attempted to decrease and control the role of political agents other than the Islamist state and the sympathising organisations and actors in local politics and development (see for example Ahmadi 2003, Nageeb 2004, Haider 2004). The Islamist state had completely controlled and monopolised development orientation, the agricultural sector and social services, whereby NGOs saw themselves driven to adopt global development visions and working mainly in urban areas.

On the other hand one major policy of Islamists in Sudan was to strengthen the role of NGOs which sympathise with the Islamisation project of the state. This was the result of the fact that one of the political means which the Islamists attempted to utilise in order to crystallise and implement the Islamisation project was to limit the power of the state by expanding the role of Islamist NGOs (Bilal 2004: 23–24). The first Comprehensive National Strategy (CNS) that devoted a special section to the role of NGOs in economic and social development was the CNS of 1992–2000, adopted by the Islamists during the first years of their ruling. The CNS defines voluntary and NGO work as humanitarian in nature, and thus argues that it should have no political agendas or aims (Elnagar 2002). Within this context and through the expansion of the role of Islamist NGOs, the latter were almost given "free reign" and received material and nonmaterial facilities from the state, to the extent that some of them replaced the state's functions.[10] Consequently, while Islamic NGOs were positioned as major actors in the field of development, the room for manoeuvre for non-Islamist NGOs dwindled during this time.

After the signing of the Khartoum Peace Agreement in 1997 the above picture started to gradually change. While government was considering some political changes to prepare for the final peace agreement the number and volume of NGOs activities began to steadily increase. Women's NGOs and

NGO networks which were formed to influence the negotiation processes were coming into existence as a result of the support of various international organisations such as the Women and Development Desk of the Royal Netherlands Embassy in Khartoum. What is important about this stage was that different global development concepts were gaining new significance as agendas for women NGOs in the context of peace negotiation. Old agendas such as poverty, displaced women, and FGM/C—for example, received more political weight since they were the agendas linked to the political issues of regional or ethnic inequality, violence, and human rights. At the same time agendas such as women and peace, gender and conflict, and conflict resolution are global development concepts. These agendas are accepted by the Islamist state as a frame for women's organisations to engage in the process of peace negotiations. The state is instrumentalising civil society organisations to reflect to the international community, which is supporting the peace negotiations and agreement, its commitment towards the participation of the civil society, and in particularly women's organisations in the process of peacebuilding. However, what is interesting here is the fact that under the frame of peace negotiations various women's organisations, who were initially working on different issues, are coming together as networks recognised also by the state to address issues of relevance to the peacebuilding agenda of Sudan and to situate old agendas within the political frame of peacebuilding.

The local pressure to end the war was one major reason for Sudanese women activists to direct their work to the area of peace. However, this orientation towards the agendas of peace has to be understood within the frame of the international discourse on women and peace. The discourse on women and peace gained international attention as a major agenda for women's organisations during and after the UN World Conference on Women in Beijing in 1995. Peacemaking, engendering peace, and promoting the culture of peace and conflict resolution are all agendas and discourses which received special attention and support from international donors after the fifth international women's conference. The role of women as well as civil society organisations in general in peacemaking is considered to be important in influencing and applying pressure on both the official as well as the societal levels. However, according to this international discourse on women and peace, women are constructed basically as victims of war who are essentially (and even naturally) motivated and directed to making peace (Hilhorst and Leeuwen 2005: 2). The undifferentiated construction of women in the women and peace international discourse and agenda is also characteristic of the local initiatives in the area of peace and development. That is to say: local engagements, discourses, and agendas of women NGOs in peacebuilding tend to homogenise Sudanese women and pay little attention to the diversities of gender, gender division of labour, women's roles, and social positions.

Nevertheless without the support of the international community, which tried to facilitate the inclusion of women in the process of peace negotiations, the role of women's NGOs in peacebuilding would have been even more marginalised. Thus discursive proximity between the discourse of local women NGOs and that of the international development agencies is observable. Specifically the political environment was not—and is still not to some extent—conducive to non-Islamist NGOs' engagement in development, hence they operate within a frame of dependency on international donors.

The current agendas of women's NGOs focus on the process of peacebuilding in Sudan. This includes various women and gender concerns which are not necessarily new (Badri 2005). However, women NGOs are attempting to place these concerns within the context of the new peace development in Sudan. The next section of the chapter will shed light on these agendas and how women activists are situating themselves.

Women's Agendas and Organisations: Between "Gender" and "Islam"

Considering the CEDAW workshop, the processes of identifying the agendas, prioritising them, situating peace and development perspectives, and representing the political dispositions are all taking place in an interactive relational frame. Peace agendas are positioned, first, in relation to how the government approaches the implementation of the CPA; second, while interacting and relating (or othering) to the perspective of others in the workshop; and third, in the context of an event financed by an international development agent. To analyse how the peace and development agendas of women's NGOs are situated in the peacebuilding process it is important to link them to the relations between women's NGOs and the state, and how this relation is shaped by an othering process based on the relation of women's NGOs to global gender discourses. To do so the current agendas of women's NGOs will be discussed by referring to two types of NGOs: NGOs which are adopting a global gender frame and discourses locally referred to as *munazmat elgender*, meaning the "gender organisations," and NGOs which sympathise with the state Islamisation politics locally known as *elmunazmat elisslamia*, meaning the Islamist organisations. This is rather a rough categorisation, since not all women's NGOs which are classified as gender-related have a unified approach to women and gender issues. In addition, many of the so-called Islamist organisations are not adopting an Islamist frame of politics. Some might be Islamic and not Islamist: meaning their work is dominated by an Islamic charity approach rather than focusing on directly supporting the local politics of Islamists in Sudan. However, for the sake of analysis this categorisation of women's NGOs will help in drawing the general picture about the situatedness of the different women's organisations and their agendas at the local level.

To discuss the agendas of the first type of women's NGOs, namely gender organisations, it is worth referring to the local discussion on CEDAW which is representative of one of the agendas of these organisations. The discussion on CEDAW is currently taking a new dimension and importance. It had been an issue for "gender NGOs" for a long time, though due to the government's repressive policies and practices during the 1990s this discussion remained relatively limited. Today, particularly in relation to the peacebuilding and the drafting of the new constitution, it has gained special importance. Discursively, the state has attempted to reflect an affirmative position with that of the international community in issues related to human and women's rights, conflict resolution and political participation. Thus women's NGOs gained more space to elaborate their perspectives regarding these issues. However, due to the structured oppositional relation between the gender NGOs and the state, the peace and development discourses of women's NGOs are oriented basically towards advocacy of global development concepts and discourses, and are dependent on the considerable political and financial support of international donors (see chapter 8). Thus, human rights, engendering the constitution, democracy, and the peace process are some of the major agendas for women's NGOs which are today advocated by adopting a gender perspective in Sudan. These agendas represent a counterhegemonic discourse which seeks to defy the domination of the state and its ideology by emphasising agency, participation, and equality of rights. The discourses of women's NGOs are thus largely shaped around the principles of human, as opposed to economic, development.

The discourse of these gender NGOs tends to construct Sudanese women within a homogenising victimisation frame, yet these organisations position their perspective in the public sphere by emphasising the role of women's agency in building peace. These largely undifferentiated discursive practices are means to claim knowledge about (the) Sudanese women, and presentation of this knowledge means power. Through this power, gender NGOs present the concerns of different Sudanese women as united and similar. Particularly within the context of peace, these discursive practices tend to be intensified. The women and peace agendas are presented by referring to women as sharing the same experiences as mothers and wives, suffering more (than men) from war and violence and being more (or even naturally) inclined to peace. The construction of women as victims is at the same time linked to their role as agents in creating peace. Despite the limitation of these discursive practices, it represents a significant strategy for situating women's agendas at the political level. These discourses help women to unify their perspectives and agendas. Through this discursive strategy gender organisations tend to counter the state hegemony by claiming power to represent the needs, problems, position, or agendas of (the victimised) Sudanese women. While doing so they advocate a more democratic and horizontal development and peace.

It is interesting to observe the similarity of the agendas of the different—according to the ethnic or religious background—gender organisations within the frame of peace. Indeed there exist variations in the way the different organisations prioritize their agendas. However, the discursive practices are largely based on a generalised gender frame. The global development concepts such as good governance, political participation, gender mainstreaming, or women and peace, which represent funding priorities for international development organisations working in the area of peace in Sudan, are thus framing the definition of the local agendas of gender NGOs. Because of this discursive approximation between the discourse of gender organisations and that of the international development agents, the agendas, discourses, and orientations of these types of organisations are often locally perceived as foreign, or not really Sudanese, specifically by Islamists and their sympathisers.

To constitute a space for their activities, one dimension of representing, legitimising, and positioning the agendas of gender organisations in the local context is by relating it to a progressive discourse on Islam. The role of the sheikh in the previously presented event is an example speaking to this effect. To combat Female Genital Mutilation/Circumcision (FGM/C), raise the awareness of HIV/AIDS, implement a reproductive health programme, advocate adult education activities, or discuss CEDAW, a progressive Islamic opinion is considered as a means to legitimise these agendas. Accordingly, one way through which global development concepts are situated in the context of peace and development is by Islamically legitimising these concepts.

Another strategy which the gender NGOs adopt in order to be able to manoeuvre within the legitimised space is to avoid politicising socially controversial issues such as sexual rights. Such issues might be discussed as part of the agendas of FGM/C, HIV/AIDS, legal aid, reproductive, or maternity health. Nevertheless they are not conceptualised nor discoursed as agendas of rights, be they human, sexual, or reproductive rights. Both of these strategies of legitimising the agenda of gender organisations by linking it to a progressive Islam interpretation, and the avoidance of politicising and problematising socially controversial issues are important for constituting a space and situating the agendas of these organisations. Through these strategies gender organisations ensure the embodiment of a certain public morality in their discourse. In addition they localise their global discursive frame by making it sensitive to the social gendered morality ideals.

A third (and reversed) strategy of politicising women and gender issues is also reflected by the example of the workshop. There are various other issues, such as unequal regional development and the problem of the marginalisation of some regions like Darfur, violence against women, conflict resolution, or illiteracy and poverty. All of these issues are gaining special importance within the frame of building a peaceful Sudan. Gender NGOs raise these issues while linking them directly to the local political agenda; for example, the drafting of the new constitution, conflict in Darfur and unequal regional development, and the policies and activities of the UN in Sudan, particularly the United Nations Advanced Mission in Sudan (UNAMIS), which is a mission reporting directly to the secretary general of the UN on the implementation of the peace agreement and the conflict in Darfur. In other words, gender NGOs situate their agendas, which are not socially controversial, by politicising and linking them directly to the main peace and development agendas of the state, a strategy which they avoided in the 1990s, during the phase of implementing the Islamisation project (see chapter 8).

The second type of women's NGOs, which support the state Islamisation project and are locally known as Islamist organisations work in various fields that include peace, health, education, poverty, and income-generating activities. Their work is principally characterised either by charity or WID approaches. That is to say: their approaches do not explicitly focus on questioning or addressing the social gendered structure as a foundation to enhance women's role in development. Nevertheless the idea of *tamkieen*[11] (literally meaning empowerment) is widely used by these organisations. According to the director of one of the biggest NGOs collaborating closely with the state, *Umm Elmumineen*,[12] who was interviewed for this study, *tamkieen* means enabling underprivileged and marginalised women to manage their lives in a better way. This includes also knowing their religion and their rights and duties better. Like this, women cannot "be played with" in the name of religion. Islamic knowledge and religious empowerment is considered to be central to improve the social status of women. To do so most of these NGOs are combining income-generating activities, credit programmes, health care and health awareness, child care, eradication of harmful traditional practices, and adult education with missionary programmes. The religious and missionary components of their activities are implemented through activities such as Quran and religious classes, support of widows and orphans, and financial assistance for poor students. The systematic and intensive religious programme and orientations of these NGOs played a considerable role in changing and addressing the gendered social perspectives and positions of women, particularly since these missionary activities focus explicitly on raising women's awareness of their rights and duties according to Islam. Further, Islamic knowledge and awareness are used to combat and question some traditions, external cultural influences, and to establish the former as the guiding principles for social transformation. Therewith, Islamist NGOs might provide women with a culturally legitimate frame to question their gendered social position, notwithstanding the fact that they load women with historical responsibilities of representing the Islamic nation and family honour as well as protecting the society from the Western influences and cultural invasions (see for example Willemse 2005, Nageeb 2004, Elbatahani 2004).

Filling the gaps of the state in the sense of acting as providers of health, social, and educational services is one of the clear objectives of Islamist organisations. They collaborate closely with the various governmental bodies, in particular with, for example, the Ministry of Social Welfare, the Zakat Council or the National Council for Orphans, or the Humanitarian Aid Commission (HAC), which is the governmental body responsible for coordinating the work of nongovernmental organisations. The support these organisations receive from the state enabled them to act as partners of the government and play a significant role in implementing its social policies. For instance the GUSW as well as Umm Elmumineen are conducting various social programmes such as communal weddings or boys' circumcisions to assist the poor families and individuals to meet some of their social obligations and needs. Within these programmes young couples receive material and financial support to meet the need (at least in part) to establish a marital home. In addition a communal wedding party is organised for them. Likewise arrangements are made to support families who plan to circumcise their sons. Such types of activities are advocated and conducted as parts of specific agendas such as social peace or poverty alleviation. Consequently these organisations play a central role in implementing the state's social welfare policies which aim at subsidising the cost of everyday life—such as weddings, education fees, orphans' care and the like for some of the poor families (see Ahmadi 2003). It is thus not surprising that these organisations have branches in the different regions of Sudan, reach a wide sector of the population (compared to organisations which are situated in an oppositional relation to the state), and create a popular basis for the regime and its Islamist orientations.

Women's NGOs, Othering Relations, and Social Space

The othering relations between Islamist and gender NGOs—such as represented by the discussion between the representative of the GUSW and a gender activist in the example of CEDAW workshop—certainly reflect how different actors are competing over the social space to represent and situate the agency of women in the peacebuilding phase. Obviously the agendas advocated by the different types of women's NGOs bear many similarities; however, the important difference lies in the approach rather than the agenda itself. While gender organisations attempt to situate their agendas by adopting a global gender frame that emphasises rights and agency, Islamist NGOs offer (a translocal) Islamic frame for addressing social and women's problems. The religiosity and transformative potential of the Islamist NGOs are often questioned by gender organisations. Islamist NGOs are viewed as partners of the state whose civil activism is basically directed to stabilise the regime by spreading its ideologies at the societal level and translating these ideologies into social practices and discourses. Thus to work with the same agendas as the gender NGOs is perceived by the latter as an attempt to coopt NGOs' work and decrease their influence at the public and local levels.

On the other hand the translocality of the discourses and networks of the gender organisations is often used, particularly by Islamists and Islamist NGOs, as grounds to accuse these organisations and their agendas as lacking cultural and Islamic sensitivity. Specifically the intensity of the translocal networking of the gender organisations, in terms of participation in international and regional conferences, workshops, meetings, and the like, as well as their link with international development donors are frequently pointed at to question the agenda of the gender organisations and to even promote conspiracy theories around them. An incident speaking to this effect is a Friday sermon delivered by a well known sheikh in a local mosque in the capital in December 2004. In his sermon, the sheikh, who is appointed by the Ministry of Religious Affairs as an Imam for Friday prayers, focused his sermon on CEDAW. He accused women who advocated CEDAW as "blind followers of the West," and urged the crowd to "defend Sudanese and Islamic values from these women." This othering relation is also supported by the fact that the work of gender organisations is more focused on advocacy than outreach programmes, whereas Islamist NGOs, as the director of Umm Elmumineen explains, "reach the poor in their place, in the different regions of Sudan." The structural conditions which shape the difference in the programmes and accessibility to the field (such as the logistics and financial support of the state to Islamist NGOs, and the lack of these conditions in the case of gender organisations) are all factors which are not considered in this type of othering relation.

These othering processes between the two types of organisations do not, however, lead to a clear division of who represents which agendas. With the exception of violence against women and CEDAW, which are more associated with the gender organisations, all the other agendas such as women and peace, social peace, poverty, reproductive health, FGM/C, or conflict resolution can be adopted by different types of women's organisations. The boundaries (of who addresses what) are often crossed; gender mainstreaming is obviously related to the gender discourse. Nevertheless the term is Arabised as *insiab elmara*, and used by Islamist organisations. The same applies to empowerment, Arabised as *tamkieen* and advocated by Islamists. Similarly, as has been previously argued, legitimising women's agendas by linking them to discourses on Islam is not only a discursive practice of Islamist organisations. Also gender NGOs have to seek a progressive religious frame in which to situate their agendas. One must hasten to add that the Islam discourses of these different organisations differ qualitatively. Yet what is important to highlight here is that these othering processes are based on the position of the different organisations concerning the Islam discourse of the state, and lead to the differentiation of local discourses on Islam.

Despite the different strategies that gender organisations adopt (which were discussed in the previous section) and the commitment of the government to institutionalise peace and democracy, the relation between gender organisations and the state remains oppositional. The policies of the HAC are in many ways especially obstructing for the work of human rights NGOs. In April 2006 the assets of the Women's Awareness Raising Group, an NGO working in the area of women's rights, were frozen after HAC issued a letter of notification for the organisation. The latter stated that the organisation had violated the 1998 HAC act by submitting a funding proposal to the European Commission in Khartoum without first seeking the approval of HAC (http://allafrica.com/stories/200604190549.html). Different incidents of obstruction and intervention in the work of NGOs in addition to the arrest and harassment of human and women rights activists are made public among NGOs activists, but hardly officially announced. Because of these state practices, forty African NGOs, including the South African Centre for the Study of Violence and Reconciliation, opposed Sudan to becoming the next chair of the African Union (http://sangonet.org.za/portal/index).

Hence the space for gender NGOs continued to be limited, despite the adoption of the CPA, Sudan's Interim National constitution, and the adherence of Sudan to the African Charter on Human and Peoples' Rights and the international Covenant on Civil and Political Rights. The limitation of space for gender NGOs severely affects the accessibility of these organisations to the social field. The adoption of the Organisation of Humanitarian and Voluntary Work Act 2006, to whose proposal my companion in the workshop had referred, grants an excessive regulatory power to the government over NGOs. The work of non-Islamist women's NGOs in Darfur, for example, is limited by undue restriction that hinders women from direct interaction with the different social groups there. Thus a burning issue like the conflict in Darfur and its gendered consequences are basically discussed by gender organisations at the advocacy level. The number of women's NGOs which have accessibility to the refugee camps and the affected areas of the region in conflict are extremely limited. NGOs need government permission before they can operate, particularly in Darfur. Even if this permission is granted, the work of NGOs is treated with a security mentality. A case speaking to this effect was the arrest of staff members of Sudan Social Development Organisation (SUDO) while conducting training on human rights monitoring in South Darfur in late February 2006. Many gender NGOs and activists have access to Darfur only through an international development agency or NGO (see chapter 7). Two consequences can be highlighted in relation to this conflictual interface with the government: First, the gender NGOs constitute spaces for their activities more at the level of political advocacy than at the societal and everyday level. Second, the relation between the government and gender NGOs is leading to the latter being even more politically dependant on, or at the least related to, international development agencies and NGOs to be able to approach the social field, specifically in the case of Darfur. Symbolically the location of the CEDAW workshop, presented in the first part of the chapter, sheds light on the relation between the triangle of state, gender organisations, and international development agencies.

The use of the (physical) space of the international development agencies for conducting a CEDAW workshop is not accidental. Gender NGOs often utilise spaces such as those of the UNDP, UNICEF, the Friedrich Ebert Foundation, and the Royal Netherlands Embassy for networking and situating their agendas. The use of this space is partially embedded in the (also financial) relation to such organisations which represent donors' organisations. The use of the space of international organisations—such as the high level of facilities as my companion at the CEDAW workshop indicated when contrasting the hot

weather outside with the cool air inside the UNDP facilities—symbolically reflects the political significance of this physical space. This (free) space of the
CEDAW workshop contrasts to the (restricted) space for NGOs according to
the government's new regulation for NGOs. However, there are dimensions
to this space, other than the freer political atmosphere, which are central to
understand how gender NGOs use the (physical) space of the international
agencies to constitute social space.

To elaborate on the above issue of how gender NGOs constitute space for
their agendas by using the physical space of international organisations, it is
worth referring to a local workshop on engendering the constitution which I
attended in Khartoum in 2005. The workshop was organised by a local gender NGO who was funded by the UNDP to carry out four weeks of gender
training for women in political parties. The gender training for women active in political parties was conducted in the premises of the NGO. However,
the training also included a two-day workshop on engendering the constitution to which men from the political parties were also invited. For this
mixed-gender workshop the NGO asked UNDP to allow them to use its seminar hall. According to the organiser if they carry out this session in their
own offices "men will think 'aha' this is a 'women's thing'. But if we send
them an invitation to a meeting at the UNDP they will think 'this must be
an important political activity'. They will fix their tie, shine their shoes and
carry their managers' bags and come." In the end male representatives from
more than fifteen parties attended the workshop. The convenors did not let
this chance go without providing basic gender training for men. During the
two-day workshop about engendering the constitution various civil activists,
both men and women, were actively involved in networking, exchanging information, and strategising. In the physical space of the UNDP gender activists gave their agenda more weight as a political programme rather than
only a "women's thing" according to the general male perception. They also
objectified their agendas by relating and framing them with international
right regulations and discourses and by doing so they strategically avoided a
subjective presentation of their agenda and confrontation with the government or traditional authorities.

A second type of space widely used by gender organisations is the space of
universities and research and educational institutions. Various gender and
human rights activities are conducted at universities, such as Ahfad University for Women. The latter is one of the leading institutions in introducing
the concept of gender to both academic and development circles. The conduct of gender activities at universities reflects a historical relation between
gender activism and universities in Sudan. Universities, especially Ahfad,

mediated and transmitted gender concepts and discourses to the local fields of development. Consequently, universities represent an important agent in rendering global gender concepts as a crosscutting issue, firstly, because of its historical role in introducing the concepts of gender. Secondly, during the 1990s, when the Islamist regime was intensifying its grip on the NGOs, universities and research institutions represented a (legitimate) space for debating issues which were otherwise suppressed by the regime, such as gender, women, and human rights. Under the umbrella of academia a relative freedom was exercised,[13] the gender epistemic community was established, and universities became a source for dissemination of gender knowledge and skills. The space which universities provided for localising global gender concepts led to close relations between gender activism and academia which is still observable today. A considerable number of female university staff belongs to gender organisations and represents a gender epistemic community. As shown from the example of the workshop, such affiliation does not go uncontested from other gender activists. The position of the university gender expertise as an epistemic community and the close networking between this community and international development agents[14] is often a source of comparative interaction and competition between gender activists. However, universities and research institutions remain an important space for gender organisations and activists to localise their global development concepts.

The spaces which gender organisations constitute at the local level are limited and are leading to these organisations and their agendas being situated more at the intellectual and political level than at the societal and everyday life levels, especially if one compares this with the spaces which the Islamist organisations occupy.

As reflected by the comment of the representative of the GUSW during the CEDAW workshop, many of the Islamist organisations have branches in the different regions of Sudan. The facilities which are made available to them by the HAC show the attempt of the government to maintain its power at the local level, despite the protocol on power sharing of the CPA (Human Rights Watch March 2006/1). Islamist organisations operate at the societal, practical, and everyday levels with programmes directed to specified sectors of the population which they can indeed reach through the logistic and financial support of HAC. The agendas of Islamist organisations reflect a conception of peacebuilding as a process of partial political transformation that should not shake the power of the Islamist regime at the local level. In contrast to the gender organisations who view peacebuilding as essentially entailing a fundamental change towards a political frame of democratisation and human rights, Islamist organisations are acting in accordance with the

regime. The focus of these organisations is how to penetrate the different social layers. Spreading their branches all over the country is one strategy—
subsidising living costs for the poor, and providing (religious) education, particularly for women. While doing so local media, mosques, schools, social
occasions, refugee camps, and prisons are all accessible channels through
which to situate their agendas and constitute spaces for reshaping the process
of social transformation. These spaces are still restricted for non-Islamist
NGOs, including gender organisations.

The division of spaces according to the type of organisation is also linked
to the transformative nature of the agendas of women NGOs. Islamist NGOs
basically adopt a socially accommodated approach to women issues, for example, WID or charity, which do not challenge the social gender order and
traditional social authorities of the Muslim majority. Thus it is much easier
for these organisations to reach a wider section of the society compared to
gender organisations. The gender organisations, on the other hand, address
women and gender issues by raising fundamental questions about the gendered social order and political structures. The critical nature of the social
transformation embedded in the agendas of these organisations is also a factor that contributes to the concentration of gender discourses and agenda at
a more urban and intellectual level. However, for the sake of the analysis this
distinction between the spaces occupied by the two types of organisations has
been put in sharp contrast and does not reflect various nuances. For example, Islamist organisations are also concerned with the urban intellectual levels to which they have freer accessibility than gender organisations have.
And gender organisations never stop attempting to situate their agendas at
the level of everyday life. The strategies of accommodating codes of public
morality and de-politicising agendas that are adopted by gender NGOs as discussed previously, reflect these attempts to reach a wider sector of the society. Further, the incidents of confrontation between gender organisations
and the HAC reveal situations where these organisations attempted to penetrate deeper in the society.

Women's NGOs: Actors and Agencies

The workshop was a space for the representation of various cultural and political dispositions of female activists. In addition it was a space that hosted
both globalisation and localisation forces at a local level. One important aspect of this workshop is that it reflected the changing nature of women's
agency in general and the Islamist women in particular, specifically within

the context of democratisation and the peace process in Sudan. Here I will shed light on some of these actors.

As in the case of the workshop, one finds some activists who belong to the 'closed Islam' discourse and whose civil engagement is largely framed by a conspiracy theory and othering of the West. This type of women's activism can be found working with the different issues raised in the workshop, but not in any engendering activities. Moreover their work is largely shaped by a vulnerability rather than a rights approach to women's issues. Their work is framed by a specific vision of social development based on the discourse of the strong Muslim supporting the weak one. Hence they focus on social categories which are classified according to this discourse as vulnerable or weak. In addition, one of their clear objectives is to "compete with the influence of the West that comes through the media and foreign aid," as one of these activists explained during an interview. In the same interview, which was conducted for this study, it became clear that the agency of these women corresponds to the state's discursive practices in the sense that "defending Islam and Muslims" or "pushing away the influence of the West" are still playing an important role as discursive practices of the state for political mobilisation. For these types of women activists they try to translate these discourses in specific social programmes. This type of agency is framed around Islamic charity and welfare concepts; thus the social gendered structure is hardly questioned and their activities are directed to support the everyday sustenance of disadvantaged groups.

A second type of Islamist women activists is represented in the example of the workshop by the young Islamist woman from the youth administration of NIF who described herself in the workshop as "Islamist but progressive." The agency of this type of activists is shaped, on the one hand, by embracing all global development concepts and issues, even debatable ones like those related to sexuality and reproductive rights. At the same time they do not place the West in an oppositional stand against Islam. Rather they emphasise the need to "work together with the West if one wants to compete with it" as the progressive Islamist woman expressed in explaining her position. One could relate this internal change in the Islamist discourse in Sudan to global politics and changes particularly after the events of 11 September 2001. In the first place this transformation in the Islamist thinking might be related to the subjugation of Islamism to critique and questioning of its own bases of legitimacy both by its followers as well as opponents. Though this type of activism is limited, the qualitative shift it represents in the discourse and practices of Islamism is very significant. This shift is characterised by placing value on individual choice, rights, freedom from rigidity, and democracy. On the other hand their belonging to Islamist organisations gives them the space to talk about Islam and criticise other Islamic discourses without running risk of being categorised as bad Muslims. Hence they represent in many cases a very liberal position concerning women's issues.

Bayat (2005: 5) in his article about post-Islamism describes a similar shift in Iran. He argues that the term "post-Islamism," which he proffered to analyse the tremendous transformation in the political and religious discourse in Iran, emphasises religiosity and rights "whereas Islamism is defined by the fusion of religion and responsibility." Post-Islamism can thus be used to explain and analyse the agency of the so-called progressive Islamists. In Bayat's analysis post-Islamism is neither anti-Islamic nor secular. The shift in the discourse of some Islamists in Sudan is similar to what Bayat (2005: 5) describes in relation to Iran as "attempt to turn the underlying principles of Islamism on its head by emphasising rights instead of duties, historicity rather than fixed scriptures, and the future instead of the past."

However, due to the hostility between Islamist and non-Islamist women activists, the latter are very critical about the shift in the discourse of some Islamists. Progressive Islamism or post-Islamism is perceived by many other civil activists to be an attempt of a faction of the Islamists to increase its power by coopting the secular discourses on rights, freedom, democracy, individual choice, and consequently the women and gender discourses of women's NGOs. Thus the relation between these two types of agencies, the progressive Islamists and the progressive activists, remains hostile.

There is also the type of actor who is locally known among the NGOs, intellectual, academic, and political communities as *niswan elgender*: the "gender women." Gender women are associated with progressive, left-wing politics, the communist party, or those who do not belong to a political party but clearly do not sympathize with the Islamist politics. The two terms, progressive and liberal, might be used interchangeably to describe this type of actor. However, the term liberal has locally some negative moral connotations, specifically when it is used by Islamists. One of the famous women activists who belongs to the gender women explained this type of agency, saying sarcastically: "You know when the NIF people came to power they sent all those who do not sympathise with them out of their jobs for 'the public good'. They sent them out of their jobs, only to meet them again from the other door in the civil society organisations." This remark reflects how the gender women, like the gender organisations, are placed in oppositional relation to the state. Their agency is framed by intensive networking, particularly at translocal levels with donor organisations including international women's NGOs. Their activities hardly reach the level of research, advocacy, and training programmes and their room for manoeuvring is limited compared to those who sympathize with the state's orientation and politics. Actors who belong to this category are mostly educated middle-class women. Questioning of state policies and discourses, the social gendered structures, traditions, and Islam discourses are embodied in the practices and discourses of these activists. However, the extent to which these questions are evoked in their discourses differs considerably.

The agency of the gender women includes different standpoints: WAD, GAD, and feminism. The significant variation in the feminist standpoint compared with the other two is mainly discursive. As revealed in the workshop by the contribution of the activist who identified herself as a feminist, she differentiates between feminism and women activism in the following way:

> Feminists are different; they accept no compromise in women and gender issues. They see the roots of the problem and they say it directly. Others tend to focus only on the political situation in Sudan, but women's problems are deeper than that. They [the women activists] compromise on many issues which they think are not important or are not culturally acceptable or I don't know what.

Feminists are engaged in more radical discursive practices, which explain, relate, and address local social and political issues by reference to a general frame of patriarchy, women's oppression, and male domination. Yet their agendas, approaches, and activities are similar to the other 'gender women' and are structured by the same social and political conditions.

The categorisation of women activists according to their different religious background is rather inaccurate, since non-Muslim women's NGOs and activists do not identify their peace and development agendas on the basis of religion. Religion plays a minor role in shaping the agency of women's activists. It is rather the types of agendas, approaches, and the relation to the state and Islamist discourses and practices which can typify women's agency and activism. Women activists who are not Muslims and come from regions like Nuba Mountains or the South are also found participating in a different type of activism. They advocate the same agendas explained in the previous part of the chapter which include peace, poverty alleviation, combating violence against women or health and education. The approach they adopt, rather than sticking to their religious identity, is the important factor for typifying their agency and analysing the way they position their agendas in the field of peace and development. Thus non-Muslim women may represent the different types of women agencies. Those whose agency is framed by questioning the social gendered structure are viewed as translocally oriented, while those who work with charity and WID approaches are not necessarily positioned in an oppositional relation to the state. Hence a form of cooperation between the two can be observed. An example of these organisations is the South branch of the GUSW or women and peace network.

Conclusion: Competing Agendas and Discourses

The peacebuilding phase in Sudan provides a view on how the different social actors are resituating themselves and their agendas in the field of peace and development. The analysis of a typical women's NGO event shows that the current stage of peacebuilding in Sudan is a social field where multilevel negotiations and struggles among different stakeholders takes place (Nederveen, 2001:72–74). These stakeholders represent a diversity of positions and agencies; accordingly the relation between the various structures and actors who try to situate their perspectives of peace in the field of development is also significant in understanding how the agendas of women's organisations are shaped. Hence peace and development represents a discourse or a variety of discourses on how to create peace and accordingly restructure the society. In this chapter NGO events have been used as a stage to discuss gendered views on peacebuilding, follow the diversity of perspectives and representations, analyse the ways through which social spaces are constituted, and observe the relations between the various actors and between the local and translocal structures.

Agendas of women's NGOs, though considerably similar, can nevertheless be differentiated on the basis of the type of organisation, the approaches and discursive practices it follows, and its relation to global development concepts and discourses. The interface between the NGOs and the state seems to be a decisive factor in the process of attributing a specific identity to the organisation, its actors, and agendas. Women's activists who are critical of the state's policies and practices are oriented more towards global gender discourses and translocal networking. This orientation is also supported by the state's controlling practices which try to limit the political agency of women that is shaped by the global gender and rights discourse. Nevertheless this type of agency gained a limited and mainly discursive space after the adoption of the CPA.

Simultaneously, the interface between the state and the gender organisations and women strengthens the othering relation between this type of women's agency and the Islamist organisations. The latter, who gained a wide social space within the context of Islamisation, set a discursive practice in the field of development that was different from the global gender frame, namely an Islam-guided discourse on social change and transformation. Hence situating the agenda of women's organisations becomes a process of competing over whose agendas and approaches are legitimate to represent Sudanese women. This competition over the social field is marked by border crossing: gender organisations that link their discourse to Islam in order to legitimise their agenda and embody public morality, and Islamist organisations that are open to (or cooptive in the view of gender organisations) global discourses like empowerment and gender mainstreaming.

The spaces which are constituted by women's agencies vary: There are discursive spaces which are constituted by shifting discursive practices as discussed above. While international NGOs and the local epistemic community are central to understand the constitution of social space by the agency of gender women, Islamist women constitute space by focusing more on the reshaping of social spaces at the everyday life and social level.

Notes

1. NCP is a faction of the National Islamic Front (NIF) which is the Islamist party governing the country since 1989. NIF became politically divided in 2002 into NCP, the faction which is currently ruling, and Popular Congress Party (PCP) which is now in the opposition.

2. The CPA consists of different protocols: security arrangements, power sharing, and wealth sharing in addition to two protocols on the contested areas which are the areas of Abyei, Nuba Mountains, and Southern Blue Nile.

3. The Khartoum Peace Agreement was signed in 1997 in the capital of Sudan between the two conflicting parties. Various protocols were signed and some others, such as the protocol on the conflicting areas, were still subject to negotiations. However after signing the Khartoum agreement the political atmosphere started to slowly open up and the Islamisation project was slowed down to prepare the implementation of the agreement.

4. The empirical research conducted in Sudan for this study was largely structured by my background as a Sudanese, academic, and activist who is identified by most of the participants of this study as belonging to gender women as called in this chapter. My accessibility to the field was rooted in these identities and in my relation (acquaintance or friendship) with many women active in nongovernmental organisations. This shaped my participatory observation in many ways: for example, on the basis of my acquaintance with the women and organisations many participants insisted on drawing clear boundaries between what is private knowledge and information, and what should be considered public and hence can be published. A considerable part of my knowledge about the participants of the study is considered by them to be private

issues. This included some dimensions of the family and social relations as well as some strategies used by the organisations to face the government control of NGOs. The border between private and public, which the participants of this study emphasised, is basically embedded in the relation of NGOs to the state as described in this chapter. My participatory observation was also rooted in the way women activists identify me as a gender specialist and sociologist/social anthropologist who worked at a faculty of sociology (at Bielefeld University) with a known tradition of research methodology. Hence I was often asked to assist organisations by conducting research methodology sessions or workshops for the staff, evaluate project proposals or ongoing research projects and facilitate workshops, and conduct training programmes on gender empirical research. In addition I was also asked to give talks or papers for certain activities. Active involvement in NGOs' everyday work was thus my main channel to conduct participatory observation.

5. In 2006 this "Organisation of Humanitarian and Voluntary Work Act 2006" was adopted by the government and was strongly criticised by NGOs.

6. To anonymise persons and events all names of persons and places are changed. Slight changes and reconstruction of the event was also applied to present the workshop in a way that does not reveal much about the persons involved. This is considered upon the request of most of the participants of this study.

7. For further discussion about the different veiling styles of Muslim women see for example Werner 1997, Nageeb 2004, and Willemse 2005.

8. In relation to the different anticolonial movements and starting from the middle of the twentieth century the term *Isslamyeen* started to be used in different Arabic speaking contexts, such as Egypt and Sudan, to refer to members of the Muslim brotherhood movements. Particularly in Egypt, where the movement was born and led by Hassan Elbana early in the last century, the term *Isslamyeen* was first adopted to refer to Muslim brothers and classified a political movement in an othering relation to *Shyoa'yeen* (communists) or *Yassaryeen* (leftist). The Muslim brotherhood movements in Sudan was/is also referring to itself with the term *Alharka Elisslamya* (the Islamic Movement). However, particularly with the growing of Islamist politics among the so-called Islamic movements such as the Muslim brotherhood, academic and scientific discourses on the subject—in Arabic-speaking societies—adopted a clear differentiation between Islamic (*Isslamy*) and Islamist (*Isslamoy*) notions. The two different Arabic notions are basically used among intellectuals and academic circles. Islamic (*Isslamy-Isslamyeen*) attributes Islam as an adjective to something, such as Islamic resurgence, Islamic modernity or Islamic law, where as Islamist (*Isslamoy-Isslamoyeen*) are notions used to refer to discourses, movements, and their members who advocate and adopt the politicisation of Islam as their main political and indeed social, economic, and even military and security, agendas. In everyday language of both Islamists and non-Islamists only the term *Isslamyeen* is used to refer to members of the Islamist movements and parties.

9. Foundation linked to the German Social Democratic Party.

10. An example of this are the organisations of Popular Committees distributed all over the country. These organisations were advocated by the Islamists as a means to care for security and basic social services in living quarters, however they also acted as political and security agents of the state who were responsible for eliminating any possibilities of opposition to the regime (see Nageeb 2004: 15–29).

11. The concept or idea of *tamkieen*, however, is not only used by NGOs, rather it represents a political slogan used by NIF political activists in general to express their view on political, social, and economic transformations, i.e., enabling those who are not able to change their economic and social conditions.

12. The name of the organisation *Umm Elmumieen* literally means the mother of the believers which is used to refer to Aìsha, the youngest wife of the Prophet Mohamed.

13. This does not eliminate the fact that universities were also subjected to intensive programmes of Islamisation and Arabisation. These programmes severely affected the academic and political freedom of the universities, which were also subjected to security mentality of the regime. Nevertheless universities were able to maintain a relatively bigger space, in comparison to other (political) agents such as non-Islamist organisations, because of their educational and academic role (see Amnesty International's Sudan Report 1995, 1996).

14. Regarding international academic networking the Ahfad Humboldt Link Programme supported by the German academic Exchange Service is one outstanding example.

CHAPTER FIVE

~

Women's Organisations and the Reshaping of the Public Sphere: A Comparative Analysis

Petra Dannecker and Anna Spiegel

Issues and Contexts

The empirical studies conducted in Senegal, Malaysia, and Sudan have illustrated the rich empirical diversity of how social spaces are constituted through the activities of women's organisations and activists to position their agendas in contested public spheres at the local level. As the three preceding chapters showed, this diversity of the activities and agendas of women's organisations is both between the countries as within different social spaces in one country. The aim of this chapter will now be to condense the empirical complexity in the sense of developing an empirically grounded theory (see chapter 1) and to work out the underlying modes of constituting social spaces (see Lachenmann 1998c; 2002 and 2004c; Nageeb 2004). The special focus of this endeavour will be on processes of social interaction and communication, which are adopted and developed by gender activists to position themselves in the respective social contexts, their organisations in the public spaces and their agendas in the political spheres. We assume that gender is "crucial in the production of differences in global/local dynamics" (Davids, van Driel 2005, 4) and the aim of this chapter is therefore to show that the different practices in local settings produce different meanings of gender in the sense of interactive negotiating, a perspective hardly ever taken up in writings about the contradictory ways in which global processes and local transformations come together. Although the focus in this chapter is primarily on the local level it is not intended to dichotomise between local and global. Rather the aim is to explore the ways through which global development visions and concepts are mediated by local structures and vice versa. To do so the analysis is committed to the deconstruction of categories such as local/global, Islam/West, and private/public spaces.

Four modes of constituting gendered spaces which are leading to the restructuration of public spaces and which were combined in different and context-specific ways can be detected from the case studies. These are networking, the popularisation of certain modes of social interaction and communication, alliance building between actors in different fields of knowledge, and the redefinition of places. Focusing on these modes and thereby going beyond the analysis of the specific and different development agendas of women's organisations allows us to analyse the processes of social transformation through interactions and everyday practices of women activists. We thereby hope to open a dimension hardly ever focused on so far. The social agency of women activists and their ability to position their organisations, agendas, and discourses within a particular contested context will be in the centre. Agency is more than an act of resisting male domination. Agency rather entails constant engagement in processes of negotiation and shifting of boundaries and meanings while making sense of the different and changing global and local context in which it is embedded. Thereby the dialectical relation between (the) local/global can be observed in the making.

Before indulging in the discussion of the different modes of constituting spaces and the processes of social restructuration, it is necessary to contextualise the empirical analysis by briefly summarising the relevant political and religious constellations, development discourses and the position of women's organisations in the three cases under study.

As has been highlighted in the introduction to this book, Malaysia is a multiethnic and multireligious country. Despite this diversity national culture is identified with Malay beliefs and practices based on Islam, a development that has increased significantly since the 1980s, after Islam was given a prominent place on the political agenda (see Nagata 1994; Evers 1997; Kheng 2002, Case 2002). The Islamic modernization project led to a more assertive presence of Islam in Malaysian society and culture and to a plurality of Islamic movements challenging not only the meaning and the content of Islam but also gender relations (Othman 2003; Mohamad 2002a and 2002b). But despite this process the government was and is still the main actor in the construction of a national Islamic identity and in shaping the texture of ethnic and gender relations (Tan, 2001, 967). The economic growth as well as the level of development have for the past decades been the foundation of the government's political legitimacy and have masked the gender inequality as well as the social inequalities especially between the different ethnic groups. The reinforcement of separate ethnic spaces is an intrinsic part of the Islamization project. Furthermore the state has monopolised the classical development arena within the framework of the authoritarian democracy, and has left hardly any space for NGO activities in general and women's organisations in particular (Weiss and Hassan 2003a, 2003b). Therefore hardly any cooperation between NGOs and the state in the classical development fields, like socioeconomic development or poverty reduction, as very typical for countries like Senegal, can be observed. Instead most NGOs studied take up human rights discourses which are considered by these organisations as the most and urgent aspect of development and which allow a critical dialogue with the state. Because of the delegitimation of an interethnic and interreligious public sphere it is nevertheless nearly impossible for non-Muslims and their organisations to talk about issues such as Islam, gender relations, and social change related to Islamisation. Therefore the focus of the research was predominantly on women's organisations actively taking up these issues.

In Sudan the National Islamic Front (NIF) seized power in the late 1980s and was changing the state, social, political, and cultural institutions in order to achieve its aim of imposing a particular vision of Islamic sociopolitical restructuration in all domains of life (see Nageeb 2004; Beck 1998). The early phase of the Islamisation project, during the 1990s, was characterised by political repression which specifically targeted civil organisations and activists who were not supportive of the Islamist politics. The events of 11 September 2001 and their global consequences, the signing of the peace agreement between the government of Sudan and the Sudanese People Liberation Army/Movement (SPLA/M) in January 2004, and the acceleration of the situation in Darfur are indeed currently putting Sudan and the Sudanese regime more and more under the focus of the international community, forcing the Islamic state to negotiate its Islamic outlook and identity vis-à-vis the global politics. This poses new questions related to the nature of political, social, economic, and cultural development of the country and lead to an opening of the political environment, although some restrictions and very authoritarian modes of governance continue to be in place. The presence of international organisations and the engagement of a huge number of national NGOs especially in the area of conflict resolution and peacebuilding reveal that new spaces were constituted which are reshaping the social, political, and civil society map in Sudan even further (Nageeb 2006). Especially women's organisations are very active in formulating the new development agendas such as the engendering of the constitution and the peace process as well as advocating the adoption and ratification of CEDAW. Thereby questions like whose development and whose Islam are becoming more and more a civic and public concern. The empirical research concentrated especially on women's organisations actively trying to reshape the public sphere through localising the new development agendas. Most of these organisations are located in the capital Khartoum. As in Malaysia also women's organisations exist working in rural areas in fields like poverty reduction or health-related issues. But due to the specific contexts, in Malaysia the monopolisation of rural development by the government and in Sudan the restrictions which organisations working on these issues have to cope with, these organisations are not only less in numbers but also tend to follow a conventional Women in Development approach. This means more recent approaches or gender discussions which might question the definition of power of the state are hardly taken up. This is not to say that the activities are not radical in a sense or in a specific context but the organisations are not, at least not openly, questioning the development visions or the gender order promoted by the respective governments.

In Senegal the state stands, in contrast to Sudan and Malaysia, for a decidedly Western-oriented modernisation project. However, traditional local culture and society are not entirely excluded from this project. The relationship between the state and the dominant forms of local Islam, the Sufi brotherhoods, can be described as a "social contract" (Cruise O'Brien 1992) binding together very different social spheres. The internal differentiations of the Sufi brotherhoods contribute to a sense of religious pluralism that is part of Senegalese national identity, which is indeed characterised by cultural pluralism and ethnic and linguistic diversity. The local brotherhoods influence to a large extent the relations between the mostly rural population and the government, even in terms of adherence to political parties, votes, or paying taxes. In return they receive from the state political protection and economic advantages that are partly redistributed to the population. This system of patron-client relations, based on a consensual strategy of nonconfrontation, has been a guarantee for stability—although the societal projects of the two actors of the contract seem quite incompatible: the Western and more and more globally oriented modernisation project pushed forward by the secular state with the support of international donor agencies on the one side, and the maintenance of local Islamic traditions by the dominant Sufi orders on the other. Within this framework of classical feminist movements on one side, and secular peasant movements on the other, a broad variety of women organisations have developed (see Lachenmann 1998b). Most Senegalese women are active in various forms of local female associations on the basis of kinship, affinity, or field of activity—like age groups, neighbourhood or village associations, mutual savings associations or associations based on shared religious practice like the *dahiras*. Alongside informal patterns of social organisation a range of formal structures and organisations exist, which are recognised and even created by the state. These organisations play an important role in the negotiation of development concepts especially with regard to women on a national and local level. They link up global development concepts and planning documents with local social practices, although the state official development discourse does not reflect the orientations and achievements on the ground. Recently translocal Islamic reform movements are spreading which criticise un-Islamic practices of the local marabouts but in particular the secular state and its modernisation project which they made responsible for the virulent economic crisis and the resulting problems of social development (Loimeier 2000a, 183). Thus whereas in Malaysia and Sudan Islamisation is not only but primarily a state project making gender and the social position of women a central topic, in Senegal gender has only recently became a site for contestation with the raise of the new Islamic reform movements. They are confronting the state-promoted project of modernisation in general and in the domain of the family law in particular. Thereby they criticise not only the Western-dominated concept of gender equality but also the (particularly in the rural society) dominant forms of traditional gender order. The tendency of state politics to make women's own spaces and their active participation in economic and social processes a matter of appropriation of discourses but not of policy orientation (Lachenmann 2001) is an important factor for understanding why the reformist movement has a special appeal for women. Within this complex setting the empirical case study focused on secular as well as religious women's organisations working locally on highly contested gender issues like the family law.

These complex and different contexts in which women's organisations are embedded in and are part of, do not allow to categorise or to classify the organisations studied along conventional categories such as conservative, liberal, or progressive as often done in academia as well as development politics, because these categorisations are highly politicised as the case studies reveal. They are used by the different actors, be it state institutions or women's organisations themselves for othering processes or for positioning themselves within highly disputed frameworks. Thereby these categories become labels and get a situational meaning by being used in a flexible way which does not allow any generalisation. What is meant locally or in a certain situation by conservative or progressive varies to a great extent as the empirical data re-veal. To illustrate the argument the young women in the so-called reformist Islamic organisations in Senegal can be taken as an example. They define themselves as progressive compared to other women's organisations whereas in the Sudan case the category progressive is used to describe women's or-ganisations which are working closely together with international organisa-tions or donor agencies and are therefore seen as Westernized. The labels and categories therefore are important as they provide insights about the respec-tive context, power structures, and discourses and they can turn into param-eters in order to define what is locally meant by conservative, progressive, or liberal. But they are hardly able to describe the organisations and their agen-das often clustered in these categories.

Therefore and in accordance with the theoretical endeavour outlined in the introduction chapter it is not intended to categorize the organisations or their agendas in the following chapter but to elaborate on the modes of con-stituting spaces for the negotiating of gender relations and development dis-courses and agendas. Even though the modes of constituting spaces do vary and are context specific, the constituted spaces are important for formulating or reformulating and negotiating not only gender relations but also national "identities" and developments. Whereas the organisations under study can-not be subsumed under certain categorises, as stated already, the modes which will be introduced below can to a certain extent be generalised, like the role of networking, alliances between different fields of knowledge or the redefining of places.

Modes for the Constitution of Spaces
for Negotiating Gender Relations

Networking

Networking locally as well as translocally is, as the three cases have shown, an important mode of constituting spaces in which the negotiation of gender relations takes place. Social networking between activists and women's or-ganisations is of course not a new phenomenon and is more than a mere link-ing and connecting of women's organisations (Klein-Hessling 1999). It is a form of social organisation, used for the mutual exchange of information, ideas, strategies, and knowledge as well as for common action (Müller 2005). All women's organisations studied are actively involved in this kind of social networking. Nevertheless the organisations can be distinguished according to the type of networks they have established or are actively participating in. Whereas some of the organisations are mainly locally networking others are members of transnational networks. The kind of networking thus allows drawing conclusions concerning the agendas of the organisations but also allows specifying further the relevance of the respective contexts concerning the modes of constituting spaces.

It can be argued that in Sudan and Malaysia due to the state-based Islamisation processes and the difficulties civil society organisations in general and women's organisations in particular face, translocal networking developed as an important mode of constituting spaces locally for negotiating gender relations and the meaning of religion. Thereby gendered public spaces have been constituted. Especially the advocacy women's organisations in Malaysia are actively, and more explicitly than organisations in Sudan, participating in global human and women rights discourses through their networking. Reembedding and negotiating the global discourses and visions is thereby an important aspect of their activities. Thereby, as Spiegel shows, they try to challenge the monopoly of knowledge production of established networks of Islamic thought as well as the knowledge production and the power of definition held by the Malaysian government concerning the right Islamic development. In Sudan and Malaysia, but in the latter case in a more established form, women's organisations seek transformations of societies through localising global development concepts as compatible with Islam thus presenting alternative visions of Islam. This is in contrast to the social work–oriented organisations which are working more issue-based on the local level and which are often networking with government institutions. Nevertheless also networking between these organisations and more secular organisations can be observed on certain issues such as violence against women in the case of Malaysia or Female Genital Mutilation/Circumcision (FGM/FC) in Sudan.

Especially in Sudan, where the state is controlling and monopolising development orientations and visions, women's organisations saw themselves driven, as Nageeb highlights, to strategically adopt global development visions through translocal networking. But whereas in Malaysia the organisations which are translocally networking do openly question the Islamic interpretations and development visions of the state, in Sudan these organisations are using global development concepts, like the gender agenda and peace and conflict resolution, to negotiate and challenge state's definition of power in general and gender relations in particular. Women's organisations negotiating global development concepts seek to position their agendas and organisations between the state and international donor agencies. For their everyday politics this means that the gender agendas of these organisations are situated and discussed in a way which is not openly challenging the state's political or religious orientation. Simultaneously these women's organisations seek to follow the interest of international donor agencies on whom they are financially dependant. Currently the women and peace agendas are one of the most popular middle ground which women's organisations try to occupy in order to create more room for political manoeuvring within the local political context while at the same time securing international funds. The financial question is of special importance for these organisations, their activities, and networking since alternative financial strategies as developed by organisations in Malaysia could not be observed yet. In both countries the organisations networking translocally are hardly ever active in rural areas or are connected to local contexts; instead they are urban based and advocacy oriented. The women's organisations and groups which are more or less merely networking on the local or national levels on the contrary are the ones implementing selectively social development projects predominantly with the aim to create gender equity within the given context. In comparison to the urban-based advocacy organisations, these organisations have a stronger link to local communities through their mainly Women in Development approach. Simultaneously they are, as stated already, more accommodative of the state's Islamisation projects. Especially the religious organisations and their networks are often closely linked to state agencies and tend to, as the Sudanese case study reveals, construct women's organisations which network translocally or globally as the others influenced by so-called Western visions of development.

In the case of Senegal no such clear pattern of translocal networking of women's organisations could be observed. The secular agenda of the Senegalese state as well as the influence of the international development agencies, who acknowledge the engagement of the Senegalese state und civil society in defence of human rights, leads to local networks of women's organisations and groups which are trying to negotiate these rights and the global development concepts, which have often been captured in a uniform gender approach by the state (see Lachenmann 2001). Strategically and in contrast to the case studies conducted in Sudan and Malaysia, networks are therefore more polycentric structured, either being decentralised into regional offices or consisting of a broad variety of organisations and associations which are locally embedded and are representing different strata of society. Networking and communication between different organisations and associations representing different groups of society and other local actors shows that in Senegal the agenda of women's organisations is more locally oriented. Nonetheless some of the umbrella organisations have a tradition of networking regionally, within West Africa (Müller 2005), for building up their own structures of exchange and knowledge production.

Networking thus turned out to be an important mode for the constitution of spaces where gender relations are negotiated. But as the analysis has shown there are different kinds of networking. The fact that especially for women's organisations in Malaysia and Sudan translocal networking is of importance due to the relations these organisations have with both states and international donors and development agencies. Through networking these actors are able to acquire the social, political, and in some cases financial resources which enable them to participate in the public sphere and secure negotiation power. Through these resources and power women activists create a discursive arena which is structured around local and global development visions, where a counterhegemonic discourse is situated and gender order, developments, and in some cases Islam are negotiated. In the case of Senegal the relations to the state as well as international organisations differ from this pattern, leading to more locally oriented forms of social networking but with links to regionally institutionalised networks and organisations.

Popularising Specific Modes of Communication and Interaction

One way of analysing the agency of women's NGOs and the constitution of spaces is to focus on processes of communication and interaction between the social actors. Having highlighted networking relations and their significance in positioning women's organisations in the respective contexts, in this section the analysis concentrates more on the patterns of social interaction adopted by these organisations. Internet and media as a form of indirect interaction, language codes as example of more face to face or direct interaction and dress codes which stand for a form of symbolic interaction will be used to discuss the agency of women's activists. While interacting and adopting particular modes of communication the actors position themselves as well as their organisations culturally and politically in the respective local contexts. At the same time these modes of interaction and communication are popularised by situating them in public and using them as means of inclusion and exclusion and othering processes.

For the women's organisations which are translocally networking the Internet as a medium for communication and a strategic tool for development is of increased importance (Spiegel, Harig 2002; Youngs 1999). This is not surprising. Since the expansion of the communication geographically and during the aftermath of the UN Decade of Women between 1975 and 1985 women's organisations worldwide are using the new communication

possibilities to connect different localities, to transcend the diversity of local realities, and to negotiate differences (see Gittler 1999; Wichterich
2000). Most of these organisations are urban-based advocacy organisations
and intensively indulge in translocal networking via the Internet. Often
the representatives of these women's organisations became brokers and
mediators in channelling information along and between the local-global
scales. On a national level they try to establish issue-based networks with
organisations which are not actively part of the 'global net' to negotiate
and popularise global development concepts and visions, as the studies in
Malaysia and Sudan have shown. These processes can also be observed in
Senegal. But as the relationship with the state in this case is much more
like a complementary partnership, the focus is more on the negotiation
and popularisation of national development issues and approaches within
the country.

The local media is also an important channel through which agendas are
set up and spaces constituted. In Malaysia especially the advocacy groups are
using the local media like the popular television programmes 3R or the radio, to create a societal basis for debating gender relations. They furthermore publish on a regular basis letters to the editors or other columns in national newspapers to bring their issues into the public sphere. Even though
space for civil society is limited in Malaysia (Weiss and Hassan 2003a,
2003b) these organisations have the technological possibilities as well as established networks with representatives from the media enabling them to
communicate their agendas. In Senegal the media, particularly the community radio, the press, but also the Internet is used intensively by women's organisations and networks for the constitution of spaces. But whereas in
Malaysia the spaces created by the women's organisation are used to criticise
government's policies or Islamic interpretations concerning gender relations, in Senegal campaigns and agendas are communicated often in close
cooperation with the government or ministries like the Ministry of Family.
The empirical research in Senegal reveals that women's organisations focusing on the local and national level nevertheless use globalised strategies
for communicating their agendas. The example of including a theatre company for the diffusion of texts concerning women's rights is a well known
global development strategy for popularising certain issues. This strategy
gets localised by embedding the performances in popular imaginations. In
Sudan only women organisations which are closely linked to the state have
access to the local media to situate their agenda, as the example of the General Union for Sudanese Women (GUSW) shows. They have actively used
the different local media to support the position of the state concerning for

example women's participation in elections, human rights violations, or poverty alleviation. For organisations which are critical about the state politics these spaces are restricted.

In face-to-face or direct interactions globalised modes of social interaction such as the use of a global language like English, French, or Arabic becomes an important marker of the specific cultural and political position of the actors involved, hence of the type of women's activists. In the case of Senegal and Sudan it could be observed that the use of French or English by women activists or in the publications of the organisations they are representing is very important. Through the use of language, which Nageeb's description of the workshop on the Convention for the Elimination of All Forms of Discrimination against Women (CEDAW) in Khartoum shows, one can distinguish between the different actors and how they are positioning themselves in the given context. Especially the use of European languages is related to educated and translocally connected actors whose development agenda can be defined as 'modern'. Modern in this context indicates not only the actors' access to modern education but furthermore their being familiar with global development concepts and visions. In Senegal the use of French represents symbolic distinctions between social spaces: the social spaces where French is used and the social spaces where Wolof (or other local languages) dominate. The former is more related to secular and Westernised modernisation discourses which also the government pushes forward; the latter are used much more to relate to rural settings and the majority of the rural and urban poor women who have very little schooling, and mostly belong to traditional Sufi structures. In Sudan the use of English language and the mixing of English terms with the local Arabic is a feature of the social interaction of activists who belong to categories locally defined as progressive or liberal. The development agenda advocated by these types of actors is perceived to be of a Western nature and orientation. In Malaysia English is primarily used by the advocacy groups for translocal networking. But in the multiethnic context English is also very often the language used in issue-based networks especially with women's organisations which are secular oriented and whose representatives are not ethnic Malays despite the fact that they are often fluent in Malay.

However, European languages are also used by another type of activists whose development agenda is basically competing with the Westernised modernity, namely activists belonging to Islamic reform and Islamist movements. The example of Ibadu Rahman in Senegal and the so-called progressive Islamist women in Sudan are cases speaking to this effect. Both of these groups are using European languages to communicate and activate their modern Islamic projects as opposed to traditional Islam(s). Traditional Islam is perceived by these activists as unpure, backward, and hindering development defined as changing the position of Muslims worldwide. Hence their social and development agendas are modern in nature addressing mainly issues of education but also technological knowledge and information technology to compete with Western modernity. Simultaneously, Islamic reform and Islamic activists in general are also introducing the use of classic Arabic to achieve sociopolitical and religious renewal. Arabisation of certain global development concepts and terminologies is an important strategy for interacting and competing in the global space. The importance of the use of a so-called globalised language as a means of social interaction is that it marks a specific cultural position, the claiming of specific—modern—knowledge and power. Knowledge and accordingly power claims are getting articulated, enabling women's activists to constitute spaces for negotiating their development agenda.

At the level of symbolic interaction dress represents a symbolic code for communicating one's status, cultural position, and political orientation as well as the belonging to a certain community or group. Douglas (1970) defines dress as part of the 'social imagery' and an important means for the construction of group boundaries and identities. Dress is furthermore also subject to shifting interpretations across space and time as current debates in Muslim countries show. As Othman (2006, 341) argues, dress, especially veiling, became a particularly sensitive and controversial issue in Muslim countries all over because projects of Islamisation or movements aiming to Islamise societies try to first of all reach their goals through a change of gender relations and the control of a woman's body. Abaza (1998b) shows that not only in public or political spheres but also in social science and in feminist discourses the wearing of Islamic attire is controversially discussed. Whereas arguments are put forward that the Islamic attire is used actively by women to participate in public life and the working force, others still define the Islamic dress as a symbol of oppression (Werner 1997). Without getting into the heated political discussion whether the Islamic attire in general and veiling, the covering of women's hair and sometimes even face and form in particular are progressive or reactionary phenomena the empirical findings indeed show that also within female spaces dress plays a significant role. But it is not the Islamic attire, which figured also prominently in colonialist, orientalist, and current representations of Muslim societies (Secor 2002; Kandiyoti 1991; Ahmed 1992), instead the traditional dresses increasingly became an important means for border drawing between women's organisations in the countries studied and a mode of constituting spaces within the respective contexts. The 'traditional' dress has been used by women's organisations as a means for negotiating gender relations, especially in interactions with the state but also with other women's organisations. This is a more recent trend in Sudan and Malaysia where the governments have enforced the wearing of the so-called Islamic dress for women as a marker for their authentic Islamic identity and the depth of their faith and piety (Othman 2006, 342).

Nageeb's analysis of a workshop on CEDAW in Khartoum shows that dress is more than a public expression of personal religious faith; it is a mode of articulation. Wearing a traditional Sudanese dress, for example, can be interpreted as a means to indirectly criticise the enforcement of the veiling regime by the state by positioning the respective woman and the organisation she represents as aware of her cultural pride and difference. Wearing a so-called Western style dress and combining it with using English language, on the other hand, is a much more open strategy to situate oneself and the organisation within the arena of political and ideological competition between Islamism and secularism. Nevertheless the event analysis displays a broad variety of combinations between traditional, Islamic, and Western dress which gives evidence to the different agendas and strategies used by the women's organisations and their positioning vis-à-vis the state and other women's organisations. Of special interest in Malaysia and Sudan is the fact that the women's organisations which are networking translocally and are trying to localise global development visions are promoting increasingly the so-called traditional dress. But women of these organisations do not only wear these dresses, like in the case of Sudan, even fashion shows with 'traditional' Malay dresses for women are supported by advocacy organisations like Sisters in Islam in Malaysia. Thereby the intention is, as the empirical material by Spiegel shows, to constitute spaces for critically reviewing the Arabic Islamic identity overtaken by Islamic political parties. Thereby, as in Sudan, the so-called traditional dress became a symbol for highlighting that within the Islamisation processes traditional dress and as such cultural modes and codes got replaced by Arabic modes and codes (see also Othman 2006). The reinventing and reconstructing of tradition as a mode of constituting spaces allows to legitimise the negotiation of gender relations and is strategically used as a symbolic mode of interaction to stage the female body back in the public without being blamed as Westernised. Thereby the women's organisations create new forms of local, gendered, and Islamic knowledge legitimised through the reinvention of tradition. Thus dress codes mirroring the cultural positioning of activists and women's organisations are combined with a selective appropriation of specific discourses and their political significance in a particular space and time.

In Senegal the situation is different since no homogenized dressing regime on the national level exists. Neither has the secular state ever demanded any dress code for women, nor have the dominant Sufi authorities showed a serious interest in restricting the strong local tradition of female fashion and erotic art expressions of female sexual attractiveness, being highly valued in local cultural traditions. The question of the right dress only recently became a political and religious issue, especially since the new Islamic movements use women's bodies and dress codes to position themselves within the public sphere. For a growing number of young Senegalese women and organisations who do support the *Ibadu* reform movement (in a broad sense), veiling as well as the Islamic attire became a practice to express their rejection of the Western-influenced national development policies in general and the repercussions of globalised feminism in particular. This "rebellion of the daughters" with regard to Islam and personal visions of gender in society is directed against the generation of the mothers being active in modern secular state institutions and/or defining themselves as feminists whose wearing of traditional African clothing is part of the independence and postindependence struggle. Some of the young women who define themselves as Muslim feminists use the Islamic attire to challenge not only the established gender but also age hierarchies, particularly the authority of their parents' generation.

In Sudan and Malaysia a lot of women's organisations studied are promoting traditional dress to distance themselves from Islamic interpretations of gender relations as forced by the respective governments while at the same time distancing themselves from so-called global or Westernised practices and images. On the other hand, the adopting of global styles of Islamic veiling for the young women, as observed in Senegal and Sudan in the new Islamic organisations, is one way to identify themselves as part of the global cultural force Islamism.

Connecting Different Fields of Knowledge

Our case studies also indicate the importance of links created by women's organisations among different knowledge spaces and knowledge carriers. Through connections with carriers of "traditional" and "local" knowledge, such as traditional religious authorities, and with carriers of "modern" knowledge, such as universities and development organisations, new public spaces where gender relations can be successfully negotiated are constituted. Especially the case studies on Sudan and Senegal reveal the intensive relations of women's organisations with local religious authorities and their strategic integration into the negotiation of gender relations and women's rights. As the examples of the two different events, the UNDP-financed workshop in the

Sudanese capital Khartoum on women's rights and CEDAW and the cele-bration of International Women's Day in a Senegalese village show, renowned Islamic scholars were invited by the women's organisations. Both chapters highlight the efforts of women's organisations to create a shared dis-cursive space with activists of Islamic movements to connect women's rights to progressive or alternative discourses on Islam. In both cases the Islamic scholars offered religious argumentations for the need to transform gender re-lations and support women's organisations. However the contexts of such al-liances differ significantly in Sudan and Senegal. In Sudan, with an Islamist state, the Islamic framework of programmes and agendas of women's organisa-tions which is established by such alliances, is in the first place about providing the women's organisations with a legitimate basis for acting in the public sphere and for integrating topics such as Female Genital Mutilation/Circumcision (FGM/C), HIV/AIDS and reproductive health into the public debates and negotiations. In contrast to Sudan, where the connections to a progressive Is-lamic discourse structure in the first place the interface between women's or-ganisations and the Islamist state, in secular-oriented Senegal it is rather the interactions between women's organisations and specific parts of the local population influenced by Islamic revivalism, which are the background for strategic alliances between women's organisations and religious authorities. As Sieveking highlights, the decision of Senegalese women's activists to or-ganise a public event like the International Women's Day not within the very abstract frame that was suggested by national gender bureaucrats but on "Gender and Islam" and to invite Islamic scholars to this event was seen as an effective strategy to adapt the government vision of gender equality to the way social reality is reflected and articulated by the local population. Also the other International Women's Day celebrations at the local level that were analysed in the chapter on Senegal were carried out in collaboration with local Islamic scholars and authorities. By building up such alliances women's organisations have engaged in the endeavour to negotiate develop-ment from below and to mediate between Western-oriented and Islamic vi-sions of development. In Senegal the motto "Islam is the solution" can be seen as an expression of the intention to translate technocratic state policies on gender equality into a popular frame, whereas in Sudan Islam and Islamic authorities are used as a mean to smoothen the tense relationship between women's organisations adopting global gender discourses and the Islamist state.

Harcourt and Escobar have correctly pointed out that women's move-ments have been entering the social public sphere "in redefining what counts as political" and that "at the heart of the politics of place, is a challenge and renegotiation of what is discussed and valued in public" (Harcourt, Escobar 2002, 9). However our research has shown that the *ways* of *how* issues can be politicised and negotiated in the public sphere are shaped by social and cultural contexts. Thereby it turned out that social and cultural transformations are more difficult to achieve than political transformations.

On the other hand the case studies reveal the intense relationship of women's organisations to the epistemic community of gender and social researchers. In the three countries we found the type of activist-scholars, women who move both within academia and the social movements and who act as mediators between these different fields of knowledge and experience. In Senegalese some very globally oriented female academicians are moving back and forth between French and Senegalese universities while being at the same time renowned feminist activists. A relatively small epistemic community on gender which is composed of female academics, researchers, and university staff belonging at the same time to "women's organisations" can be identified in Sudan.

In Malaysia the interfaces between women's movements and Islamic scholars on the one hand and academic institutions on the other hand takes a particular form. Through inviting lecturers of the International Islamic University and religious scholars belonging to a progressive Islam from Malaysia but also from Indonesia or Pakistan to their internal study and training sessions, the organisation Sisters in Islam has over the years managed to establish a significant body of knowledge and expertise on women and Islam themselves, conducting their own research on polygyny for example. Out of the three country examples Sisters in Islam is surely the case with the highest degree of academisation of gender activism in the field of women and Islam. Leading feminist activists of women's organisations belong to the nationally and internationally researching and publishing epistemic community on women, development, democratisation, and Islam.

Building alliances with different fields of knowledge certainly plays a significant role in positioning gender discourses and women's activists in the public sphere. Through building alliances gender epistemic communities as well as women activists are no longer isolated communities. Rather gender discourses become more and more integrated in different fields of knowledge. Thereby discourses on women and gender as well as the global discourse on Islam become more differentiated depending of course on the actors involved.

Redefining Places

In all our empirical case studies women's organisations and female activists are engaged in the redefinition of places revealing that places are not fixed unities but contested and reconstructed by the intersection of global and local processes (Massey 1994; McDowell 1999). This is equally the case for places to which traditional meanings are attributed like mosques, traditional female associations and for places which have emerged out of modernisation processes like shopping malls, universities, international development organisations, and which stand for development and modernity. This redefinition of places has to be considered as one important mode of constituting spaces for the negotiation of gender relations and gender equality within a global frame. In Malaysia the redefinition of places plays a significant role for women's organisations. Shopping malls, the "empires of consumption," are used by women's organisations as places where gender relations are put into the public and are negotiated. Shopping centres become laboratories for the development of new ways of doing politics in a highly consumerist and at the same time highly politically restricted society. Women's groups strategically use the lifestyles of the consumption-oriented middle classes and politicise consumption in order to politicise the public space.

In Sudan, meeting rooms and seminar halls belonging to international development agencies, such as UNDP, UNICEF, the Friedrich Ebert Foundation, or the Royal Netherlands Embassy are included into the politics of place of women's organisations. Conducting their workshops and conferences in these places instead of in their own offices the gender activists achieve to upgrade their agendas which are now recognised as complex political programmes rather than only a women's thing. Framing their activities with international right regulations and discourses which the international development organisations stand for, also contributes to an objectification of their agendas within the confrontation with the government or traditional authorities.

As Nageeb elaborated, also universities and other research and educational institutions where a variety of gender and human rights activities are conducted, belong to those places which are integrated into women's place-based politics in Sudan. This is due to their role as mediators and transmitters of gender concepts and discourses to the local fields of development and as a hideaway for a critical gender epistemic community in times of a suppressive political system. But also the mosque is increasingly appropriated by women, who were not traditionally the main users of this space. The mosque, both in rural and urban areas, is currently used by women groups to conduct their religious programmes, and therefore is an important site for negotiating development concepts (see Nageeb 2007).

In her chapter on women's organisations in Senegal Sieveking describes the redefinition and reconstruction of places which are related to tradition and religion and which are embedded into specific local forms of gendered social organisation within place-based women's politics. The *mbotaye*, informal local female associations embedded into local village and community structures, are redefined in the light of development activities and turned into the local basis for microfinance or microcredit or other development activities of women such as the promotion of women's rights. Nevertheless this entails the danger, as Lachenmann (2001) has shown that through the redefinition and the integration of some of these associations into development policy and the formal finance sector the former logic of agency changes leading to their exclusion or invisibility in the rural areas. The *dahiras*, originally religious associations formed by male migrants in the urban areas, are more and more appropriated by women in urban but also rural areas, with some *dahiras* becoming female dominated. Women have successfully renegotiated the gendered structure of these traditional spaces and managed to place their development activities within traditional social and religious dimensions by (re)appropriating certain organisational forms.

Concerning the politics of place (Harcourt, Escobar 2002; Harcourt, Rabinovich, Aloo 2002) this means that not only women's politics are place based within the four domains of place: body, home, environment, social public sphere, but that places themselves become the object of women's politics. Women's organisations and women's activists strategically occupy specific places which are highly loaded with symbolic meaning within their local context. Within globalisation processes the importance of such specific local places does not vanish, "concrete places" do not "disappear under the unavoidable advance of things global" as Harcourt and Escobar have rightly pointed out (2002, 7), but on the contrary places are used strategically to ground claims for gender equality: within consumerism and middle-class culture, local religious traditions, or translocal movements of Islamic revival. Giving globalised places like malls or media centres new meaning or using traditional places like mosques, neighbourhood associations, or saving groups, women's organisations are contributing to the reshaping of public spaces and to the process of social restructuration both at the local and global level (see also Dannecker, Spiegel 2006, or Nageeb 2007).

Constituting Spaces and Gaining Room for Manoeuvre

As the comparative analysis of the three case studies has shown women's organisations have developed a wide range of modes for the constitution of social spaces. They have developed modes of local and translocal networking in order to strengthen their negotiation power vis-à-vis the state or other actors. They make use of specific cultural and linguistic repertoires in order to facilitate the negotiation at multiple interfaces and engage in the redefinition and reconstruction of places for embedding their agendas in the local context. They creatively combine academic knowledge and everyday knowledge to negotiate and to question local gender norms and structures and they provide women with a socially and religiously accommodated frame for gender equality through alliances with Islamic authorities. Though the context-specific ways of combining the discussed modes of constituting spaces women's organisations reshape their interaction with both the state and local communities and are able to increase their room for manoeuvre for the negotiation of gender relations and gender equality. On the one hand local epistemic communities become more differentiated and specialised on the basis of gender knowledge and knowledge on women issues, on the other hand religious knowledge and discourses become more differentiated. By these processes rights and gender discourses are getting increasingly part of development as well as academic and public local debates restructuring the public spheres in significant ways.

At the same time the various modes of constituting spaces used by women activists and their organisations show the dynamic processes accompanying the ways actors position themselves in the public. This means linking, shifting, and negotiating constantly the boundaries between global/local, traditional/modern, Islam/Western and private/public institutions and spaces characterise the processes. The various modes of constituting spaces discussed in this chapter show the different patterns of everyday interactions and practices of the actors involved in the specific contexts. These everyday interactions and practices are thus standing for "the double strategy of no-silence and no-violence" (Bayat, 2004, 5), which enable women's organisations to assert their public presence. At the same time it is nevertheless important to highlight that social restructuration is not always explicitly seen as a transformative approach by the actors studied. However it can be interpreted as a result of their activities in development fields like poverty reduction, institutionalising democracy, and human rights and/or building peace in which women's organisations are involved differently. Our empirical cases therefore allow the conclusion that positioning women's agenda in politics and in the public spheres cannot be understood as the outcome of an intended, strategic, conscious, and organised process. Nor can it be understood as only an act of resisting male domination. Instead while constituting spaces for their agendas these actors are combining different cultural forces, redefining spaces and places, shifting boundaries, and sometimes even using the structural limitations of their social position to sustain their presence in public and produce their alternative development discourses. This leads clearly to the social construction of societal change.

III

NEGOTIATING DEVELOPMENT: NETWORKING AND STRATEGIES OF WOMEN'S ORGANISATIONS

CHAPTER SIX

~

Negotiating Women's Rights from Multiple Perspectives: The Campaign for the Reform of Family Law in Senegal

Nadine Sieveking

In the process of establishing women's rights in contemporary Senegalese society, diverging visions of development are negotiated by different actors, connecting globalised concepts to local discourses and social practices. This chapter analyses this process by means of a case study in the context of a nationwide NGO campaign for the reform of national family law. The latter has constituted a battlefield since its enactment, confronting the positions of civil society actors, the Senegalese women's movement, Muslim authorities, and the secular state. These different positions will be analysed with a special focus on women's organisations and their relations with representatives of distinct social spheres. Pointing to the networking between various actors on the one side, and their differentiating strategies in the process of negotiating and localising global concepts on the other, the complexity and the often contradictory dynamics characterising the processes of social transformation can be understood.

In a first step the problems and challenges in implementing the official politics of women's advancement (see chapter 2) are shortly discussed, introducing thereby the institutional framework of gender policies in Senegal. Second, the ongoing debate concerning national family law is outlined. Then the main part of the chapter focuses on the localisation of the global concepts of women's rights and gender equality. The practice of negotiation is analysed as a process through which new discursive spaces are created, allowing the diverse actors in the field to question existing social boundaries and redefine their cultural legitimacy. This kind of analysis challenges the established discursive divide between the domains of religion, local tradition, and state-promoted modernity. The case study shows that the significance and implications of the symbolic confrontations (Cruise O'Brien 2003) between religious authorities and the secular state are highly contextual. And they indicate how the distinctions between different development visions and the apparent opposition between modernity and tradition are shifting, according to the interpretations of the various social actors and their respective agendas, as well as with respect to specific interactions. The appropriation or rejection of global concepts in local discourses thus calls for a consideration of the "many different modes of practical glocalisation" (Robertson 1995, 40) shaping new social spaces in the process of cultural transformation.

Sketching the Conditions for Women's Advancement in Official Development Politics

In April 2005 I interviewed Ndeye Soukeye Gueye, a leading representative of the Directorate of the Family, which is part of the Ministry of Family, Social Development, and National Solidarity in Dakar. The position of Mrs. Gueye, such as expressed in this interview, could be summarised as follows: Poverty reduction is the aim, women's advancement the means, gender equality the necessary condition, and religion no hindrance for development.

Mrs. Gueye had just come back from the international Beijing +10 conference at the UN headquarters in New York, where she led the official national delegation of the Senegalese government.[1] I asked her for a statement about what she considered as the most important issues of the conference in New York and what would be their implications for development policies concerning women in Senegal. In response Gueye spoke at length about the difficulties in the process of implementing the international conventions (such as the Convention for the Elimination of All Forms of Discrimination against Women, CEDAW) and the national development policies that had already been decided accordingly. She emphasised that the main challenge in the Senegalese context remains poverty reduction, with serious problems in the domain of health and education. In these domains women are considered as particularly vulnerable groups. Gueye considered the politics of women's advancement, in the framework of a multisector approach, as a way out of the impasse of the persistent social and economic crisis. Yet the conception of women's vulnerability, persisting in national as well as in the global development discourses, could be considered in itself as an impasse.

The Vulnerability Discourse: "It Blocks the Women"

Women's effective contribution to agricultural production and ensuring food security stands in contrast to the discourses and policies brought forward by the state and other national and international development agencies. The fact that women are continuously classified as one of the most vulnerable social categories enforces this contradiction because it tends to render women's own spaces and their active participation in economic and social processes invisible (Lachenmann 2001, 85 ff.). Thereby women's socioeconomic marginalisation is enforced (see chapter 2). At the same time the actors of the international development community find themselves in a position where they can easily follow their own agenda without really considering the capacities and needs of the local female population. This logic has been systematically repeated through multiple development programmes, as Khadija Doucouré, the director of the African Centre for Women's Entrepreneurship (CAEF, see chapter 2) stated in an interview:

> The problem is that there are organisations, discourses, and contents which are auto-paralysing. They see the woman only in terms of her vulnerability. Finally this destroys any kind of creative spirit, it blocks the women . . . but it helps certain NGOs, it helps certain bilateral co-operations, it helps the consultants. I am a consultant myself. It helps everybody. No one has to question oneself, and the same thing is repeated over and over again. (Khadija Doucouré, Centre Africain de l'Entrepreneuriat Féminin, 11.05.2004)

Doucouré harshly criticises the labelling of women as a "vulnerable group" within mainstream development policies and discourses, as such labels tend to "infantilise women" and put them "in a situation of extraordinary precariousness" (interview 11 May 2004). A main reference for this kind of discourse is the official Senegalese Poverty Reduction Strategy Paper (PRSP; République du Sénégal 2002) where the concept of vulnerability is made explicit with a definition followed by a list of groups characterised as vulnerable.[2] Moreover, the discursive pattern of women's vulnerability is also perpetuated implicitly through national development programmes such as the National Action Plan for Women or the official CEDAW report. The first official CEDAW report by the Senegalese Ministry of Family was published in August 2004 (République du Sénégal 2004). To a certain extent this applies equally to the above-mentioned National Strategy of Gender Equity and Equality and the National Report of Evaluation of the Beijing Platform for Action. Even if these papers do not make use of the term vulnerability as extensively or explicitly as the PRSP, they reproduce the same conceptual pattern by focusing on women's subordination without analysing their social position as producers and active economic agents. In this context their subordinate position is mostly explained by stereotyped formulations concerning patriarchal structures, traditional practices, social and cultural demands, or so-called sociocultural burdens.

Religion is rarely mentioned in the context of national development discourses. Representatives of national development institutions, such as the coordinator of the National Federation of Groups for Women's Advancement (FNGPF, see chapter 2), resort rather to the generalising statement that "Islam is no hindrance for women's development" (Mouslymatou Ndiaye, 14 April 2004). In a general way, cultural conservatism and the "backwardness" of local traditions are held responsible for women's oppression and limited space of action—for example, girls' early marriage and lack of education, which are often cited as the most detrimental aspects of traditional society. This corresponds to the official position concerning the secular character of the state as defined in the first article of the Senegalese constitution.[3]

The Role of Religion: A Stabilising Element

Rather than confronting and criticising religion, underlining its positive aspects in the process of social transformation is a recurrent discursive pattern in the articulation of national development discourses on various societal levels (see chapter 2). It can be clearly discerned in the following passage on the first pages of the official CEDAW report which introduces the issue of women's discrimination in the frame of a larger sociocultural context where religion figures as a factor of social cohesion:

> Due to a long standing tradition of tolerance and to a religion shared by large parts of the society (94% of the Senegalese population) and because of urbanisation, which has transformed the modes of life, the representatives of diverse ethnic groups respect their differences and have learned to live and work together. This social peace, in addition to political stability, has favoured the flourishing of the state under the rule of law and the recognition of legal equality. Nevertheless some important inequalities remain between men and women, between rural and urban citizens, between regions, between poor and rich. (République du Sénégal 2004, 7)

The last sentence of this passage, following the ideal of equality and unity, indicates some quite contradictory aspects of national identity construction while at the same time recognising cultural diversity and social differentiation processes.[4] The idea of legal equality (*égalité de tous devant la loi*) on the one side, and the recognition of social inequalities on the other constitute the basic references for actors in the field of development and women's rights.

Another important aspect influencing negotiation practices and discursive strategies in the field of women's rights is the growing weight of religious identity compared to the blurring or vanishing of ethnic identities in the process of "Wolofisation" (Cruise O'Brien 2003), which can be interpreted as an effect of urbanisation and as a condition that enables different ethnic groups to live and work together peacefully. However, in the CEDAW document, like in other official policy papers, such as the National Action Plans for Women or the recent National Strategy of Gender Equity and Equality, this process of cultural homogenisation is somehow taken for granted and not given much attention. Nor is the role of religion with respect to persisting structures of women's discrimination and their remaining "sociocultural constraints" in any way specified or analysed.[5]

A rare exception among the papers published by the Ministry of Family is the study on "Senegalese women by the year 2015," funded by the ILO, the World Bank, and other bilateral agencies such as USAID. The study was coordinated by two renowned Senegalese social scientists, the feminist sociologist Fatou Sow (see chapter 2) and the historian Mamadou Diouf, and supervised by the regional representative of the Population Council. The text presents an analysis of women's situations, starting with a historical perspective in which the development of Islam in precolonial Senegambia is mentioned as a factor which "seemed to have increased the marginalisation of women in public life" (followed by the colonial regime, which is considered to have reinforced the exclusion of women: République du Sénégal 1993, 4). Considering the possibilities of redefining gender relations "in the face of social and moral crisis" due to the breakdown of the "material and spiritual foundations" of the family, the study criticises not only culturalist but also religious "mechanisms of defence." The statement that religions "have never held such a central position in all the social strata as they do now" is followed by a critical comment: "Religions will not be able to bring about the emancipation of women as long as the exegesis of the texts continues to belong to men's domain and as long as their subordination is believed to have a religious basis and men and women are not considered as equal partners" (République du Sénégal 1993, 28).

The analysis of the mechanisms of women's marginalisation and the clear statement concerning religion indicates that this study is more linked to the epistemic community of academic researchers and sociologists than to the sphere of official development discourses represented by the state. Most of the national and international NGOs in Senegal share the standpoint of the government, holding local cultural traditions as the major constraint for women to claim their human and civil rights. This argument is all the more popular as it avoids any direct confrontation with the religious powers and does not contradict the position of those who see Islam as an emancipating force in favour of women's rights. Among state officials as well as among women's or human rights activists this position is quite common.

A typical example is Maïmouna Kane, founding member of the Association of Senegalese Jurists, former Minister for Social Development, and one of the first female representatives in the Senegalese government. In an interview with a women's NGO network she said: "Muslim religion, in contrast to what people think, defends the rights of women. It has set up a revolution in relation to the situation women had before. Islam is not opposing itself against progress, in fact it urges us towards science, towards progress" (Réseau Siggil Jigeen 2005, 12). This statement goes along with a critique of feudal structures and traditional patriarchy rooted in local culture. It does not, however, give an explanation for the intermingling of power relations between the state and religious institutions. And it transmits a certain ambivalence concerning the legitimacy of the secular constitution and Western-oriented national legislation expressed thus: Is it actually supported by Islam or not? This question has become most acute in the debate concerning the national family law.

The Debate on the National Family Law

Senegal has acceded to all the relevant international conventions for the elimination of discrimination against women (most recently to the Protocol to the African Charter on Human and Peoples' Rights on the Rights of Women in Africa, ratified in 2005) and has also adopted laws penalising violence against women. Nevertheless in the national legislation various clauses still exist which contradict CEDAW (ratified without reservations in 1985) as well as the principle of equal rights stipulated in the current constitution voted for in 2001 (Sow 2003, 75). Women's rights activists and NGOs point out some contradictions, mainly concerning the Senegalese Family Code. The latter has been hotly disputed ever since it was presented to the public in 1972, constituting the major bone of contention between the feminist movement and various Islamic forces. It was called the "Women's Code" by its opponents because it strengthened women's legal position, determining conditions for marriage, inheritance, and custody which were formerly regulated by diverging legal practices including customary, Quranic, and French law (Creevey 1996, 297; Loimeier 1995, 197; Sow 1996, 150 ff.).

With the Family Code the government intended to establish a unified law to be applied to all citizens, no matter what their religious denomination. However, it contains some options for Muslims to adopt a version of Islamic law corresponding to Quranic dispositions concerning, for example, inheritance (giving daughters one-half of their brothers' share) or marriage (dowry is accepted, polygyny possible). The Islamic prescriptions were altered to enhance women's rights—that is why at the time of its enactment the Senegalese state assumed an avant-garde position in terms of a Western-oriented modernisation, compared to other Muslim countries of the West African region (Sow 2003, 72). But it always encountered strong resistance from within Senegalese society. Senegal's first president Léopold Sédar Senghor, himself a Christian, used the Family Code to strengthen secularism and promote women's emancipation as an integral part of his vision of an African socialism. With the official enactment into law in 1973 Senghor overruled the objections of many elements of Senegalese society, notably the marabouts (Loimeier 1995, 197 f.). Without their support, however, the Code is rarely applied and continues to be widely ignored by the population, particularly by women in the rural areas (Creevey 2006, 157).

The arguments used by the state to convince its citizens of the need to abandon local legal practices and accept the application of the national family law currently refer to "international standards" as opposed to local traditions (Villalón 1995, 98 f.). Recently this discursive strategy, representing the state's efforts as a kind of civilising mission, has changed slightly. The government has tried to maintain its position while retreating from the arena of conflict and symbolic confrontation with the Islamic authorities. Because of this it has come to rely strongly on women's organisations and NGOs who are promoting the code and sensitising the population at the grassroots level. And what they bring to the fore is less the idealised vision of secular modernity, but an argumentation that refers explicitly to religion, in particular to Islam, in order to enhance the legitimacy of the national legislation.

This attitude change can be interpreted as a sign of the awareness of an increased relevance of religious issues in national politics, where "everybody is manipulating religion" (Fatou Sow in: Nageeb, Sieveking, Spiegel 2005b, 17). It also indicates a situation in which the state is trapped by its own symbolic representations and strategies. Cruise O'Brien has pointed out that "the state loses more by being ignored or avoided [by its Muslim population] than it does by confrontation" (2003, 26). However, concerning the claims for a reform of the national family law, the new government refrains from confrontation. It seems reluctant to engage actively in a public debate where secular state power is challenged from two sides: by local religious authorities as well as by secular civil society organisations and women's networks.

As indicated above, the debate concerning a reform of the national family law has been ongoing. Since the mid-1980s, when the UN women's decade and the newly emerged Senegalese feminist movement strengthened the position of women's organisations, NGOs and trade unions, as well as the secular-oriented peasant movement multiplied their efforts to improve women's rights and advance the notion of gender equality in public discourse. The discussions heated up when in 2003 a new Islamic association (Comité Islamique pour la Réforme du Code de la Famille du Sénégal, CIRCOFS) was founded, demanding a reform of the Family Code in the sense of adapting it more to the Sharia.[6] Claiming to defend the Muslim identity of the majority of the population, CIRCOFS calls for a restoration of Muslim courts (abolished by the Senghor regime) and a modification of several articles of the Code concerning marriage (conditions of its validity and obligations of husband and wife), divorce (legitimacy of repudiation), and issues of filiation (including adoption) and inheritance.

While president Abdoulaye Wade pronounced himself in public clearly against the initiative of CIRCOFS, he did not take measures to turn this statement into concrete and effective policies on the national or local level. Trying to link up with global development discourses on women's rights and gender equality on the international scene in a rather symbolic way, the government left the task of communicating these concepts and negotiating their meaning with the Muslim population at the local level to women's organisations and networks, like the Siggil Jigeen Network (see chapter 2). The publication of policy paper concerning the new National Strategy for Equity and Gender Equality in Senegal (République du Sénégal 2005b) and the two accompanying booklets containing a "religious argumentation for gender equity" in January 2005 can be seen as part of this kind of alliance based on a strategic division of labour.

At the same time the RSJ (which had participated significantly in the elaboration of the strategy paper; see chapter 2) started a nationwide campaign for the modification of the Family Code. In this context discussions with local women's groups were organised all over the country, in order to popularise knowledge about the Family Code and elaborate arguments for its reform that would reflect women's own perspectives. The central topics of the campaign concerned the notion of family authority, specifically the change from "paternal authority" to "parental authority," addressing both father and mother as responsible for the children. An important strategy in the campaign was the use of religious arguments in favour of women's rights elaborated by progressive Islamic scholars (see chapter 2) such as the author of the above-mentioned booklet, Abdul Aziz Kébé.

Kébé is Secretary General of the Islam and Population Network (Réseau Islam et Population, RIP), founded at the instigation of the Ministry of Finance and Planning and the UN Population Fund in the aftermath of the Cairo Conference on Population and Development (1994). RIP is one of the few Islamic NGOs recognised by the state (Renders 2002, 73 f.). It claims to be an autonomous organisation, bringing together experts in Islamic religion, Imams, and researchers, as well as representatives of different maraboutic families. RIP diffuses progressive interpretations of Islam, illustrated with examples from the Quran, mainly concerning reproductive rights. In this domain it has gained notoriety, such as in the case of an AIDS awareness campaign where it promoted the use of condoms for which it was virulently criticised by a range of religious leaders. Kébé, who holds a doctorate in Arabic, asserts that although Islam explicitly forbids certain roles for women, a knowledgeable interpretation of the Quran still leaves "enough room to manoeuvre" (ibid., 74 f.). In his "Argumentaire Religieux Musulman sur l'Équité de Genre" (République du Sénégal 2005a), written in French with some Arabic quotations, Kébé introduces the term equality as one of four directive principles: the principle of ease (*aisance*), meaning that nobody is forced by Islam to transgress the limits of his/her possibilities, the principle of constructing the social well-being, the principle of universality, and the principle of equity (to guarantee the universality in the construction of the well-being).

Campaigning for Women's Rights and Gender Equality

The text written by Kébé does not contradict the global development concepts embodied by the UN institutions, to which the RIP is affiliated. Yet, the religious arguments for gender equity as such have so far not been taken up by the Western-oriented national or international development discourses. Neither have they been connected to popular discourses within local Muslim society. Thus, to be effectively communicated and used for the purpose of women's organisations on a broader societal level, the religious argumentation for gender equity needs to be translated. In this respect, the carefully chosen notion of gender equity seems not to be as problematic in the Senegalese context, the main challenge in the context of the campaign to reform the family law being the concept of gender equality. Whereas the notion of women's rights is well established in public discourses at many societal levels, the concept of gender equality is perceived as alien to the cultural and religious foundations of local society (see Schulz 2007). Moreover gender equality is strongly associated with Western feminism and economically powerful but morally questionable development agencies, exercising an acculturating force on the Senegalese population. The discussions concerning women's rights within family law, organised as part of the national campaign launched by the RSJ, illustrate this problematic.

The Setting: Discussing the Family Law
with a Women's Group in Medina

"We don't want equality—we want to be given our rights!" This statement was articulated by the NGO activist Ndeye Diagne during a discussion with a local women's group in Kaolack in March 2005. The discussion was organised by the Association for the Promotion of the Senegalese Woman (APROFES; see chapter 2), one of the most active members of the network RSJ. The meeting with the local women's group took place in a small courtyard in Medina.

Medina is a popular quarter of the city that has been growing around a big mosque, representing the spiritual centre for adherents of the *Niassene* branch of the *Tijan* Brotherhood. It is among the most ancient parts of the city, not very far from the big market and the modern administrative centre, but relatively isolated and difficult to reach because of the bad condition of its dirty, bumpy, and sandy streets, which turn into impassable mud during the rainy season. Nevertheless the mosque attracts large streams of pilgrims from all around the country and the neighbouring regions, as well as from further abroad. The sheikh who presides over the religious community of the *Niassene* is Imam Hassane Cissé, a cosmopolitan intellectual and charismatic spiritual leader. Hassane Cissé, who studied at the Al Azhar University, Cairo, and obtained a masters in philosophy in Oxford, is very popular—people within the local community proudly point to his ability to speak "many languages." Promoting Quranic education with a strong transcultural emphasis, he attracts pupils from the neighbouring countries of the West-African region but also from abroad. Many of his supporters live in the United States of America, where he directs several branches of the African American Islamic Institute, an organisation founded by himself in Kaolack in 1988 and recognised as NGO by the United Nations, with affiliations in various West-African countries.[7]

On the basis of his transnational relations and networks sheikh Cissé is actively supporting local development. He is particularly engaged in the domain of healthcare and has established, with the support of UN agencies and the American NGO AmeriCares, a sociomedical centre in Medina. Mortality at childbirth has recently been an issue of special concern, where he has been networking with midwives' organisations on the national as well as on the local level.[8] Another emphasis of his activities is on sustainable rural development and local self-help organisations. In all these domains he strongly promotes women's rights issues—in Kaolack he frequently collaborates with APROFES and other local women's organisations.

Ndeye Diagne is a founding member of APROFES and part of the permanent staff. As a trained secretary with knowledge in French and English, she is in charge of the domains of rights, HIV/AIDS prevention, and the NGO's centre for female victims of domestic violence. She is also the local representative of Women in Law and Development in Africa (WILDAF), a pan-African network for women's rights. During the campaign for the reform of the family law she coordinated the discussions with local women's groups and supervised the NGO's local agents, trained as para-juristes (paralegals). The latter work as intermediaries between the NGO and less formalised women's groups from the local communities. Apart from the various training they received from the NGO (in the domain of rights, adult literacy, economic management, female leadership, HIV prevention, and reproductive health) their social and economic background is similar to the members of the women's groups from the communities they come from: most of them are illiterate or have a very low level of formal school education. All of them maintain some small-scale businesses in the agricultural and informal economic sector to secure a livelihood for their families. The majority of the women live in polygynous households.

In contrast to other women's organisations affiliated with APROFES, which include also members with a Christian background, in this case all the women were Muslim, although most of them had a rather low level of religious education and a restricted knowledge of the Quran. Moreover, there were only very few people with a concrete knowledge about the content of the Family Law, let alone the conflicting secular and religious positions and the respective claims and objections concerning its reform. To open the discussion Ndeye Diagne thus had to explain first of all the basic aim and the central concepts of the campaign. To this end she introduced some French terms in her speech, which was otherwise held in Wolof. Thus she used the term gender (*genre*) to explain that after mobilising the women, the men should get involved, because the issue concerned both sexes equally. Then she underlined the importance of getting into contact with the religious authorities, to tell them that the campaign was not aimed at "making politics."

Diagne reported how a group of women activists from the RSJ had talked with the highest representatives of the local Sufi brotherhoods to explain their intentions. Remembering the experience, she cheered up: "To talk with the marabouts directly—that's a good thing!" Describing the women's standpoint towards the religious authorities, Diagne pointed out that instead of calling for equality in terms of a radical change of the existing social and gender order, they had rather argued on the basis of an everyday logic of reciprocity: "We want to be given our rights, because we are giving money." To explain this argument she mentioned that women have to pay more taxes than men, because the state attributes to the wife the status of single, whereas the husband is considered as the "head of the family" in charge of his wife and the children. However, the statement could also be understood as a hint to the fact that women's financial contributions to their marabouts in the context of *dahira* activities (see chapter 2) are considerable.[9] This sense of the argument was left implicit, but could be well understood in the everyday context of the women present in the courtyard in Medina, where few people had formal employment or paid taxes. Yet, everybody was familiar with the institution of *dahiras*, which are proliferating in the local communities and neighbourhoods (see chapter 2).

In the course of the discussion with the women in Medina, which was then opened for all the participants and became very lively, further arguments were brought forward to call for a modification of the actual Family Code: Women suffer during pregnancy and during childbirth, without having the right to declare their children for tax or insurance purposes. They care for the members of the family, for the education and health of the children, and often as well for their husbands, but cannot assume this responsibility officially, apply for family allowances or health insurance coverage for their children, etc. The concept of rights became the crystallising point for the arguments supporting the women's claim for change. The inequalities and injustices women have to face in their everyday life were exemplified by individual accounts of the difficulties of their position in polygynous settings, their responsibility for securing livelihood for the whole family, frequently facing male unemployment and out-migration, domestic violence, and humiliations. Commenting on the examples given, the women concluded that their situation was "not normal" (Wolof: *jaaduwul*). Thereby they referred to a set of locally established cultural norms and values concerning women's duties and obligations in the framework of the traditional family on the one side, and an ideal of social solidarity and a moral economy based on reciprocity on the other.

Defining Equality: Identity Construction and Social Differentiation
As the above-cited statements indicate, the term equality, quite in contrast to the notion of rights, is introduced by the NGO activists with a disclaimer. During the discussion, one of the local agents, Aissatou Mbodj, put it like

this: "When we speak of equality it is not equality in general, but the equality of rights, because God has created us different." With this formulation, pointing to the essential differences between men and women as something given by God (to question them would be immoral for a believer), she asserts the women's Muslim identity. At the same time she contextualises the notion of equality by restricting its meaning to a discourse on rights and entitlements in the framework of women's position within the family. In a separate interview[10] she clarifies her notion of equality and explains how she translates the French term into Wolof: "We don't talk of being equal but we talk of the rights of mother and father concerning life with the children in the house. . . . Of the two, who is more tired? It is the woman who is more tired but she is not given the rights that are accorded to the father. . . . This is not normal, you know, it is not normal! This is why we women have to stand up—not to fight, but to demand satisfaction" (Aissatou Mbodj, 10.02.06).

The Wolof term *jaadu*, usually translated by Wolof speakers with the French adjective *normal*, also carries the signification of convenient or logic. This means that the claimed *satisfaction* (French in original) aims at being given a convenient position in the family on the basis of rights or entitlements which would correspond to a logic of solidarity, respect, and mutual recognition, including the acknowledgement of women's responsibilities and the fulfilment of their duties. Concerning the responsibilities, Mbodj confirms the culturally established differences between men and women:

> For the child the mother is the model. . . . The woman has to know that she has huge responsibilities. If you make a fault, everything is spoiled. In a household, if the man is bad but the woman is good, the faults of the man will not be known by the others. But if the woman is bad, the people will not see that the man is good, they will just know that the woman is bad. And the children who are born by a bad woman will probably be bad too. (Aissatou Mbodj, 10.02.06)

Having fulfilled the social demands within this framework, women are more tired than men; this is why they feel entitled to demand satisfaction. Mbodj is not questioning the fact that women's obligations and moral responsibilities are different from those of the men. This is why she prefers not to talk about equality, but about women's rights (Wolof: *sañ-sañ*). From her perspective this kind of reasoning is also the appropriate way to address the religious authorities, whom she sees indeed as crucial in the negotiation of women's rights:

> If you want to succeed, you have to start with the marabouts because the real problem is with them; with the others, there is no problem. But if you succeed to negotiate with the marabouts you will get on with everything. . . . They

think that women want to push the men from their position, whereas women and men cannot be equal. But they are mistaken, because this is not what we want, we just want rights. (Aissatou Mbodj, 10.02.06)

There are further aspects which need to be highlighted in order to understand the meaning of Mbodj's statement with respect to local identity constructions. Mentioning the differences between men and women as something created by God, she refers to specific discursive modes of presenting oneself as a good Muslim believer. And even more importantly, she links up the issue of rights and equality with a cultural ideal of female qualities according to which women's strength lies in the capacity to accept and bear the hardships and injustices of life without openly contesting or fighting (Wolof: *xeex*). Comparing Mbodj's position with Ndeye Diagne's it is important to take into account that she articulates her statement from the perspective of a collective actor, embracing the whole women's group as a moral community. While her statement concerning equality could have sounded quite different in the context of an individual communication, in this case she assumes a conservative position according to the popular image of women as the keepers of traditions and assumes the persistence of local cultural values and morality.

Diagne speaks from a different position, representing another kind of moral and epistemic community. She belongs to an economically more privileged milieu and is able to participate in social spaces that are much more translocally and globally connected. This background provides her with the ability to use certain discourses, concepts, and arguments. Talking as a representative of WILDAF or as a private person in an informal situation, she would defend a much more radical feminist notion of gender equality and also assume a more critical attitude concerning local norms and values. Her rejection of the notion of equality in this concrete context has thus to be understood as a communicative strategy and rhetoric device for specific situations, including the present discussion with the women's group in Medina as well as the women activists' encounter with the marabouts.

In the context of Senegalese Sufi Islam, the appropriate behaviour in addressing a religious authority is generally characterised by a strong hierarchy and an attitude of respect that expresses the formal acknowledgement of the spiritual power and moral superiority of the marabout by the ordinary believer. However, similar hierarchies also characterise the culturally established intergenerational and gender relations. With respect to the very complex social stratification of Senegalese society, the rejection of the concept of equality thus has to be understood as a pragmatic device concerning the appropriate behaviour which is necessary to successfully communicate with other social actors, particularly if they come from different social milieus.

A similar attitude towards the concept of equality was expressed in the context of a training session on "Gender and Leadership" carried out by APROFES in February 2006. During a group discussion concerning the meaning of gender, different concepts were mentioned, among them the terms equality and equity. While equity was explained by the participants as an illustration of the principle of complementarity, the notion of equality was explained by the idea that men and women can do the same work and have the same responsibilities in everyday life. Yet, this idea was perceived as a contradiction to social reality and a challenge to the established hierarchies of male authority. Therefore many of the participants did not consider the term equality as a good means to bring about a consensus concerning female leadership, and some even rejected it categorically: "Don't mention equality. It will only bring more problems!"

Women's Rights Within the Family: A Local Perspective

The discussions in the context of the campaign for a reform of family law show that women often assume an ambivalent discursive position to enlarge their room for manoeuvre—such as Mbodj, who underlines that the rejection of the principle of equality by the local women's groups is actually only partial. From her point of view there is a notion of equality which needs to be defended—not the idea of "equality in general" (*égalité tout court*) but the "equality of rights" (*égalité de droits*). This differentiation calls for a more thorough consideration of the aspect of language.

The discussion in Medina was mainly in Wolof, but some concepts had been introduced in French, among them the notions of gender, equality, and rights. It was the task of the local agents of the NGO to translate these terms into Wolof in a way that could be understood by all the members of the local community. The most recurrent rhetoric formula used in this context was the assertion that women are tired. To promote the concept of equality within the local women's group it has to be contextualised. This was done by relating it to the way in which the discriminations and inequalities characterising women's daily life are articulated in popular discourses. The notion of women being tired is a widespread discursive pattern in Senegal. It reflects women's ambivalent social position of bearing most of the work and responsibilities concerning subsistence and the well-being of the family, without being recognised in this position in terms of corresponding rights and entitlements (be it in the framework of national legislation, as fixed in the Family Code, or of customary law, based on religion or legal tradition).

To explain the reasons of women's tiredness Aissatou Mbodj (10 Feb 2006) described the recurrent case of women who work hard and invest all their money in the education of their children, culminating in a ticket to send them off to Europe, but finally have to give up their plan because the father refused his authorisation "just to put the woman down." At another point in the interview she referred to the situation of women in the times of her mother who had been much more tired than herself. Compared to those times the situation had considerably improved in terms of the alleviation of women's physical workload, but also in terms of rights: "Every generation has its privileges. I am very happy of my generation and I am sure that my daughter will be even more happy with hers. My generation has more rights than that of my mother. What existed in the time of my grandmother and grandfather is continuing until today—but we don't want it anymore!"

Another local agent of APROFES, Fama Niang (14 Feb 2006), who had also worked as a paralegal during the campaign for the reform of the family law, embraced the notion of equality as a means to call for a change concerning the share of responsibilities and workload: "Women are the most tired within the family. This is why we have stood up to explain the meaning of equality to the other women. . . . Equality, in the way we explain it to the women in Wolof, means '*yemale ci biir kër gi jekker ak jabar nyu yem dogal ci biir njaboot*' (equilibrate/share/bring into balance the decision-making power of husband and wife within the family)."

To explain why the notion of equality is often rejected in local discourses Niang refers to the idea of male physical strength that legitimises the traditional gender order: "We have a tradition, an ancestral belief, that God has created men and women in a way that men have more force (Wolof: *doole*), and are thus able to do the kind of work women are not able to do." However, from her point of view these traditions and beliefs are "not really verified," and were perpetuated simply "because they are so ancient." While she concedes that on the grounds of religion men and women cannot be conceived as equal in all respects, she is still convinced that the aim and reason of their fight are noble, and that the women's demand "is perfectly in line with the Quran." Without having profound religious knowledge herself, she leaves this field to the Islamic authorities that support the women in their campaign. And to further strengthen her own position she also refers to the case of Morocco where family law has been changed already, replacing the notion of paternal authority by parental authority.

Negotiating Social Change and the "True Meaning" of Equality

Fama Niang's main argument for the promotion of gender equality is based on pragmatic reasoning which concerns the anticipated outcome of reform: "Some people have understood that this could make their life easier." Taking her own experiences as an example, she communicates her vision of gender equality according to the principle of ease (such as promoted by Kébé) to the people in her neighbourhood. In contrast to Aissatou Mbodj, who is the third wife in a polygynous household, Niang considers herself lucky to be the only one. She says that through the training she received by APROFES she has considerably improved her social and economic situation. Before, she was "doing nothing," now she is teaching an adult literacy class and is running a small restaurant:

> Even here in my restaurant I often discuss with my clients and talk with them about gender and equality between men and women. I explain to them that it serves our interest, as well for the women as for the men, the children, and the whole family. . . . Thanks to the discussions [those organised by NGOs in the community or transmitted through the radio] people now know that it serves the interest of the men, because it can also help in the management of the household. (Fama Niang, 14.02.06)

Niang reports that she addresses in particular the single men among her clients, telling them that they would profit if they married an intellectual woman (meaning a woman with a higher level of Western education) because the knowledge of such a woman could facilitate the achievement of a better life for both of them. However, she is aware that the association of the term equality with Western development agencies and Western lifestyle is problematic, particularly in relation with the identity constructions of local Muslim society:

> There are some men who have studied the holy Quran well and they apply it at home. If their wives want to put into practice the notion of gender or equality without explaining to their husbands the true sense of these terms, they refuse categorically. One has to explain to these men the notions and clarify their meaning, and little by little they will accept. They just think the tubaab have implanted in our heads the idea of equality between men and women like over there. (Fama Niang, 14.02.06)

With her last remark Niang refers to the way the campaign for a reform of the family law is perceived by large segments of the population: As the result of Western influence, embodied by international development agencies, NGOs, as well as by the secular state administration, that tries to impose a model of development that is alien to local culture. The concept of gender equality is rarely understood in the sense of a universal principle, but rather interpreted as an expression of specific Western habits and lifestyle, which are seen as a contradiction to the local African sociocultural values and the institution of the traditional family. The notion of gender equality evokes the fear of acculturation and moral decay (particularly in the domain of sexual behaviour). At the same time it stands for an anti-Islamic attitude which is transmitted on the level of global discourses and politics.

While Aissatou Mbodj argues for women's rights in a way that avoids challenging the established social and moral order, Fama Niang explicitly calls for a change in society. She has appropriated the notion of equality as a key concept for development. From her perspective the implementation of gender equality would bring about the changes that are necessary to achieve the common good. Therefore, she is convinced that the idea of gender equality would be well accepted if only its true meaning could be transmitted, that is, the achievement of the common good in the sense of improving life for men and women.

The Common Good in Terms of an "Equality of Rights"

The common good, however, is defined very differently by actors from different social and religious spheres. Progressive Islamic scholars such as Aziz Kébé or Taha Sogou are very much in line with the state and international development discourses. Yet these scholars represent only a tiny minority among the various trends in Senegalese contemporary Muslim society. Other religious authorities, like those associated within CIRCOFS, assume quite different positions. A leading representative of the Islamic reform organisation Jama'aatu Ibadu Rahmane (see chapter 2), for example, emphasised that his organisation completely rejects the notion of equality such as promoted by the state and "the feminists" because "the man is always superior to the woman." In his eyes development and women's advancement can only be achieved through religious education (according to the principle of men's superiority).

The processes of social differentiation, represented in the interaction between the various social, political, and religious actors, are reproduced in the women's strategies to negotiate their rights, notably in their partial rejection of the concept of equality. The latter illustrates the significance of the speaker's position in the concrete context of social interaction. In contrast to the concept of equality, the concept of rights seems much more appropriate in dealing with these differentiation processes and prevailing social hierarchies. The latter are characterising not only the gendered relations on a local level, but also communication between the grassroots level, the state level, and the national and international development agencies, as well as between representatives of diverse Muslim organisations and institutions. The discursive construction of an equality of rights illustrates the appropriation of global development concepts in terms of a process of constant recontextualisation. Looking at this process at the local level, it becomes clear that language is an essential means to contextualise and redefine the meaning of development. The case also points to the important role of religious discourses as part of local cultural realities as well as of global cultural flows.

Although the discussion had been opened with an explicit reference to the national Family Code, these rights were understood as something acquired through women's social and economic engagement in their daily lives as wives and mothers, but not as something given automatically to everybody in terms of citizenship by the national constitution or by the government acceding to an international convention. During the above-described event women's rights were thus not discussed in terms of national or international legislation. While the relevant articles of the Family Code are mentioned and the numbers of the relevant paragraphs (§152 and §277) memorised, the concept of legal rights is hardly taken up in the discussion. Rather the term *rights* is related to customary law, concrete social practices, and locally grounded logics of reciprocity which characterise the interactions of the participants.

As the cases of the two local agents of the NGO in Kaolack show, their vision of change is reflected in the use of particular concepts and communication strategies. The way these women try to enhance their agency by appropriating the global concepts of equality and rights goes along with considerations concerning their appropriateness in specific contexts. More precisely, for the women in Medina it seems much more important to consider the question of appropriateness than to join in a general call for change. This can be understood by analysing how women's agency and negotiating potential is related to their capability to strengthen their social position in terms of a public recognition and affirmation of their moral integrity and cultural identity.

Female Activism between Concession and Contest

An important aspect in this context is women's certainty that the claim for a reform of the Family Code brought forward by the representatives of the NGO does not contradict the principles of Islam. Ndeye Diagne's report of the encounter with the marabouts contributed to this conviction. But even more significant in this respect is the general reputation of the NGO as expressed by Fama Niang, who repeatedly assured that all activities undertaken with APROFES "correspond exactly" to the prescriptions of the Quran. The way she came to know about the NGO tells a lot about how the organisation is socially embedded and how it creates space for local women to articulate their visions of development and social change.

Ten years ago in a neighbouring quarter a nine-year-old girl had been raped by a sixty-six-year-old local politician. Someone had called APROFES for legal help. Through their intervention the man was sentenced and put into jail for ten years. But the contact with the NGO did not stop at that point. APROFES encouraged the women of the neighbourhood who had joined together in their effort to support the raped girl and her mother to organise and become registered as a formalised women's group—thereby they could involve themselves in development projects, receive training, and also funding. According to Fama Niang, who worked as an adult literacy teacher for this women's group and was also active in managing the community centre and the mill that had been constructed in the meantime, these achievements had significantly changed the gender relations within the community. Before, "women were not respected by their husbands" and always had to keep silent when a man was talking. But since then, things have changed: "Now we are proud to be women!"

The NGO's intervention and its success in defending the women's case against a locally influential representative of the male political establishment had a strong empowering effect on the local women's group and helped to legitimise their activities on moral grounds. Moreover Niang emphasised that the economic success that had come along with the NGOs engagement, due to the women's improved management skills and the possibility to receive small credit loans, was important in "getting more respect": "They [the NGO activists] worked until the husbands knew that APROFES does not turn away the women. It is an NGO which helps the women and their husbands."

In Fama Niang's eyes, respect and esteem are constitutive elements for women's agency. And in this sense, the good reputation of the NGO is essential. The idea that Western development institutions want to "turn away" (détourner) Muslim women from the "right way" is a recurrent pattern, not only in Senegalese Islamic discourses. Niang's statement is thus related to globalised discourses on how development can be achieved without losing one's cultural and religious identity. However, for the women in Medina this global dimension is only relevant insofar as it strengthens the position of local Islamic authorities who maintain that the reform of the code as well as the state's effort to establish gender equality in terms of legal rights is perfectly in line with the Quran. In this context Imam Hassane Cissé plays an important role. In an issue of the RSJ newsletter dedicated to the revision of the Family Code he is quoted with the following statement:

> The whole society must join this movement which consists in reinstituting the working women's rights. This is a disposition from which the whole society will profit. In Islam the woman has to have the same legal rights as men. The responsibility has to be executed by both parents to the benefit of the child and the woman has the right to aspire to social coverage [family allowance, health insurance, etc.] by the state. (Réseau Siggil Jigeen 2005, 9)

This statement comprises different arguments which are important elements in the strategy of the campaign for the family law. Brought forward by a religious authority and member of an important traditional maraboutic family, they represent a multiplicity of voices and perspectives, which cannot be identified with the stereotypes of an anti-Islamic, Western-oriented feminist position. The Imam particularly points to working women and their rights. He links the notion of legal rights to the issue of social security. Thereby he legitimises the claim for a reform of the Family Code not only by the Quran but also by essential elements of the national agenda of poverty reduction. Nevertheless he insists on the title of "head of the family" for men and argues for a compromise which would keep up the principle of a single authority embodied by the husband. This position is not only held by male authorities, as can be seen with the example of the jurist and former minister of social development, Maïmouna Kane. Concerning the articles of the Family Code defining the status of the man as head of the household, she states: "This doesn't bother me. It would be unjust to say that the woman must be head of the family. In life one has to make concessions. It's like going in an office where one finds a boss who embodies the authority, but this doesn't mean that the others are harmed or 'damaged' in their rights" (Réseau Siggil Jigeen 2005, 11–14).

Negotiating Women's Rights while Maintaining Cultural Identity

The Senegalese Family Code has actually always been a compromise. When it was established, several articles (concerning for example the age of marriage and the prohibition of forced marriages) were quite revolutionary (Sow 2003, 72). In the above-mentioned interview, Maïmouna Kane explains the historical signification of the Family Code as a tool for the implementation of the state's policy of women's advancement which could respond to the needs of social and economic change while still preserving cultural identity: "I think we have our own values and that the women should not try to copy the Western model" (Réseau Siggil Jigeen 2005, 14). She stresses the ability to make compromises, to negotiate women's rights corresponding to a shared moral code concerning the well-being of children, the family, and of the society as a whole. This ability is conceived by her as a female quality and at the same time as an integral part of Senegalese cultural identity. Her emphasis on "our own values" corresponds to an emphatic notion of culture that is typical for the intellectual elite of the first postindependence generation, and reflects Senghor's vision of the Senegalese nation as a kind of combination between the essential qualities of *Négritude* and the political ideal of an African Socialism.

Implementing Gender Equality: A Problem of Communication?
It is interesting to compare Kane's position with the attitude of the coordinator of the FNGPF, Mouslymatou Ndiaye. In an interview conducted in April 2004 she talks about the "backwardness" of local culture which she holds responsible for women's disadvantaged social position and difficult living conditions, especially in remote rural areas: "Religion is not very restrictive—it is Senegalese culture which has established women's oppression." And she believes that once "the continuity of cultural practices is interrupted" (*"le lien culturel cassé"*), Senegalese women could acquire an "equal status" with men. Dressed in Western clothes and ostentatiously smoking cigarettes during our interview, she expresses her rejection of the established image of the traditional Senegalese woman and her supposed essential Africanness not only on the discursive level, but also on the level of bodily symbolism. Quite in contrast to Kane, she conceives of local cultural traditions as a bondage, as a hindrance on the way to women's liberation, and not as a possible resource in negotiating women's rights.

Like many other government and NGO representatives in Senegal, Mouslymatou Ndiaye strongly resorts to globalised development discourses and a rather universalistic concept of women's rights, thereby rejecting cultural particularism. Still, she does not reflect on the problem of how these global concepts could be effectively communicated and translated into local discourses. Conversely, in analysing the problems of communication between different political groups and institutions and across heterogeneous sociocultural milieus, the difficulties in the implementation of national legislation as well as international conventions concerning women's rights can be better understood. At the same time some inherent contradictions of national development politics come to the fore.

From the perspective of Ndeye Soukeye Gueye, who represents the Directorate of the Family, the problem has to be traced back to the fact that programmes intended to implement the politics of women's advancement are conceived by "economists who do not take into account the cultural realities." Furthermore the ministry of family is de facto a rather marginalised institution in the Senegalese government and the postulated multisector approach is far from reality. Aminata Kassé (29.04.04), then director of the NGO COSEF (see chapter 2), who can look back at frequent collaborations with the ministry of family, holds that that the human resources and material equipment of the ministry are poor and its capacities for conceptual analysis limited. According to Kassé it has been and continues to be the most politicised ministry in the government. Through its related structures, like the FNGPF, it is able to use women's organisations for the purposes of the ruling political elite. The Directorate of the Family is specifically named by Kassé as an institution that is in itself "completely void" of any executive power or political conception independent from party politics.

As a way out of this impasse Ndeye Soukeye Gueye (06.04.05) underlined the need for a "programme of communication."[11] Responding to my question of how far she saw religion, or more precisely Islam, as being part of those "cultural realities" that are perpetuating women's discrimination, she presented me with the leaflet containing the "religious argumentation for gender equity" written by Aziz Kébé (see chapter 2). Referring to the new National Strategy of Gender Equity and Equality, Gueye emphasised that "gender equality and equity are something fundamental," constituting a basic condition for development which "is not opposed by the holy books." However, she conceded that the high ambitions of these official documents did not solve the problem of communication. Given the high rate of illiteracy among women, in addition to the fact that the majority of women have rather restricted access to religious knowledge and difficulties in actively participating in religious discourse, she admitted that this religious argumentation for the state's gender policies could not easily be communicated.

To be able to engage in a dialogue with the population at the local level, she argued, it is useful to include nondiscursive means of communication, such as theatre plays or other performative or visualising strategies. As an illustration she showed me a big booklet containing plates on which various situations of everyday life were depicted that exemplified the existing inequalities between men and women. She explained that in consciousness-raising campaigns these images were used to discuss the notion of equality and question the given gender order and its foundation in local culture. Yet a direct confrontation with local beliefs and customs were to be avoided, as Gueye underlined: "Instead of confrontation we have to work on the unconscious of the population."[12] And after all, this work of communicating with the population and translating the meaning of the state-promoted development concepts into local discourses could not be done by the state institutions alone: "We need the NGOs!"

Concerning the position of women's organisations, their different perspectives have to be considered. State-promoted structures and globally connected NGOs, as opposed to locally grounded social networks and traditional forms of organisation, constitute different social spaces (although they may partly overlap). They bring forward divergent ideas of development and do not conceive of themselves as agents of development in the same way. While leading the national campaign for the reform of the family law, the RSJ for example assumes the role of an intermediary between civil society and the state. In its publications the RSJ is giving voice to progressive Islamic scholars and thereby linking its vision of development based on a globalised discourse on women's rights and gender equality to a moderate religious ethic. Its relations with the state are ambivalent. The main focus of RSJ activities is characterised by its role as a watchdog, pushing the government to implement women's rights in order to avoid a state of illegality with respect to its own constitution but also to the diverse international conventions to which it is a signatory. But at the same time RSJ is also collaborating with the state authorities and its campaign is supported by state representatives.

In this collaboration one can observe a kind of division of labour that also applies to the state's attitude towards other organisations defending women's rights. The government officially promotes gender equality in order to appear as a progressive and avant-garde state in the eyes of the international community, but it does not combine this attitude with concrete policies, least of all concerning the reform of the Family Code. Thereby it avoids any direct confrontation with the religious authorities, leaving this field for the NGOs. Joining in this strategy, the secular women's organisations assist the government in order to avoid conflict which would imply a further politicisation of religion (as intended for example by the CIRCOFS). Emphasising that Islam supports women's rights and the equality of all human beings before the law is thus an important step in achieving a consensus with representatives of diverse Muslim groups (who would nevertheless rather argue that the defence of women's rights by a secular family law is "unnecessary").

The above-presented cases of different women's groups show that their strategies to build up networks by resorting to various types of social organisation, diverse modes of communication, discursive and nondiscursive forms of articulation, as well as popular cultural practices are essential means to strengthen their position and enlarge their room for manoeuvre. Through the negotiations between actors with multiple agendas, social space is recreated in a way that allows women to act as knowledgeable social agents instead of being reduced to a particularly vulnerable group of the population.

Notes

1. From 28 February to 11 March 2005 the UN Commission on the Status of Women conducted a ten-year review of the Beijing Platform for Action, focusing on national-level implementation. The Beijing Platform for Action is the outcome of the fourth World Conference on Women held in 1995. It is the most comprehensive document produced by a United Nations conference concerning the subject of women's rights incorporating the accomplishments of prior conferences and treaties such as the Universal Declaration of human rights, CEDAW, and the Vienna Declaration, and also including a paragraph on human rights in general.

2. The first category on the list are children, followed by women, handicapped, elderly people, the youth, displaced persons, and refugees (République du Sénégal 2002, 35).

3. "The Republic of Senegal is secular, democratic and social." The meaning of secularism (laïcité), as explained by the former president Abdou Diouf, has to be understood as "neither atheism nor antireligious propaganda," but as a protection of religious values and beliefs (Loimeier 2006, 191).

4. This picture of the Senegalese citizen neglects the lines of political differentiation between social groups.

5. Religion is mentioned as an obstacle to family planning and health consultation (République du Sénégal 2004, 42), as contributing to the sociocultural, administrative, and political constraints for women to have access to farming land (ibid., 44), and as reinforcing the interiorisation of women's subordination to a "patriarchal order" (ibid., Annexes, 14).

6. The president of the CIRCOFS is Babacar Niang, a lawyer and former Marxist and militant member of the RND.

7. The African American Institute has chapters in New York, Atlanta, Detroit, Memphis, and Washington, D.C. (http://home.earthlink.net/~halimcisse/aaii-2.html; download 1.12.06).

8. The region of Kaolack had one of the highest rates of maternal mortality in Senegal but through the effort of women's organisations and their networks this has decreased by about 50 percent between 2000 and 2005 (http://www.lesoleil.sn/article.php3?id_article=6763; download 4.12.06).

9. Salimata Thiam highlights women's considerable influence on the male religious and political establishment through their participation in religious organisations and in constituting networks with strong translocal and transnational connections that are used for trading activities (Nageeb, Sieveking, Spiegel 2005b, 13 f.).

10. The research situation in spring 2005 did not allow the registration and transcription of the whole discussion in Wolof, but only an ad hoc French translation. In order to analyse the

negotiation of the meaning of rights in local discourse in a more detailed way separate interviews in Wolof with the local agents who had participated in the discussion were conducted in 2006.

11. *"Rien ne vaut plus que la communication—les programmes ne règlent pas le problème"* (Ndeye Soukeye Gueye, 06.04.05).

12. *"À la place de la confrontation il faut agir sur l'inconscience de la population"* (Ndeye Soukeye Gueye, 06.04.05).

CHAPTER SEVEN

~

Negotiating Women's Rights in a Translocal Space: Women's Organisations and Networking in Malaysia

Anna Spiegel

A significant number of civil society organisations in Malaysia work within the framework of global development concepts and the relevant UN declarations. Especially for the women's movement, the concept of rights—be it women's or human rights and the respective Convention on the Elimination of All Forms of Discrimination against Women (CEDAW)—is gaining importance. However, the meaning of these prominent concepts is neither static nor uniform. Rather it is subject to manifold negotiations at the local level which lead to a diversification of the discourse on rights. The localisation of the global concept of rights is shaped by different discursive battles around contested sites such as *state, culture, tradition,* or *religion.* Within these sites the boundaries of rights are negotiated and new forms of meaning, translation, and localisation emerge. The approach of highlighting the often conflicting and ambivalent perspectives of different actors, their "strategies, manoeuvres, discourses, speech games, and struggles over social identity" is chosen in this chapter in order to "tease out the intricacies of how knowledge is internalised, used and reconstructed" (Long 1996, 56) within the process of negotiating global development concepts.

These negotiation processes, however, are not restricted to the local or national level, but are shaped by the fact that all civil society actors presented in this chapter are to different degrees part of global networks. It will be argued that these localisations are shaped by the process of contesting gender, rights, and development discourses put forward by the strong developmentalist Malaysian state. The Malaysian state promotes Islamisation and is moving towards an increasingly authoritarian political system. In this context networking is one way for civil society actors to enlarge their room for manoeuvre as well as their space for imaginations (Appadurai 2000), and global conventions, treaties, and concepts are important instruments to pressure governments to change its policies.

The chapter will start with the presentation and analysis of an event that stands for the specific translocal discourse on women's rights, the National NGO Conference on the Convention on the Elimination of All Forms of Discrimination against Women in 2004. In a second step the sites such as *state*, *tradition*, and *religion* where the concept of women's rights is contested and its boundaries are negotiated will be discussed. In a third step the translocal dimension will be brought into the picture discussing the ambivalent processes of negotiating women's rights within a culturally diverse global women's movement. Here the focus will be on the significance of intercultural interactions at conferences and on intercultural comparison as a means of translocal networking.

CEDAW and the Process of Writing a Shadow Report in Malaysia

Around forty Malaysian women from different ethnic backgrounds—Malay, Chinese, and Indian—are gathered in a seminar room in one of Kuala Lumpur's pleasant, air-conditioned hotels. They are representatives from different women's organisations from Kuala Lumpur, but also from Penang and Kota Bharu, who came to attend the National NGO Conference on the Convention on the Elimination of All Forms of Discrimination against Women (CEDAW). This conference was organised by the Women's Aid Organisation (WAO) and the National Council of Women's Organisations (NCWO, see chapter 3) on the weekend of the 21st and 22nd of August 2004 in Kuala Lumpur. At this conference the shadow report which had been produced by a smaller group of women activists was presented to the wider public of Malaysian women's organisations. In the introduction of the shadow report the aim of the conference was described as follows: "to raise awareness on how NGOs can use the CEDAW convention and the treaty reporting process in their work and the linkages between advocacy on the national and international level" (NGO Shadow Report Group 2004). The conference was opened by one of the main organisers with the words: "If we all work together we have like 100 years of experience." After giving a short introduction on CEDAW itself in the plenary, each chapter of the thematically organised shadow report[1] was discussed by smaller working groups. The participants were asked to document their corrections and amendments to the presented chapters in order to identify emerging issues in the respective field and to formulate specific recommendations to the government. Later, the results of the smaller working groups were presented in the plenary. During the whole conference women activists stressed the importance of the convention in general but also of the NGO shadow report again and again: "The convention is the tool in areas where we have difficulties at the national level, areas that we already work on but that we need to push forward." "This is our report. We can highlight what is missing in the government report. That's why we have to put in the reviewing of national policies. If we don't say it, they don't do it." "We are the ones who have to bring in the gender issue. We have to push the ministry to work on it. We as women have to test the government." Referring to the World Conference on Women in 1995 one activist said: "In Beijing the government agreed to 30 percent of participation of women in the public sector. We make the government responsible and we can accelerate this process." The concept of rights was very prominent in the debates. One of the activists stated: "We should use strong words. We should not say 'Women should be allowed to do this or that'. We should say 'Women have the right to do this or that.'"

The National NGO Conference on the Convention on the Elimination of All Forms of Discrimination against Women (CEDAW) is a good example of the dynamics of negotiating women's rights at the national level. CEDAW, which was approved by the UN general meeting in 1979, is one of the most important international treaties for women's organisations worldwide. State parties who sign and ratify the convention are obliged to document their efforts of putting into practice the contents of the convention and to present this report every five years to the UN commission located in New York. During the time of research, CEDAW was of special importance for women's groups in Malaysia since the government had presented a draft of the long overdue and much anticipated report. Malaysia had ratified CEDAW in 1995, but with several limitations in the application: First, the Malaysian government only signed the treaty with important reservations to some of the articles, especially concerning Sharia law; second, it was not passed as an act through the parliament, which means that it has not been included into a national jurisdiction; and third, only in 2004, six years after the first report to the committee was due, Malaysia's government started efforts to report to the UN committee.

The increased willingness of the Malaysian government to fulfil its duties concerning the process of reporting which is demanded by CEDAW is one facet of the generally growing importance of global concepts like 'women's rights and gender issues' in government policies. Since the Asian economic crisis the Malaysian government is increasingly integrating international human and women's rights discourse into its policies. In the year 2001 the term "gender" was included into Article 8(1) of the Malaysian constitution, where the prohibited grounds of discrimination are formulated. Before 2001 the enumeration comprised only "religion, race, descent and place of birth." In the same year, the Ministry of Women and Family Development was set up and important amendments to the guardianship act were carried out. In 2003 the prime minister convoked for the first time a Women's Summit, where leading women from the fields of politics and economics—but not women from the women's movement—gathered to debate issues surrounding women in the economy. In 2004 the series of women summits was continued with a summit on leadership and the first report to the CEDAW committee was submitted. Also in 2004 a Cabinet Committee on Gender Equality chaired by the prime minister was created. One can view these policy measures as a rather late concession to the growing international pressure to integrate discourses on gender equality into national policies.

The National Council of Women's Organisations (NCWO), the national umbrella organisation, initiated the process of writing a NGO shadow report in 2003, which then was coordinated by the transnational women's organisation International Women's Rights Action Watch Asia Pacific (IWRAW) and its local partner, the Women's Aid Organisation (WAO) which is explicitly undertaking the project to localise CEDAW to the Malaysian context. The shadow report is supposed to provide an alternative view and a corrective to the report presented by the respective governments. Being produced by civil society actors, it can take up issues that were neglected in the government reports or criticise the way in which issues are presented in these official reports. The CEDAW commission in New York takes into account the shadow reports in their evaluation of the government reports and even confronts the government delegations with the critical issues raised in the respective shadow report.

In Malaysia, a first meeting with interested groups and individuals was held in Kuala Lumpur in January 2003. Around thirty activists and academics participated in the meeting where issues to be covered and possible authors were discussed. The participants identified ten key areas, according to the articles of the convention and even added one, violence against women, which is of central importance for the work of women's organisations in Malaysia (see chapter 3). In the original body of the convention there is no such separate article on violence against women. On that meeting the participants agreed that the shadow report should be a collective paper, with individual people from different NGOs writing separate chapters in the areas of their expertise. After this first meeting several smaller group meetings of authors followed where critical issues of the shadow report were shared.

The activities of the NGOs pressured the women's ministry to an initial government report in February 2003. The Ministry invited civil society actors, mainly representatives from the NCWO, to give comments and feedback to the draft government report. In May 2004 the government distributed a first copy of the final government report. Cynthia, a young Eurasian lawyer from Kuala Lumpur who was one of the main activists of the CEDAW process and one of the main organisers of the national conference, described this entire process of communication among the different NGOs and writers as being very fruitful. For her not only is the shadow report in itself an important tool for the women's movement, but the entire process of negotiating its meaning in interaction with other women's groups is also of the highest importance, an innovation which was first practiced for the Beijing conference.

> This is the NGO report. I think it's interesting that one person could have written the report. We could have got one person to do the research, to gather the data from all the groups, that person could have sat down six months and the government could have looked at it. I think it really could have been a good report. But at the end of the day, that is not the point. It has been quite a process for us. Of course you have 10–12 different people working on different sections what takes a long time; everyone got their own stuff, that's why we had a delay. But the whole idea is that these 10 people in whatever areas, whatever organisations, they work with that. This actually should spill into their work or at least their organisation, that perhaps never looked at CEDAW before and suddenly says "Oh yes, we are working on this CEDAW project." (Cynthia, 28 Aug 2004)

Apart from legitimising the endeavour, the organisation of the shadow report writing as a collective process was a strategy to disseminate the contents of the convention and also to foster networking among the women's organisations working in very different areas. For Cynthia the fact that activists from various NGOs wrote the different sections and related their work to the content of the convention was already one important step to put the convention into practice. Although it seems to have been difficult, those involved felt that the process of interaction and networking was even more important than the quality of the resulting texts.

This accentuation of the aspect of networking has to be contextualised within the landscape of women's organisations in Malaysia. According to the structure and the content of CEDAW, a broad variety of topics are treated in the NGO shadow report and discussed at the national conference: education, religion, rural women, politics, health, work and employment, violence against women, and others. This combination of topics and cooperation of women's NGOs crossing thematical borders has been rather atypical for Malaysia, as the case of the rather short-lived National Women's Coalition which was created in the 1980s suggests. The National Women's Coalition was created as an alternative to the mainstream National Council of Women's Organisations and meant to be a broad network linking urban-based women's organisations with grassroots groups that were fighting for land rights, indigenous women, and women workers. But the coalition did not last very long and was not very successful. Instead networks based on specific issues have been very successful and more durable in Malaysian civil society, such as the Joint Action Group on Violence Against Women, the Coalition on Women's Rights in Islam, Malaysians against Moral Policing, and the Coalition Article 11 on Freedom of Religion. CEDAW, however, served as a connecting framework for local organisations and created a platform where women's organisations collectively discussed a wide range of important issues concerning women. Furthermore, the conference constituted a space for the women activists to construct themselves as knowledgeable experts in their areas, as was suggested in the above-quoted opening remarks of the conference organiser regarding the one hundred years of experience through cooperation between women's organisations.

Several times the activists pointed to the fact that it was the responsibility of the women's movement to monitor how the concepts of gender were used and appropriated by the government institutions, in order to identify or prevent any instrumentalisation of the concepts that would go against the needs of women. In the NGO shadow report and during the NGO conference, the state's gender concepts and the report which the government handed over to the CEDAW committee were discussed in detail and then partly challenged and deconstructed by the women activists. This deconstruction started with the definition of discrimination given in the government report. In the government report one of the basic fundamentals of the convention, the concept and definition of discrimination, had been questioned and reformulated. Despite the fact that the term discrimination is defined in detail in the text of CEDAW itself,[2] it is stated in the report by the Malaysian government that "there is no clear definition of the term discrimination" (Ministry of Women and Family Development 2004, 14). Instead, a new "Malaysian perspective" on discrimination is offered. This new definition of discrimination, as "treating women differently than men to the detriment of women" (Ministry of Women and Family Development 2004, 14) is sharply criticised by the women's movement as being less complex and insufficient to cover all dimensions of discrimination against women (NGO Shadow Report Group 2004, 2). Primarily, the "Malaysian perspective" formulated by the government contains the acknowledgement of local traditions and cultural values which may conflict with international standards of women's and human rights. "In Malaysia, there are customary and traditional practices that make a distinction between the role of men and women in the enjoyment or the exercise of their civil, political, economic, social and cultural rights" (Ministry of Women and Family Development 2004, 14). Although the government report questions these traditions which contain discriminatory tendencies to a certain extent, the culturalist undertone prevails and dominates the CEDAW report. Thus, the government report points to the fact that the Malaysian constitution guarantees basic human rights standards, which "take into consideration of Malaysia's multiracial society and are within permissible national values, traditions, religions, customs, social and economic conditions." This line of argument is also found in the Eighth Malaysia Plan, one of the most important national development policies, which explicitly states that all women's advancement has to be "consistent with Malaysian values, religious beliefs and cultural norms" (Economic Planning Unit 2006). This relativisation of the universality of the concepts of women's rights, equality, and discrimination is severely criticised by the women activists who underline the fact that "these values, as currently controlled by men, act as an impediment to the elimination of persisting gender inequality" (NGO Shadow Report Group 2004, 8). According to the women activists, the argument of cultural difference made by the government is a strategy to maintain the power of men and hence discrimination.

During the national NGO conference on CEDAW women activists pushed the notion of women's rights in a very self-confident and offensive way. The critique of the formulation that women *should be allowed to do something* and its replacement by the assertion that women had the *right to do something* indicates the rejection of a vulnerability approach and the growing importance of a rights-based approach. This remark alludes to the critique that women should be conceived as active subjects and participants of development, and not as passive receivers of benefits that the government gives them or even as vulnerable victims. The same issue was raised by women activists criticising formulations like "protecting" or "defending the rights of minority groups and women"[3] or "respecting women's rights and dignity" as they appear in a wide range of government documents about gender and development (Ministry of Women and Family Development 2004, 14). These formulations, according to the critique, assume that minority groups and women already had acquired their rights which then only needed to be protected (Shuib 2005). This, again, according to the critique by women activists, not only undermines the idea of social change but also produces the image of women being victims. At a seminar organised by the Ministry of Women, Family, and Community Development (MWFCD), women activists pleaded for the replacement of the above-mentioned formulations by the global concepts of gender mainstreaming and empowerment (Shuib 2005, 11).

The plea for strong language on rights is a remarkable fact because on other occasions women activists had reported that within the local context they preferred to avoid such strong language in order not to provoke the charge of being too Western oriented. In the context of CEDAW, however, this strong language is preferred. At this national level, NGO activists perceive the shadow report and the whole CEDAW process as a tool to put pressure on the national government. The Convention is appropriated by the local NGOs as an instrument of empowerment within their negotiations of women's rights and gender equality with the state. The process of writing an NGO shadow report became an important interface between the women's organisations and the state.

Using CEDAW and the terms *women's rights* and VAW as the framework for their work, Malaysian women's groups are connected to a global network of women's organisations. At the Asia–Pacific NGO Forum on the Beijing Platform for Action +10, which took place in Bangkok in July 2004,[4] the transnational organisation International Women's Rights Action Watch Asia Pacific (IWRAW), which is based in Kuala Lumpur, organised a special workshop on CEDAW with the title "How to Use the CEDAW Reporting Process." At this workshop two examples, Malaysia and Mongolia, were presented to the international participants from a variety of countries including Nepal, Japan, Korea, Pakistan, New Zealand, and India, to name a few. At the workshop one of the CEDAW committee members was present, the Korean women's rights activist Heisoo Shin. Cynthia, one of the women activists presented earlier in this chapter played a leading role in the organisation of the CEDAW process in Malaysia, informing the participants about the progress of the negotiations with the government. At the centre of the discussion stood the ambivalent relations towards government and state institutions of the different local women's organisations. On the one hand participants raised the question of how powerful the convention was as a tool to pressure government and what possibilities of sanctions were connected with CEDAW. On the other hand, they raised the question if and how a global convention like CEDAW was related to their own local work and to their own local issues of concern, such as women workers' rights or handicapped women's rights. What was observable in this workshop was the process of finding out the links and connecting elements between the local work and local struggles of women's organisations and a global instrument like the CEDAW convention. At this workshop networks between the Malaysian activists and Heisoo Shin were established with the result that Shin accepted the invitation to come to Malaysia and participate at the National Conference on CEDAW giving advice on how to make a shadow report more effective.

Within the networks which are built up through the process of writing the CEDAW report, knowledge produced on different levels is put together. Local NGOs use the convention to reorient their work in the light of its structure, writing their reports about the respective article of the convention. At the same time the NGO activists involved in the process of writing bring their specific local and sectoral knowledge into the global process: knowledge that then goes up to the committee and with which the government is confronted at the session with the committee at the UN headquarters in New York. The knowledge produced is also disseminated within the networks of a global women's movement as country examples which serve other national women's movements as the background for argumentation and for comparative knowledge creation.

As this analysis has shown, a global convention such as CEDAW and the underlying concept of women's rights is appropriated by local women activists as a tool to deconstruct the state's culturalist stand on gender equality and to challenge the notion of victimisation and vulnerability of women. The convention also serves as a platform for increased networking on the local and translocal level and strengthens the negotiation power of women's organisations within the local context.

State, Tradition, Religion:
Negotiating the Boundaries of Rights

For most of the female activists the concept of women's and human rights and a strong feeling of global solidarity form the foundation for their engagement in the struggle for social transformation. Nevertheless, the experience of being confronted with others who are in opposition to the idea of rights is very vivid in the narratives of many of the activists. As an analysis of these interfaces with family members, participants of training sessions organised by the NGOs, or with the state, reveals the negotiation of the rights concept is shaped by different discursive battles around highly contested fields, such as *state, culture, tradition,* and *religion.* Within these negotiations the activists develop the consciousness that a global concept of rights, be it women's or human rights, has to undergo multiple processes of translation to become effective in the local context.

In the following quotation from Su Ling, a Chinese-Malaysian women's activist, the first site of negotiation and confrontation appears: the authoritarian state.

> We find it very difficult at the local level to use the word human rights, which is such a bad word, when you are talking about women's human rights, wow! To people on the street, it is equal to anti-government. . . . And to be honest, even if you are talking to the young activists, you don't say "I am a human rights activist and a women's rights activist at the same time." Because maybe some of them are not comfortable to use the words "human right." Unless you are really meeting women friends who have been in the movement for a long time, you don't say such things. Because of that kind of atmosphere, to be able to promote that concept of human rights among the NGOs and also to certain women's groups, it is not easy at all. (Su Ling, 22.10.06)

Within the framework of an authoritarian state the concept of human rights becomes associated with the notion of being antigovernment and subversive. Civil society actors must take into account the repressive measures of the state and also, as it becomes clear in Su Ling's quotation, the reluctance of a significant part of the population to be identified with this concept. For the women's organisations one strategy to carve out space for political dissent was a translation into a terminology which was viewed as being less political, as Su Ling continues: "It took us a very long time for women to find a way. We had to find a different terminology for ourselves. Of course violence, you know, and issues like that, is an easy, very nice issue to talk about, to start with." Other activists spoke about "magic words" such as health and citizenship, which would not be as contested. Su Ling's statement underlines the difficulties of the women's movement in Malaysia which is searching for support in the multiethnic population as a societal basis of their activities and simultaneously trying to enter into a critical dialogue with state authorities to put social transformation into practice.

This approach however is heavily debated among different civil society actors in Malaysia. The organisations that focus on the area of so-called classical civil rights are especially critical about this approach. Their contention is that although the women's movement has managed to successfully influence national legislation on violence against women, for example, with the amendment of the Domestic Violence Act 1995, it has only hesitantly engaged in general debates about the economic and political development of the country. Some of the women's organisations did not participate in protests against the Bakun Dam or the Internal Security Act. In this context the negotiation of rights appears as a juxtaposition of women's rights issues as soft issues versus human rights issues, for example, the death penalty, and other symptoms of an undermined democracy, as hard issues. In the following statement from the coordinator of the "Stop Violence Against Women" campaign of AI in Malaysia, a young Chinese-Malaysian journalist, this juxtaposition is revealed:

> For me, I do coordinate the violence against women campaign but I don't think it would be my issue, I don't think it'd be my passion, something I want to do for the rest of my life. It's a very important issue but personally I prefer to tackle harder issues like the death penalty and torture that seems to be more of an interest for me than violence against women. I think the women's movement is picking up and it will always be a very easy issue to push because it appeals so much to people, you don't have to go very far. What happens to your family, marital rape and marital abuse is not right if it happens to your mother or sister. People immediately feel for that, but my interest has always been to harder issues like freedom of expression, justice in the court system, getting people aware, making them aware of the kind of violations that happen on an everyday basis. (12 Sept 2004)

The Malaysian AI group saw the participation in AI's global campaign on violence against women and the integration of women's rights into their activities as a major shift in their thematic orientation. Due to the campaign new forms of cooperation and exchange between women's organisations and human rights organisations were built up and institutionalised. Women's rights activists and women's organisations' representatives are regularly invited to give talks and training to Amnesty volunteers and International Women's Day 2004 was organised by a range of women's organisations and AI (see chapter 3). However, this new orientation of the AI group in Malaysia is not very highly regarded by some of the other so-called human rights groups. The Malaysian AI director talks about these tensions among the human rights activists:

> For us the campaign on violence against women was a major shift from our civil and political rights focus. It was very hard. So here in Malaysia people are saying: why do you talk about women? What about torture? What about death

penalty? We lost people along the way, not so much members, but NGOs working with us. They say: "You are taking the easy issue, what about the harder issues?" (David, Malaysian AI director, 19.03.04)

For the Malaysian case the question whether there could or should be any
prioritisation between differently interpreted rights is a central issue. There
is an ongoing debate about which issues are to be considered as political and
hence should be at the centre of political debate. The emerging discourse on
easy or soft versus hard issues has to be interpreted within the framework of
a restricted and fragile democratic space.

Secondly, for activists involved in the negotiation of women's rights, *culture* and *tradition* become especially significant sites where the boundaries of
such rights are negotiated. The following quotation comes from an interview
with Mira, an Indian Malaysian women's rights activist, who works in a project on violence against women especially for women from Indian origin in
Malaysia:

> We cannot go there and directly talk about domestic violence and "women's
> rights." Because a lot of people, even the women, believe that this is part of our
> culture. We have to go very slowly asking, Do your children have birth certifi-
> cate, identity card? Is your marriage registered? Does it have to be that way? Is
> our culture a culture of violence? Do we have to accept it? So we just keep it
> throwing back to them. (Mira, 02.08.04)

Mira works in the suburbs of Kuala Lumpur, where her organisation has established ten community centres. The so-called community consists of former plantation workers of Indian descent who had been relocated from the
plantations to newly built apartment blocks in the surroundings of Kuala
Lumpur. During the community meetings and workshops Mira has often had
the experience that women's rights get rejected as alien to local culture and
tradition. Even violence against women which at the national public level
served as an entry point for the women's movement becomes a difficult issue
at the very local level. The justification of the subordination of women in
terms of tradition and culture is a common phenomenon not only in
Malaysia, but also on a global scale. Confronted with this kind of argument,
activists and NGOs develop different strategies in order to "bring the conventions back home" as one of the activists said. First, the threatening term
rights, which might be conceived as alien to local culture and tradition, is
avoided and localised through translation into everyday experiences of
women, such as the registration of marriage and the birth of children in the
above-quoted example. This approach is practised by a great deal of human

and women's rights activists in their seminars, workshops, and conversations with local people.

Another feature of this approach is the strategic reinvention of the terms *tradition* and *culture*, as Mira's question whether their Indian culture was a culture of violence indicates. Some of the activists use historic examples to uncover different traditions in order to empower women and to give them the legitimacy to struggle for their rights. At a training session on "Gender, Culture and Community," which AI organised for its volunteers, an activist working mainly with Indian plantation workers had been invited to speak about his work with so-called grassroots communities. He presented his method for "putting things in their way" and focused especially on the sources of tradition. In his presentation he argued that several points of cultural and "racial" contact such as the earliest ancestral migrations of Indo-European peoples to India around 2000 B.C. and the influence of patriarchal religions such as Brahmanism, Christianity, and Islam led to changes in what until then had been Asian "mother-centred cultures" and traditions. "Before that there were no traces of a male god, it was all about matriarchy. Women led the army, the hunting team, they were leaders of clans, they were judges, priests, religious leaders, decision makers, and law makers and there were even female deities. We showed this to our women groups to show them that before patriarchy they were the leaders and to give them empowerment." Following this argument it is not against tradition to demand women's rights.

Historical reflexivity is used by many activists as a typical strategy to break the authority of tradition, especially tradition which became institutionalised in texts, be they religious or legal. Questions about the historical provenience and the social character are central elements of many workshops and training sessions organised by NGOs, as the following quotation by Mira indicates: "So, we bring it to them and say: 'Who made the law? How does it happen that they are there?' We say 'Laws are made by human beings, you know. We can totally get rid of it. It can be rewritten. It can be changed. It can be written any way. Look, who said that the men must be consulted, that the legal right of a child is with the man, but the mother can do all the custody care and control?'" The same strategy is applied in the context of religious texts as the following quotation from a Sisters in Islam member shows: "The basic idea of our training is the formation of Islamic family laws. We ask: How did they come about? We also look at the Quran and ask how it was compiled; we look at *hadith* and ask how *hadith* was compiled and how all these things became laws and how the law is affecting our lives."

This rather social approach to the construction of tradition implies not only questioning the authority of certain elements of culture but reinterpreting culture and history from a feminist point of view. The women's movement questions the authority of who can determine what the traits of a specific culture are, and what the content and meaning of culture is. This strategy aims at analysing, questioning, and redefining the content of *culture* that one specific group, composed mainly of men, promotes in order to maintain power relations, and at renegotiating the content of a specific culturally defined identity.

Thirdly, for Muslim women's rights activists *religion* becomes a specific site for the negotiation of women's rights because they have to confront the authorities of the religious courts. Within this context women's rights are translated into religious language itself. The case of Ida, a twenty-seven-year-old Muslim, who today is one of the most vocal Sisters in Islam members, illustrates this translation into religious discourse. Ida had studied secular, codified law at a private university in Kuala Lumpur and had then started her work in the civil society sector as a legal officer in one of the multiethnic women's organisations. But she soon became dissatisfied with her work. In the following quotation Ida talks about her frustrating experiences with the Islamic judges:

> Something that pissed me off was that I could assist my non Muslim clients, because there is the law and everything. But when it came to Sharia law I couldn't help. Because the judges would use Sharia verses, which are very discriminatory towards women, but which are not in the sections. And lawyers would come back to me and say: "Yes, obviously husbands can beat their wives." That started my interest in Sharia law. Because if you talk to religious authorities and scholars, using human rights discourse does not work, there is no other way to use religious discourse. (Ida, 25.04.04)

During her work she came to the conclusion that at the level of the religious courts human rights arguments were not valid and not recognised by the religious authorities. Whereas according to Ida the mediation between the secular, codified law and a human rights approach was running smoothly, the mediation between religious law and human rights approaches produced significant frictions. Because of this frustration Ida decided to adopt a religious discourse. She did a second degree in Sharia law at the International Islamic University, quit her work with the multiethnic women's organisation, and started to work with Sisters in Islam. Ida is part of a new trend in Malaysia but also in other Muslim countries, the so-called Muslim feminism or Islamic feminism (Mernissi 1992; Mernissi 1996; Barlas 2002), which in

Malaysia is propagated in particular by Sisters in Islam. Because of the institutionalisation of religion through family law and the increasing politicisation of religion in the public sphere, it seems necessary for Muslim women
activists to develop a specific form of agency that reflects these characteris-
tics of the context and that enables them to communicate successfully with
the respective religious authorities. In a presentation at the Asia–Pacific
NGO Forum on the Beijing Platform for Action +10 in Bangkok 2004,
Nurhuda, another Sisters in Islam member, called this strategy "adopting the
language of the enemy," a strategy chosen in order to deconstruct discriminatory discourses and practices that are legitimised by certain interpretations
of religious texts. The discourse on Muslim feminism emerges in a context
where religious arguments are not only very prominent but also powerful and
where to a significant extent only arguments deduced from religious texts are
recognised as valid knowledge. Although in these empirical examples Muslim feminism takes the form of a consciously chosen strategy, it also must be
seen in a wider context as one way of being feminist which has developed
historically in Muslim societies within the globalised framework of Islam.

The preceding analysis shows that the appropriation and localisation of
the global concept of women's and human rights is shaped by different discursive battles around contested fields, such as *state*, *culture*, *tradition*, and *religion*. These negotiation processes however, are obviously not restricted to
the local or national level, but are also significantly shaped by the fact that
all the civil society actors presented in this chapter are to different degrees
part of global networks. The following section will deal with the significance
of translocal networking for the negotiation of rights. Here, the practice of
translocal interaction and comparison will be of special importance.

Negotiating Rights within Diversity:
Translocal Networking and Comparison

One of the numerous workshops held at the Asia–Pacific NGO Forum on
the Beijing Platform for Action +10 in Bangkok was about "Current Issues
and Challenges in Crisis Intervention Work on Violence against Women."
At this workshop women's groups from the Philippines, Nepal, New Zealand,
Fiji, and also the All Women's Action Society from Malaysia presented their
organisations, approaches, and concrete activities. In a first step the women
shared their concrete local experiences as well as the problems and challenges that they face in their local contexts and made explicit reference to
their national identity. Women from Fiji heavily criticised the allocation of
state resources to services that are extremely conservative and the increasing

imposition of Christian fundamentalist beliefs on service providers for women. Malaysian representatives, social workers from AWAM, focused on their networks with other institutions, hospitals, the welfare department, and other NGOs, and talked about the experiences of women's groups in lobbying for a domestic violence act. Women from Nepal identified economic dependency as a main reason of violence against women in Nepal, which was reinforced by state policies, through polygyny and a lack of civic and property rights for women. Women from New Zealand, defining themselves as indigenous women, presented their warrior strategy which is based on traditional female power. They closed the session singing a song in their local language. During the discussion the participants agreed that the aim of the workshop should be to develop a common "feminist approach for crisis intervention" and made it clear that in spite of the very different contexts—Christian fundamentalism, traditional marriage systems, etc.—the underlying problems were similar. The Nepalese women argued: "Everywhere the problems and the causes are the same. Because we are women. Maybe the degree of oppression is different but the situation is the same." Another participant from Taiwan expressed her solidarity with all other participants saying: "We want to help all our sisters in the world; we are all in the same situation." The outcome of the workshop was a list of joint recommendations for all governments of the region.

As this example shows, one of the main aspects of translocal networking among women's organisations is the transfer of knowledge within these networks. Specific local knowledge on specific locally embedded issues is exchanged and a body of knowledge with multiple local sources is created. This multiplicity of sources is articulated within the ambivalent discourse on diversity and sisterhood and is manifested in the practice of comparison. At this workshop the diversity of experiences in the Asian region was transformed into the global identity of "sisters" who collectively formulate locally grounded demands to governments.

The concepts of diversity and the practice of comparison are locally employed to counteract Islamisation projects. The struggle for a reform of Islamic family law in Malaysia illustrates this process. Sisters in Islam, one of the leading organisations in Malaysia promoting a reform of the Islamic family law (Sisters in Islam 1993, 2005), is part of the international solidarity network Women Living Under Muslim Laws (WLUML). WLUML is a network where diversity is cultivated and formulated and which provides the possibility of exchange among women's organisations in more than seventy Muslim countries. Hamima, a Malaysian activist, expressed her view about the value of being part of such translocal networks:

What we did first was to compare different Sharia laws in different countries. In Malaysia, in India, Sri Lanka, Pakistan, Bangladesh. And what we saw was that the Sharia law was all different in each country. Even here in Malaysia you have different Sharia in different states. So how can this then be divine? We wanted to show that Sharia is not divine, because a lot of people argue with that. (Hamima, 04.10.04)

The diversity of existing Sharia laws in different Muslim countries is interpreted by Hamima as a sign that they are not essentially divine, but the result of human thought and interpretation and could hence also be subject to transformation. A recent example of how the discourse on diversity is implemented can be seen in the first issue of the Sisters in Islam bulletin (Sisters in Islam 2005), which is completely dedicated to the issue of reform of the Islamic family law. A great part of the bulletin contains comparisons of different national Islamic family laws from countries such as Morocco, Indonesia, Turkey, Egypt, Tunisia, and Pakistan, and of the reforms based on an egalitarian approach to which these laws had been lately submitted.

One of the bulletin articles refers to a current debate about forced marriage in Malaysia. The question raised is whether a woman could be forced by her *wali*, her male guardian, to marry a certain man without her consent. The article reports that a Malaysian university professor supported this position, arguing that "a Muslim father can force his daughter to marry a person of the family's choice against her will, and that this marriage would be legal and binding in Islam" (Sisters in Islam 2005, 3). It is also reported that the Islamic Family Law Enactment of Kelantan, the only state in Malaysia governed by the Islamist opposition party PAS, which was put into practice in 1983, also provides the possibility that a woman under certain circumstances can be married without her consent. In the article the argument that a forced marriage is in line with Islamic teaching is deconstructed by giving contradictory examples. The bulletin, for instance, mentions that Saudi Arabia's top religious authorities have banned such a practice and that also Islamic family laws in Algeria, Iraq, Syria, Jordan, and Morocco prohibit forced marriage.

The main question is formulated in the following way: "If the laws of so many countries ban forced marriages, why have the professor and the Kelantan Islamic Family Law Enactment allowed the practice to continue?" The answer lies in the differentiation between Sharia, "the infallible and unchangeable law revealed to the prophet" and the *Fiqh*, the "interpretation by man" (Sisters in Islam 2005, 4). That means a practice such as forced marriage is not based in "infallible and unchangeable law," but is rather the result of the integration of "conceptions of women's roles from pre-Islamic Arabia and other patriarchal civilisations" (Sisters in Islam 2005, 3) into Islamic jurisprudence. The argument of interpretation and the translocal comparison of legal practice open the way for rethinking and reforming Islamic family law on the basis of new interpretations.

Sisters in Islam also planned to organise an art exhibition on women in Muslim art with contributions from several Muslim countries. The activist in charge declared diversity and comparison to be the main concepts behind the idea of an exhibition: "We try to get paintings from all Muslim countries. From Iran and the Middle East, from Muslim communities in China and from Indonesia and Malaysia. Actually, our idea is to show the diversity of the Muslim world, because Muslim is not only Arab. We want to show the diversity. So there will be paintings of women showing Muslim women in their diversity."

Also for the CEDAW process *comparison* and *diversity* are used to open up room for manoeuvre. The organisers of the workshop "How to use the CEDAW Reporting Process" at the Asia–Pacific NGO Forum on the Beijing Platform for Action +10 in Bangkok encouraged the participants of the Muslim countries to look at the reservations that had been made by other Muslim countries and to compare these reservations with the ones that their own governments had made. The organiser of the workshop highlighted the fact that the range of reactions among Muslim countries towards CEDAW was very diverse and that there were Muslim countries who had even ratified the convention without any reservations. In a national context where reservations are made with the argument that to accept those articles would go against Islamic traditions, this type of knowledge can serve as an instrument to question these so-called Islamic traditions.

Interestingly, the discourse on diversity, as it is conducted in such networks, clearly refers to and deconstructs global dichotomies. Among the seven plenary sessions at the Asia–Pacific NGO Forum on the Beijing Platform for Action +10 in Bangkok there was one with the title "Asian Women in Muslim Societies: Perspectives and Struggles," with a keynote speaker from Pakistan, a member of the network Women Living Under Muslim Laws, and commentators from Malaysia, Iran, Indonesia and Turkey. These different women coming from different Muslim countries debated the consequences of political Islam and women's rights in Islam. Doing so, they also negotiated the meaning of the label "Muslim women." Nearly all speakers of this plenary commented critically on its topic and challenged the idea of "singling out" Muslim women because of their religion. Farida Shaheed, the main speaker from Pakistan, said:

I feel very unhappy that women are singled out because of their religion. Especially with Islam. . . . It creates the image as if Muslim lived in a separate world. But this is not my reality. And who are these Muslim women anyway? And where are they? In Senegal or in secular Turkey? The Muslim world is divided by race, gender, class, development. Even within Asia the traditions are so diverse that is difficult to agree on the basic fact of who is Muslim and who not. Most Muslim Asians have never heard about female genital mutilation and are shocked by this practice. Yet this practice is being promoted in some African countries as an Islamic tradition. Women of the Arab world however are shocked about the widespread practice of dowry in Southeast Asia, because this to them is completely un-Islamic. (Farida Shaheed, 1 July 2004)

This case makes clear that "Muslim women" are a category of global concern. In the last years, the categories of gender and Islam or Islamic culture have developed into one of the most contested fields for the negotiation of global development concepts. Although the organisers of the NGO Forum set up this session following this global discourse, the invited women refused this category, because in their eyes it reflected the global dualist discourse on the West versus Islam. The argument that the Pakistani keynote speaker brought forward was that treating Muslim women as a separate group meant being part of the dichotomist oppositions which dominated the global political discourse. Both Islamist groups and "Western fundamentalists à la Bush" were criticised for creating the picture of homogenised groups that leave no freedom for personal choices about dress, religious practices, and interpretations. Instead, as the above quotation shows, the diversity of the so-called uniform category of Muslim women but also the political importance of the concept of 'diversity' were highlighted. Referring to diversity, Nurhuda, the Malaysian participant, spoke about the "window of opportunities." The Iranian speaker talked about diversity in relation to the diverse approaches in Iranian women's movement towards religion: Islamist women fighting against imperialism, Muslim reformist women fighting for democracy, and secular women fighting for the separation of state and religion.

Furthermore, the women brought several examples of how at the global level conservative forces such as the Vatican and Islamist leaders cooperate concerning the limitation of women's rights. Also in the summaries and recommendations of the Bangkok NGO Forum, Islamisation or Islamism as a political force is not mentioned at all. Generally, fundamentalism, identity-based politics, conservatism, militarism, neoliberalism, globalisation, and patriarchy are named as the social forces that a women's movement must face and counteract. The social space that these women constitute, based on their identity as progressive women, is constructed against this complex syndrome.

By doing so, the dichotomising discourse between Islam and the West is partly deconstructed, a discourse where Islam alone is equated with fundamentalism and identified as the religion that oppresses women. Furthermore, 'diversity' is perceived as an instrument against homogenised versions of Islam and gender relations at the national level. The strategic use of the diversity concept reopens the public debate about the question of what is the content of the label "Islamic" and who has the authority to define this content (Salvatore 1997). Conferences like the NGO Forum in Bangkok and networks like Women Living Under Muslim Laws provide national women's organisations with arguments, evidence, and knowledge to bring this question to centre stage and to insist on the fact that women and women's organisations are equally legitimate to produce relevant and valid answers to that question.

Conclusion

The aim of this chapter was to explore how the global concept of women's rights and the Convention on the Elimination of All Forms of Discrimination against Women is appropriated and localised by Malaysian women's organisations. It has shown that within a limited democratic space global concepts and conventions are perceived by the local civil society actors as a crucial instrument to enhance their room for manoeuvre vis-à-vis an authoritarian state and hegemonic ethnicity and religion-based identity constructions, a perception which is clearly embedded into glocalised life-worlds of urban-based women activists. Nevertheless, the confrontation with different life-worlds, where the relation of the local and the global is perceived as being antagonistic, is a general experience made by women's and human rights activists. The negotiation at such interfaces leads to the elaboration of techniques and practices of translation and mediation, as the emic concepts of "magic words," "bringing the conventions back home," or "putting things in their way" show. All these approaches aim at the reinterpretation of the authority of culture, tradition, religious and legal texts, and the creation of new forms of authority of knowledge (Lachenmann 2004b, Pfaff-Czarnecka 2007).

All knowledge, especially knowledge that is produced by translocally connected social movements, is necessarily local and global at the same time. However, as Henrietta Moore has argued, this does not mean that this knowledge is somehow universal or homogenised (Moore 1996). Local women's organisations, such as the Malaysian women's organisations engaged in the CEDAW process, create specialist knowledge on a specific area, such as on women and law or women and participation. This knowledge is locally generated and also located in a specific context but can be generalised as a technique of knowledge generation (Moore 1996, 10). The Convention on the Elimination of All Forms of Discrimination against Women can be seen as such a global technique of knowledge production in the field of gender and development. Whereas women's organisations work on their own locally and nationally defined issues, they use the global communication channels provided by the convention to put pressure on their own governments. The negotiations on CEDAW can be analysed as an important interface between the women's movement and the state. Thereby they contribute to the constitution of a public sphere, democratisation, and the challenge of a state-promoted development model.

Furthermore, translocal networks with women's movements in other countries based on a regionally defined Asian or a religiously defined Muslim identity play an important role for the transfer of critical knowledge and local empowerment for the Malaysian women's movement. The practice of translocal comparison can be identified as a strategy of women activists to create a new discursive order that transcends local and global dichotomies. Malaysian NGOs make explicit use of translocal comparisons, links, and networks, as they refer to other country examples to reflect upon their own situation and to ground their demands. A prime example is the Sisters in Islam when they compare different Sharia laws in different countries to question their sacred character or when they organise art exhibitions to show the diversity of women's everyday realities in Muslim countries. Additionally, within the CEDAW process different country reports are compared in order to produce diversity. The construction of new identities such as "women against fundamentalisms" or "global sisterhood" reflects these new translocal visions of Islam, development, and women's rights. Women's organisations in Malaysia are thus contributing to the constitution of a translocal social space where alternative visions of society, gender relations, and religious discourses can be developed.

Notes

1. The report was composed of the following chapters:

   1. Definition of discrimination; law, policy, and measures to implement the convention
   2. Sex roles and stereotyping
   3. Trafficking and exploitation of prostitution

   4. Political participation and public life
   5. Citizenship
   6. Education
   7. Employment
   8. Health
   9. Social and economic rights
   10. Rural women
   11. Equality in the law
   12. Equality in marriage and family life
   13. Violence against women (NGO Shadow Report Group 2004).

   2. "The term discrimination shall mean any distinction, exclusion or restriction made on the basis of sex which has the effect or purpose of impairing or nullifying the recognition, enjoyment or exercise by women, irrespective of their marital status, on the basis of equality of men and women, of human rights and fundamental freedoms in the political, economic social, cultural, civil or any other field" (CEDAW, article 1, http://www.un.org/womenwatch/daw/cedaw/text/econvention.htm).

   3. This formulation is one of the guiding principles of the concept of Islam *Hadhari*, that was introduced by the Prime Minister Abdullah Badawi in 2004, a concept that formulated development goals in a religious language (http://www.pmo.gov.my/website/webdb.nsf/vIslamHadhari/7ADA18205EDC7C6C482570830032B65E).

   4. At this NGO Forum, which I attended as a participant observer, more than 800 women from all over the Asia-Pacific region gathered to discuss the advancement of the implementation of the Beijing Platform for Action, to identify key issues that need to be tackled in the future and to formulate concrete policy recommendations for the regional government representatives. This NGO Forum was a preparatory meeting for the official Asia–Pacific government meeting that took place in October 2004 in Bangkok.

CHAPTER EIGHT

~

Negotiating Peace and Rights in Sudan: Networking for the Agenda of "Violence Against Women"

Salma A. Nageeb

Situating Violence against Women in Local Politics: An Introduction

After the signing of the Comprehensive Peace Agreement (CPA) between the central government of Sudan and the Sudanese People Liberation Movement in January 2005 and the explosion of the Conflict in Darfur, the global agendas of rights be they human or women's rights gained a central position in the local map of politics and development. The human rights question is a critical issue which the current government has to face for two main reasons. First, the question of human rights and violence against women in Darfur bring a high level of media and international attention to the conflict in the region and to the declining of the humanitarian and security situation. Such attention leads to more pressure from the international community on the government to solve the conflict and improve the humanitarian conditions in the region, as failure to do so could lead to international military intervention in the region. Second, the international concern with Darfur not only focuses on the subject of military intervention: equally important for peacebuilding in the region is to invest in the process of democratisation and development. The interest of different international donors and development agents to contribute to the peacebuilding processes in Sudan represents a supportive environment for civil organisations, particularly women's NGOs working in the area of human and women's rights. Specifically, international development agents and donors who are involved in supporting the peacebuilding stage are explicitly targeting the enhancement of the role of civil organisations in peace and democratisation processes. Hence, whereas the women and human rights questions are putting the Sudanese government in a critical position in relation to the international community, NGOs that deal with development relate differently to this issue.

Within this context the global development discourse on Violence Against Women (VAW) is currently undergoing a process of repositioning on the local political and development maps. The issue of VAW was highly contested by the Islamist state during the 1990s when the Islamists were intensively engaged in the Islamisation project and the construction of the Ummah (see Nageeb 2004). According to the Islamist politics the discourse on VAW represents a "foreign agenda," an "anti-Islamic vision" which is not relevant to what they see as "Sudanese culture" and "Islamic society." Thus non-Islamist women's NGOs which were able to maintain activities on the issue of VAW tactically avoided the adoption of human and women's rights as well as VAW as themes to characterise their activities. Gender-related issues and problems were addressed in manners that intentionally reflected a minimum level of politicisation of the issue involved in order to insure the inclusion of these issues in local development within the context of Islamist politics (see chapter 4 of this book). This situation is currently—under the frame of peacebuilding—changing and women's NGOs and activists tend to place the agenda of VAW in a new position in relation to local politics and development. To understand the processes through which VAW is gaining more political weight it is important to analyse the relation of the agenda of VAW to both the sociopolitical context in which it is locally embedded as well as to the peacebuilding process.

This article thus focuses mainly on how women's NGOs deploy the discourse on VAW, and how this agenda of VAW represents a space for women's NGOs to network and to negotiate development, peace, and democratisation. The main argument is that in working with the agenda of VAW women activists are engaged in negotiating the relationship between NGOs and the state on the one hand, and the democratisation and peacebuilding processes on the other. In this process VAW represents an important link between the local women's agendas of peace and democratisation and the global ones through intensive translocal networking. However, in comparison to the intensity of translocal networking of women's NGOs, at a local level the link between the agenda of VAW and the different local communities in Sudan is weak. Basically this is due to the type of relationship between women's

NGOs and the state and the way VAW is placed in relation to the sociopolitical context. Indeed the questions of financial resources and the connection between women's NGOs and international development agents and donors are of a central relevance to the subject of VAW and the ways it is positioned in the local development agenda. However, as this issue is addressed in another paper published within the framework of this research project, and is also tackled in chapter four of this book, this chapter will in general focus on the relationship between the Islamist oriented politics of the state during the nineties, the resulting sociopolitical restructuration, and its relation to the ways women activists are currently networking to place the agenda of VAW in local politics.

It should be emphasised here that VAW is relatively new on the agenda of local women's organisations compared to poverty and Female Genital Mutilation/Female Circumcision (FGM/FC). Particularly after the signing of the peace agreement, women activists tend to reshape the agendas of VAW. Therefore, it is also an objective of this article to study and analyse a relatively new approach to the global concept of VAW and the role this agenda plays in the peacebuilding phase. In this sense the article also intends to document some of the significant changes in the perspectives and discourses of women's NGOs which have taken place as a result of recent political transformation.

To illustrate the above argument the paper is organised in four parts. Part one gives a general idea about how the global concept of VAW is placed in the agendas of women's NGOs and local development context after the signing of the peace agreement. The second part provides a more in-depth analysis of how the advocacy VAW is embedded in social and political structures. To do so trajectories of three activists and their perspective on the issue are analysed. To move the argument from the local to the translocal level the third part of the paper will focus on presenting a network of women's NGOs working with VAW agenda. The final part of the paper draws a conclusion from the empirical sections of the paper.

Violence against Women:
A New Space for Women's NGO?

After signing of the peace agreement and the explosion of the conflict in Darfur the human rights and VAW agendas became an integral and central part in the peacebuilding process. The government is more reluctant to accept human rights or VAW agendas of civil organisations than the women and peace initiatives (see chapter 4). In particular VAW is a rather sensitive and complicated issue as it is directly related to the questions of gender structures and state power. The political weight of the VAW agenda in the current context of Sudan is related to specific cases of violation of human rights, namely rape in the region of Darfur. The Sudanese government, which insists that rape is not an organised war tactic in the region, finds itself in direct confrontation with the international community. The latter perceives the rape cases as systematic practices of human rights violation in Darfur that should be urgently addressed by both the state and civil society organisations.

VAW is gaining specific political significance and is coming to the surface as a legitimate concept to guide the work of women's NGOs not only in Darfur but also in the capital Khartoum, where the majority of women's NGOs are located. VAW agendas are emerging as a highly politicised issue that is utilised by women and human rights activists to work with various problems from gender inequality at the public and institutional levels to sexual assaults and rape in Darfur. In other words the surfacing of the cases of rape and sexual assaults against women in Darfur at the public level both locally and internationally on the one hand, and the role of the international development agents in supporting the peacebuilding process on the other, are leading to a change in the way gender-related problems such as violence are discussed. Within this context woman NGOs and activists, who are mostly urban based, educated, professional, and middle class are, in a way, reversing their strategy. Namely the way in which they further politicise their agendas and discourses constitutes a space to negotiate the peacebuilding process. The local discourse on VAW is an example of how gender issues are further politicised to enlarge the space in which women are able to influence the local agenda of peace and development. While a number of NGOs are specifically concerned with the issue of rape in Darfur, the majority advocate various other themes under the frame of VAW. These themes vary from FGM/FC and early marriage to problems of displacement or women in the market, all of which one may find addressed under the frame of VAW. In project documents, workshops, or training programmes activists adopt flexible definitions of the concept which accommodate different forms of violence as well as wider frames of gender-based sociocultural, political, and economic problems and discriminations. This qualitative shift in the language of women activists links different gender concerns with the discourse on VAW and thereby aims at increased politicisation of women's agendas. This politicisation of VAW agendas serves as expression of opposition and critical stands towards—at the first place—the state and its gender politics. Consequently, and as the result of this oppositional relations between women's organisations and the state, the agenda of violence is manifested more at the level of advocacy in the forms of training and research and less in the direction of concrete projects addressing practically and in an interactive way the everyday problems of a specific community. The following example of how activists conceptualise and advocate their agendas related to the global concept of VAW comes from a paper presented by an organisation called the lawyers of Darfur (*Mohamo Darfur*) at a gender forum organised by a group of women's NGOs in Khartoum in January 2005. The organisation stressed that VAW in Darfur should not be only related to rape and sexual violence. The paper stated that:

> Violence against women in Darfur is not only related to sexual violence. There are different forms of violence, and it is high time to unveil the complexity and multi-dimensionality of violence women in Darfur face in their daily life. Women are subject to discrimination and male [mis]treatment in all fronts of life, economically, socially, culturally and politically. If we look at the division of work, resources and power between men and women we will find many forms of violence and we need to address all these forms. (Gender Forum, Violence Against Women in Darfur, paper No 2, 1)

Similarly in a roundtable discussion on VAW in Darfur organised by PANOS Khartoum[1] in December 2004, the participants emphasised the need to enlarge the usage of the concepts of VAW. One of the activists expressed this need saying: "We should now be more courageous and give things their real names. Any form of discrimination that leads to the increase of the work load of women, or to the decrease of resources like education or money is a form of violence against women."

Sudanese politicians and political observers, such as Alsadig Almahdi,[2] in an interview conducted for this research points at this new (local) development in the use of the global concepts of VAW:

> VAW is a very sensitive issue that should be addressed carefully, particularly by women. Nowadays there is an explosion of the use of the term without a clear definition. Is this a stage that the concept of VAW should pass through in order to get a local meaning? or in order to be able to link the origin [what is local] with the modern [what is global] (*tarbut alassle be alasr*)? Or is it only a matter of following what comes from the international community? We need a conceptual relation between what comes from the international community and what is our social reality.

Without doubt the question of international funding is very relevant. Many international donors such as, for instance, the United Nation Development Programme (UNDP), the Joint Assessment Mission (JAM), or the European

Union (EU) are interested in the human rights aspect of the Darfur conflict. In addition international funds and support directed to women and gender issues, from organisations such as Women Waging for Peace, the Women, Peace and Security Working Group, the Dutch Ministry of Cooperation and Development, and the Ministry of International Development Norway, are currently paying specific attention to the question of women's human rights including the subject of VAW. Through this international concern with the human and women's rights situation, NGOs are getting not only funded but also recognised specifically by international development agents as a major actor in the process of peacebuilding and democratisation. Through this process the agenda of VAW is adopted by various women's organisations as an urgent gender concern; the significant point to be discussed here is the way VAW is "rediscovered" and placed in the local development agendas.

At this level one could say that the global development concept of VAW is localised by resisting the limitation of its use to refer to the cases of rape in Darfur, which is the initial situation that is behind the (re)emergence of the concept. Rather, the concept of VAW locally stands for a highly politicised frame for engendering the peacebuilding process. This process of localising and further politicising the discourse on VAW is a socially embedded process. This process is to be understood within the political frame of the Islamisation project of the state, on the one hand, and the peacebuilding process on the other. To illustrate this argument, in the next section three life trajectories of activist women who work in the field of VAW are presented. These trajectories will help in analysing how Islamisation politics on the one hand and the questions of funding and peacebuilding on the other are modelling the agencies of women activists who advocate the agendas of rights in general and VAW agendas in particular.

Three Women Activists and One Agenda

The following short biographies of women activists were acquired by interviewing these women and asking them one question: How did you start including the concept of VAW in your work?[3] In answer to this question various familial, social, economic, and political issues were chronologically presented and linked by the interviewees to explain how they became engaged in the field of NGOs and specifically in advocating women's rights.

Fatma
Fatma is a forty-three-year-old married woman who started her activist career during the 1990s. She was working at an educational institute and was plan-

ning to go abroad for postgraduate studies when the Islamist-seized power in 1989. Fatma's family is of a leftist background, and her brothers were active members in the Sudanese communist party. Until the 1990s Fatma was not politically active though she "always considers Islam and religion to be a private thing that should not be used in politics or to control people." In 1991 one of her brothers was taken for security investigations because of his oppositional activities with the communist party. He was imprisoned for more than nine months during which time he was physically tortured and thereafter suffered from severe depression. During this time an institute in Europe offered Fatma a scholarship for postgraduate studies. As she proceeded with the travelling arrangements, she discovered that all members of her family including herself were restricted from crossing the borders of Sudan. She spent many months trying to get travel permission but without success. Ultimately the institute which agreed to fund her postgraduate studies abroad withdrew their offer of funding.

Fatma described this as a very depressing experience, particularly that the political situation in the country was deteriorating and the fact that the Islamist regime was practicing severe control and suppression—particularly on those who were classified as belonging to the opposition like Fatma's family. She decided to take a leave without pay from her work and to enroll at one of the local universities as a postgraduate student. However, she could not persue this plan as the registration fees for postgraduate studies were beyond the financial ability of her and that of her family. This experience affected Fatma to such an extent that she "lost the desire to work, live, and make things move."

After some months of staying at home she planned to change her job. A friend suggested to her to join a women's NGO, which was seeking volunteers, and to see if she could build a career there. She followed the advice and started working with an NGO that was focusing on gender training and advocacy. The year which she spent with the organisation was very enlightening for her. She described this, saying: "it helped me get out of the depressive moods I had, especially after the torturing of my brother. It also helped me to learn about gender and violence and to understand our suffering through new lenses." Thus Fatma continued to work for NGOs.

Currently Fatma is codirecting a women's NGO together with another activist. The organisation is working in the area of gender training and advocacy. For Fatma, who describes herself as a feminist, VAW agendas "should address all women's problems, particularly problems related to reproductive health, because FGM, rape, or marital rape are all very severe forms of violence that we don't talk about." And she adds to this "if you experience violence in your life you are more sensitive to it and you would want to fight all its forms."

Leila

"I represent the open Islam. I am Islamist but progressive"—with this description of herself began Leila, who is a forty-four-year-old married woman and a mother of three children, to tell me about her understanding of the concept of VAW and how she integrates it in her work. Leila's political activism started when she joined the students' faction of the NIF in the 1980s. She described her work with NIF as part of the struggle of Muslim women to get the rights which Islam granted them.

She is the only member of her family to belong to the NIF. The family is an active member of the Ummah party. Nevertheless this was not a problem for her, since for her family what was important was that Leila remained a good Muslim who observed the teaching of Islam in all aspects of her life. She also described this difference in political loyalties as a healthy condition which enriched the atmosphere of political dialogue and respect of the difference of others. Accordingly she grew up as a good Muslim, observing the Hijab, respecting those who are different, and practicing free dialogue with others.

Her political activism with the NIF was very remarkable. Leila is known to non-Islamist activists (see chapter 4) to be a very gender-sensitive woman who uses Islam as a frame, as she expressed, to "liberate women from all forms of dominations and suppression." Her gender sensitivity was reflected in her struggle with the male members of her party. In the 1980s Leila was engaged in her first gender-based conflict within the NIF. This took place during a preparation phase for the elections of the students' union at the university where she studied. Female candidates from the NIF were not allowed to run for election at that time. The NIF considered the hanging of posters with the photos of female candidates as a sin, a practice not admissible in Islam. In effect this meant that female students who were members of the NIF were prohibited from running for election in the students' union; they were engaged as organisers of the campaigns for elections, but not as candidates to be elected. Thus Leila was engaged actively in fighting this narrow understanding of admissibility and forbiddance in Islam. She fought for a woman's right to run for election as a representative of the NIF in the students' union.

Leila referred to the fact that she grew up in the rural area as a major reason behind her gender sensitivity. She described her life as a child and a young woman in the village as follows: "[L]ife in the village does not have this complication of the modern life in urban areas. We grew up together—

boys and girls. We went to the same primary school because there was one school there for all. We played, ate, and chatted together. There was no problem with that." However, when she moved to the city, in this case Khartoum, she realised that the gender code is stricter there and that this way of life is advocated as Islamic. Through her life in the village she knew Islam differently. Thus she became committed to changing the position of women by advocating a "progressive Islam interpretation." Leila is described by many activists as a very open-minded woman. One female activist who belongs to the communist party said of her: "[O]ne could hardly believe that she is a member of the NIF."

Currently Leila is setting up, together with three other activists from the NIF, a women's NGO, which according to her "will work with all international concepts and particularly the issue of violence to improve the position of women and to stop men from manipulating Islam to abuse women." Simultaneously Leila indulges herself intellectually in the subject of wife battery.[4] She wrote many papers on the subject arguing from a theological point of view that Islam is against the beating of women by their husbands and guardians. What is interesting about her approach is that she utilises a gender framework to develop a new interpretation of Islamic sources and to argue against the practice. Her approach receives considerable recognition, particularly from religious authorities who cannot deny that her contribution is based on a solid Islamic science of interpretation.

Igbal
Igbal, a thirty-nine-year-old unmarried woman, was working for a public sector bank as the secretary of a director of one of the bank's departments when the NIF announced its twined policies in the early 1980s of "purifying the public sector from corruption" and the "suspension from jobs at the public sector for the public good."[5] Both of these slogans and policies were used by the Islamists in very elastic ways. However, the essence of these policies was to ban all public sector employees who belonged to the opposition parties or who were not sympathisers of the NIF. The director of the department where Igbal was working, together with all his staff including Igbal, were released from their jobs. Unlike her boss, who was known to be an opponent of the NIF, she had neither political activities nor interest in politics in general. Nevertheless in the early 1990s she found herself without the job for which she had struggled. Working for a bank was one of her dreams. According to Igbal, bank jobs, unlike other public sector positions, provide employees with various facilities that help to improve their financial status. She was longing to improve her financial situation and that of her family,

which became increasingly impoverished particularly after Islamists seized power (see Nageeb 2004, Bilal 2004). Igbal found herself without a job and with no hope to join any other position in the public sector.

She spent some months at home, without really searching for a job (Igbal explained, half jokingly, that during this time she was basically hoping to find a husband who was either a migrant in the rich Gulf States or someone who lived in Sudan but was financially stable). Her search for a new job started when she became acquainted with a young Sudanese woman who worked for the UN in Khartoum. This acquaintance helped Igbal to formulate an idea about what sort of jobs she should be searching for. The high salary rate, transportation, and office facilities, in addition to some other advantages that one could get by working as a local staff for the UN, made Igbal determined to start a new career plan.

The dream of finding a job at the UN local offices or any other international organisation that were stationed in Sudan shaped Igbal's career as an activist. Igbal enrolled in an intensive English-language course and took many short-term volunteer jobs with local NGOs which were working in different fields such as gender, displaced people, or poverty alleviation. Her goal was to make her curriculum vitae look attractive to the local offices of international organisations. But successive rejections made her believe what she often heard: qualifications are not as important as having the right connections to support a job application at the UN or any other international organisation. Because these right connections were lacking in her case she did not hesitate to accept a job at a local NGO whose work focused on poverty eradication and gender equality and with which she was working on voluntary basis in any case. Although the job was administrative, Igbal was sure that in local NGOs the distinctions between administrative and activist work were not very clear. She became interested in the different concepts with which NGOs work; gender equality, empowerment, the eradication of harmful traditional practices were all new ideas for her. More importantly she was interested in the question of funding and how NGOs, using the different development and rights concepts, can formulate projects and fund their organisations.

After three years of working as an administrative assistant for a women's NGO a vacancy was announced in the local office of a British NGO. The two-year job offer was for an assistant to project director. Igbal's application was accepted though her enrollment with this organisation lasted for only thirteen months. Like many international organisations, this British NGO had to close its offices in Khartoum due to the hostility of the political situation during the 1990s. Igbal's unemployment did not last for long this time, however, and she was welcomed again in the local organisation where she previously worked. There she occupied different positions: administrative assistant, project coordinator, and deputy director. In early 2001 Igbal took the decision together with one of her friends, who also worked for an NGO, to start their own NGO.

She explained this move as follows: "We felt we have enough knowledge of women's problems and the projects they need and we also got to know which areas are not yet covered by women's NGOs. We can formulate project proposals and get funds, so why shouldn't we start our own business?" The establishment of the NGO was costly both financially and in terms of time. However, the idea of business is very strong in the way Igbal perceives NGOs' work and she was convinced that it was not a bad investment.

As a cofounder and an executive director of an NGO working in the area of gender training and advocacy, Igbal exhibits considerable skills in project formulation and fund-raising; this seems to be her professional strength. The fact that her organisation is working in various issues and lacking a clear focus was explained, for example, by one of the activists in the area of human rights as follows: "Igbal and her organisation work in whatever subject as long as this subject brings them money." Igbal sees this differently. As an answer to my question concerning the involvement of her organisation in the area of VAW, she explained a bit about the philosophy of the organisation saying: "The donors are very much interested in the area of peace, conflict, and VAW, so we also focus on these issues. Within the frame of these issues one can address variety of subjects, but first you have to get funds, after that you can adjust your project according to your ability and interest." The question of funding and sustainability of the NGO business is thus an important aspect in understanding the nature of the involvement of Igbal's organisation in the area of VAW.

VAW and the Gendered Process of Sociopolitical Restructuration

During the 1990s and under the ruling of the Islamists the role of NGOs and their relation to the state observably changed. The expansion of the role of NGOs as major actors in the field of development was beneficial only to NGOs which were sympathetic to the Islamisation politics (see chapter 4). The role of others, who were critical of the political project of the NIF in development, was severely affected.

Fatma's activism and social agency reveals how oppositional relations between women NGOs and the state are structured. The commitment of Fatma

to the agenda of VAW is very much related to the way she and her family experienced the Islamisation project. Direct violence, in the sense of imprison-
ment, physical torture, and the restriction of movement, was utilised by security forces to eliminate opposition and increase political control of the state.
However, it made global concepts of rights, such as VAW agendas, more appealing to political activists who were engaged with NGO work as an agenda
for change. Fatma, as a leftist, can be considered as a classical case of how the
agency of oppressed political actors is locally situated. A comment of a political activist on the subject of NGOs' relation to the state, which she offered
during an interview conducted for this study, explained this issue. She said,
"When Elengaz[6] came it displaced the progressive opposition. Progressive
men left the country or they were kept in prisons, and progressive women became NGO activists." The association of the agenda of VAW with the progressive, liberal, or communist oppositional movements is on the one hand a
strategy of the Islamist to disqualify this agenda as a (Western) frame for social transformation and development. On the other, the systematic marginalisation and oppression of these movements by the Islamists left little room
for activists to engage in politics. Thus NGOs and civil work becomes a space
which largely contains anti-Islamisation potential.

Women's NGOs working with the agenda of rights often represent political opposition. This opposition is either expressed in being critical of the
state Islamisation project while adopting global concepts of rights, or it is revealed in the fact that women activists are also members (or former members) of oppositional parties. Because most members of women's organisations are critical about the state politics and some are also members or
ex-members of opposition parties, opposition movements and their ideologies tend to shape the work of civil society organisations which are working
with the agendas of rights. This politicisation of civil organisation is described by many studies as one of the problems of civil society work in Sudan
(Niblock 1989, Bilal 2004).

At the same time the politicisation of NGOs is leading to the (re)shaping
of the local development agendas and discourses. Fatma's advocating of VAW
as a frame for social change and transformation is to be partially understood
in relation to the state's policies of development in general. Despite the discursive adoption of the Islamists of the concepts of human development and
social transformation, the focus of development policies of the state is still
quantitative and based on economic production. Moreover, the classical
fields of economic production as well as relations of production in these fields
are almost completely controlled by the state. Consequently both the state
and NGOs which reflect Islamisation politics have greater weight in shaping

processes of development and social transformation. On the other hand the state treats NGOs which are critical of Islamisation politics and whose politics are shaped by global development concepts with a security mentality, thus such NGOs have little room to influence the classic areas of development such as the agricultural sector.

It is interesting here to note that the oppositional relation between the state's development discourse and that of non-Islamist women's NGOs is reproduced by two mechanisms. First, the oppositional politics and the critical relation between the state and non-Islamist NGOs leads to the ideologicalisation of the agenda adopted by certain women's organisations. Aba Seed (2001, 60) argues that most women's NGOs which advocate women's rights and/or feminism as a perspective to address the women and gender questions are more occupied with political opposition to the state and its Islamisation project than with how to link up with women and women's spaces and how to adapt their feminist perspective to the experience of the majority of Sudanese women. Hence feminist activists, argues Aba Seed, tend to use a fixed and uninteractive approach when dealing with women's rights agenda. Second, this ideologicalisation of the women and gender agenda is supported by the hostile political environment in which NGOs operate, and this affects the institutional capacities of NGOs. The policing by the state of political and civil actors, particularly those who are considered to be oppositional, affects the possibilities of direct interaction between NGOs and the various social groups and communities and weakens the mobilisation of research as a strategy for change. NGOs such as Fatma's thus often focus on advocacy as a strategy to work with VAW agendas. In addition, their work is lacking the needed interaction with the target groups and communities and focuses mainly on (negating) Islamist politics and practise. Consequently the oppositional stance between these two actors is reproduced. This does not mean that there is no cooperation between the state and non-Islamist NGOs; however, NGOs' involvement with the state is often shaped by critical engagement and a lack of trust between the two sides (see chapter 4).

The case of Igbal is comparable: her situation resembles that of thousands of Sudanese who were deprived of their jobs as a result of the policies of the state. Her role as an activist in the field of VAW is based on a commitment to women's rights, as well as her need to secure a career outside the public sector. NGOs, as the case of Igbal illustrates, become a space which absorbs those who lost the chance of employment in the public sector due to the problem of unemployment or the state's policies of clearing the public sector of the opposition.

The case of Igbal's engagement in NGOs activism sheds light on the process of the diminishing of the middle class[7] which is rooted in politics of Sudan since the 1950s. The various development policies of the (independent) Sudan (Niblock 1989, Bilal 2004) inherited a colonial system which is the root cause of the diminishing of the middle class. However, the deterioration of the civil service due to many factors that include the structural adjustment programmes in addition to the NIF politics, particularly those directed to the public sector employment, were the main factors that led to the shrinking of the middle class during the 1990s. The suspension of all of the employees in the specific bank department where Igbal was working is a case speaking to this effect. Igbal's case illustrates what happens to those who were suspended from the public sector. Migration, private sector employment, self-employment, and NGOs are some of the options left for people like her.

Unlike the case of Fatma, who to a large extent represents the further politicisation of NGOs and the ways through which VAW agendas become an oppositional discourse, Igbal's activism could be described as the business(isation) of NGOs. NGOs become an employment or self-employment option either because of the lack of opportunities to secure employment in the public sector, or due to the attraction of NGOs' work in terms of flexibility of the working conditions, exposure to other societies and culture through networking, or the (relative) independence from the state's bureaucratic systems. Activists like Igbal and their NGOs have a sort of oppositional relation to the state and its political agendas. However, the work perspective of these activists is mainly of a business nature rather than political opposition.

The domination of the business mentality of some women's NGOs can be understood within the frame of two main factors: First, the Islamist policy of clearing the public sector of active or potential political opposition. Second, the lack of funding for NGOs, particularly those working in the area of rights, which makes this sector seek financial support from international development donors almost exclusively. In this way a relation of dependency is developing between these two actors—namely NGOs working with the agendas of rights and international donors—on the level of local politics. These NGOs are preoccupied with the question of how to "hunt funds." The agendas of the organisations are very elastic, flexible, and largely determined according to the funding priorities of the donors. The result is shallow interaction with the target social groups and weak programmes and mechanisms of implementation. Hilhorst and Leeuwen (2005, 11–13) noted similar observations about some Sudanese organisations working in Nairobi with the agenda of peace. Activists who set up these organisations are fundamentally interested in leadership experience and a career. This in turn leads to strong identification of the NGO discourse with that of the donors' organisations.

Nevertheless the competition, networking, and mobilisation of resourses to secure funding make these NGOs a significant agent in channelling global development concepts to the local setting. As argued before, these NGOs lack the needed technical and conceptual capacities to act as a middle point between the majority of Sudanese women and the local and global development agendas. However, through these NGOs global development concepts, and particularly women's rights, currently become an important discourse in negotiating the state's development politics and agendas.

The analysis of the case of Fatma shows how an oppositional relation to the state can shape the ideological framework of women's NGOs; the case of Igbal reflects the relation between the business(isation) of NGOs and diminishing of the middle class. Both of these types of organisations and activism address and interact with the educated decision and policy makers on both urban and political levels. At the same time these agencies play an observable role in the current process of political transformation and peace thus linking the local agenda of peace with the global development concepts. Important to mention here is that these two types of women's NGOs can be found in one organisation and are not necessarily separated as presented here.

Interestingly the case of Leila highlights an often ignored dimension of the process of Islamisation, namely the gendered struggle within Islamist political organisations. The instrumentality of Sudanese women to Islamist discourses and nation- or state-building projects is a well studied phenomenon (see for example, Hale 1996; Ahmadi 2003; Nageeb 2004; Willemse 2005). At the same time many studies show that belonging to an Islamist organisation granted some educated Sudanese women upward mobility on the political career ladder (see for example Al-Affandi 1991, Lowrie 1993, and Westerlund 1997). However, little is revealed about the gendered interaction and conflict within the Islamist organisations (Hall 1996, Westerlund 1997). Leila's case demonstrates the gender conflicts in Islamist organisations and politics as well as the change in the Islamist discourse, particularly after the events of 11 September 2001. Hale (1996, 213) argues that in their political discourse Islamist women activists are coopting the language of leftists' discourse.[8] This opinion is also shared by many Sudanese academics who were interviewed for this study. Cooption of the discourse of leftists is still used to explain the observable change in the discourse of some Islamists today. Cooption can be used to explain the change in the discourse of the (Islamist) state, which tries to maintain its political power within the context of peace and democratisation by embracing global development concepts. However, there are other forms of transformation in the perspectives and practices of many Islamists that could be observed by following the various Islamist discourses in Sudan and not only of those who are in power.

Leila's perspective on women's rights and gender questions represents an emerging Islamist discourse which is inclusive of (many) global development concepts. This type of discourse, that Leila calls "progressive and open Islam," is observable in many other contexts (see chapter 4). Leila's intellectual engagement in the field of women's rights and VAW agendas demonstrates a strong, gender-sensitive approach for dealing with Islamic sources. Her activist involvement in the area of women's rights is classified by many non-Islamist activists as progressive, liberal, and particularly confrontational towards religious and traditional authorities.[9] Further her activism is not based on rejecting global development concepts. Instead it consciously integrates and uses them for a better understanding of Islam as a rights frame.

Leila's approach to VAW agendas and particularly the issue of wife battery is based on Islam and nevertheless supportive and complementary to that of liberal and progressive activists, as this antiviolence and gender-sensitive Islamic perspective is very useful for addressing traditional and state authorities. At the same time her activism reflects how Islamist perspective, discourses, and strategies might transform over time as a result of social and political changes at both the local and global levels. Although this transformation is applied to the discourse of a minority of Islamists, it is nevertheless important in the context of peace and democratisation which allows for more political interaction.

Whether VAW is a framework to express political opposition, a means to secure funds from international organisation for local NGOs, or a way to express an open Islamist discourse, it remains a significant concept to understanding how (global) agendas of women's organisations are linked to the (local) social and political structures. Up to this point the discussion in this chapter emphasised that VAW is gaining a new political weight within the context of peacebuilding in Sudan. However, due to the ways in which political and civil activism in the areas of rights and women's rights are embedded in the sociopolitical structure as shaped by the Islamisation project, VAW remains an oppositional discourse. In the coming sections we shall see how activists in the field of VAW enlarge their space of action and negotiate local development agendas through translocal networking.

Networking: A Strategy for Working with the Agenda of VAW

In 2004 the Sudanese Humanitarian Aid Commission (HAC) issued a bill concerning networks of civil society organisations which has posed a challenge to women's networks. According to this bill, networks of NGOs must be registered with the HAC in order to be able to officially function as a network according to the vague definition of networks in the bill, namely a group of organisations working to achieve the same objective, implement the same programme(s), or advocate the same agenda(s) with one or different sources of funding. Because the legal, administrative, and financial requirements for the registration of networks are complicated and expensive, very few networks of women's organisations are officially registered. Activists due to the mistrust between NGOs and the state argue that this bill is only beneficial for organisations which sympathise with the state Islamist orientation. To others, who are critical about the state and its development policies, the bill is basically a means to enhance the control of the state over NGOs and the potential of solidarity between groups of NGOs which are networking or intending to form a network. Through the required system of reporting and renewal of registrations and the control of the financial sources, the bill gives HAC power over networks. For all of these reasons many networks of women's organisations remain unregistered, hence officially unrecognised as networks.

Through the implementation of this bill and the reaction to it by many women activists, the definition of a network at the level of Sudan takes two forms: The first, registered (or intending to be registered) networks of women's organisations which make up the minority and, accordingly their network's status must have a defined physical space (network's office(s), administrative structure, budget and programmes), and the second, unregistered networks consisting of groups of women's NGOs that have strong networking relations and in many cases network infrastructures such as common funding and physical meeting location, and network equipments (e.g., computer or fax machine) despite the lack of the official network's status. Women who are involved in this kind of networking strategically refer to it with the English term "partnership" or the Arabic term *taa`wn*[10] meaning "cooperation" to avoid using the official term "networks." However, they define the relationship among themselves and between their organisations as a network.

Since there is not a single registered network of women's organisation which is explicitly focusing on VAW as its network's thematic issue,[11] the next part of the paper will be devoted to discussing the network relations between women's organisations working with the theme of VAW, characterised above as the second form of network.

Partnership for the Agenda of Violence[12]

Shams is a local women's NGO specialising in the general area of gender training and advocacy and receiving funds mainly from organisations based in the Netherlands and Scandinavia. After the signing of the CPA and the relaxing of the political atmosphere, the team of the organisation decided to consider some changes in the programmes and activities of the NGO in order to be able to meet the challenges of the peacebuilding phase. VAW, sexuality, and sexual rights are to guide the process of transforming the NGO from an organisation working within a general framework of gender to an NGO specialised in the area of VAW. Violence and sexuality is regarded by the director of the organisation as "a very important field because very few NGOs and activists want to talk about these issues." She also argued that "many NGOs consider violence and sexuality within the framework of FGM/C. Thus Shams—as a long term plan—should work explicitly with the agenda of violence and sexuality to unveil these culturally sensitive issues."

During the conduct of this research Shams received the approval from a Dutch donor organisation to fund their first project on VAW. Shams is the initiator of the programme; however, the project is funded according to the project document as "a partnership on VAW which is a network of local organisations working together to implement this project." Two other organisations are involved in this network, one is a local office of a regional NGO specialised in the area of VAW, and the other is an organisation working in the area of gender research. The project includes the classical components of research, training, awareness-raising activities, and documentation. The target area for the first phase of the project is the capital Khartoum and subsequently the project is planned to cover other regions. What is interesting about this project is the networking relations between the involved organisations as well as between these organisations and other regional ones. In the next sections three levels of networking will be introduced to discuss how this partnership project on VAW came to existence and how the network between the organisations involved functions.

Diaspora's Connection

To achieve their objective of specialisation in the area of VAW and sexuality the director of Shams decided to seek the advice and support of other activists who have experience in this field. Sudanese activists living and working in asylum were the first to be contacted. This category of activists, according to the director of Shams, is well acquainted with the social, political, and cultural conditions of Sudan, and their activism outside the country enabled them to address culturally sensitive issues and to collect experience in this field. Shams addressed a U.S.-based international organisation specialising in the area of sexuality and sexual rights and closely working with international development and funding agents such as UNIFEM. The Shams director contacted one of the founders of this organisation, a Sudanese living and working in U.S. for more than fifteen years. The proposal which was sent by Shams to the U.S.-based organisation was a three-year project on VAW. During a visit of the Sudanese founder of the U.S.-based organisation to Sudan in 2004 the director of Shams had a meeting with her to discuss the possibility of funding the project on VAW. The project proposal was not rejected, but the funding was delayed. The meeting between the two parties took on more the shape of counselling. The Sudanese activist advised the director of Shams to focus first on the institution building of the organisation in order to be able to carry on with being specialised in the area of VAW and sexuality. She also suggested that Shams should submit another (smaller) project proposal to support the institution building of the organisation.

A few months later Shams received funding from the U.S.-based organisation to purchase office, communication, and media equipment to enhance its institutional capacity. Most importantly this incident formed the first networking relation between Shams and Sudanese activists abroad for the purpose of working with the VAW agendas. Aside from the material support, the U.S.-based organisation included Shams in their list of African partner organisations working in the area of VAW and sexuality. The networking relation with a Sudanese activist in diaspora was, thus, a vital step for Shams to realise its aim of becoming an organisation specialised in VAW, to prepare the organisation for the peacebuilding phase, and to facilitate networking with other African organisations.

Translocality of Local Networking

Late in 2004 Shams' new offices, complete with the new equipment and office facilities, were well established, though there was not yet a project on VAW under implementation. During this time representatives of a Dutch organisation, which funds many small projects of Shams, was visiting Darfur to carry out projects there. The Dutch organisation contacted its local partners to implement projects on health, human rights, and postconflict traumas for

workers at the refugee camps in Darfur. Shams' director was in the implementation team for the project of the Dutch organisation in Darfur. During
a one-week stay in Darfur she introduced an idea for a project on VAW to
the Dutch donors. The idea was provisionally accepted and the Dutch organisation suggested that the project proposal should be submitted before the
end of their financial year.

Upon arrival in Khartoum the representatives of the Dutch organisation
conducted meetings with the various local NGOs which received funding
from the organisation. The meeting with the Shams team was very successful. The representatives of the Dutch organisation developed a positive im-
pression about the progress of the organisation, the office facilities, the commitment of the team to the agenda of VAW, as well as its network with other
African NGOs. Accordingly they confirmed their preliminary approval of
the idea of funding a three-year project on VAW, particularly because the
Shams project was based on networking with other NGOs which were also
partners of the Dutch organisation.

According to one of the representatives of the Dutch organisation, who
was interviewed for this research, the involvement of other partner organisation is very important. In her opinion networking strengthens the capacity
of organisations and makes them more able to face the state and traditional
authorities. Furthermore, the suggested organisations for the implementation
of the project on VAW already formed a network and had strong working relations, which the donor organisations have to support by financing and in-
stitutionalising processes.

Within two weeks Shams and two other local organisations had to finalise
an application for a three-year project and send it to the Dutch organisation.
Several meetings were conducted for this purpose. Participatory observations
of these meetings reveal much about how global development concepts get a
local shape.

The feminist director of Shams believes that there should be no further
compromise in addressing the issue of VAW and sexuality and that Sudanese
activists have to make use of the political transformation and the relaxation
of the Islamisation politics taking place in the country in order to upgrade
their approach and agenda of women and gender. The adoption of "uncom-
promised feminism," according to the director of Shams, who used this English term to express her opinion, is the only way for women activists to meet
the challenges of the peacebuilding phase. According to her, "uncompro-
mised feminism" means "that we don't have to be shy or hesitant because of
cultural or political reason in fighting all forms of patriarchy, and women
oppression—even the sexual ones." The peacebuilding phase for her is a po-

litical stage that should lead to transformation "from a WID and charity mild approach to a more courageous and confrontational approach" of women's NGOs. Hence she believes that "one of the main problems of women's NGOs in Sudan is that they are not feminist, or not feminist enough." With this perspective she argues the position of her organisation concerning the formulation of a VAW network and project.

The other representatives of the two organisations involved in the partnership had a different standpoint concerning the network and the VAW agenda. They both considered the position of the director of Shams as "unrealistic" in focusing more on the adoption of feminism without considering the suitability of this approach to Sudan. They argued that women activists should not ignore the fact that Islamist politics and influence had become deeply rooted in the society. They both suggested that the partnership project should address the question of Islam explicitly and should include activists like Leila, who are accepted as a religious authority. Feminism, as one of these activists expressed in English, is "a personal conviction, but strategically speaking should not dominate the discourse of women activists in the time of peace," and added in Arabic "for real peace civil society organisations in general should try to reach the wider society and to do so this feminist language is not suitable."

The final project idea moves from a local to a translocal network. An Asian feminist and women activist, with whom the director of Shams got acquainted during a workshop in Southeast Asia, was invited to conduct the gender and VAW training programmes. Asian feminists are considered by Shams' director as "feminists of the South: they are more close to the nature of our society than European feminists who don't have to consider issues like religion and ethnicity any more." For the part of the project which addresses the component of policies and VAW the partners decided to consider the experience of activists from the Maghreb region in reforming the family code and engendering the constitution. The contact with the activists from the Maghreb area was already taking place through one of the activists involved in the partnership programme. She was attending a series of workshops in North Africa focusing on introducing and discussing the draft of the family bill suggested by the women's movement as a unified law for the region. Leila was suggested to advise the partners on how to formulate and address the question of religion.

Networking at the Regional and International Levels

As mentioned earlier, through a U.S.-based organisation Shams became a member of an African network[13] connecting organisations working to fight—across the continent—social norms, cultural practices, and states' policies leading to all forms of violation of women rights with a special focus on the area of FGM/C, sexuality, bodily, and reproductive rights. Through this network's status the director of Shams got invitations to participate in various events addressing issues of relevance to VAW and sexuality. She also took part in many of these events as a representative of her own organisation as well as of the partnership programme on VAW. One of these meetings was organised in Ethiopia in December 2004 as an outcome of the launching of the first sexuality institute in Africa in Nigeria in 2004. The meeting in Ethiopia was a training programme for women's organisations working in the area of sexuality and bodily integrity and rights. One of the main objectives of this meeting was to introduce the issue of the sexual rights of youths and women in the agenda of the African Union. Hence a one-day session of this training programme was organised on the premises of the African Union in Addis Ababa to carry out a dialogue between representatives of different African women's organisations and the members of the Union.

The local network on VAW is also connected to the North African region. A member of the partnership programme was participating in the North Africa meeting of the African Federation for Sexual Health and Rights organised in Egypt also in 2004. The meeting was organised to coordinate the African movements in the fields of sexuality, health, violence, and rights. It also aimed at preparing for a conference organised by the African Federation for Sexual Health and Rights and the African Union in 2006.

At the same time the Oslo Donors' Conference (ODC) on Sudan which was taking place in Norway in April 2005 was an event around which women's NGOs intensively networked. One of the NGOs involved in the partnership project on VAW was even taking the initiative of coordinating a series of meetings between different women's organisations to prepare for this important conference. During these meetings women NGOs were tactically discussing, prioritising, and formulating their agendas and vision on how to address the ODC and to engender the peace-building process. The meetings also facilitated intensive networking on the subjects of fund-raising and participation in ODC. One of the NGOs involved in the partnership project was represented as a member in the delegation of women's organisations to Oslo. VAW and gender-based violence were among the major issues addressed to the ODC by women's NGOs. In the common document "Sudanese women's priorities and recommendations to the Oslo Donors' Conference on Sudan" different women's organisations from both the North and South of Sudan as well as representatives from the government of Sudan and the SPLM/A presented their recommendations. The urgent priorities for the Sudanese women's delegate included gender-based violence. Hence, through networking and networks of women's organisations VAW became integral to the agenda for engendering the peace process.

The above discussion shows that VAW as a global development concept was addressed as an agenda of women's organisations in Sudan during the peacebuilding phase through various network relations. These translocal networks played a major role in shaping the local perspective on VAW. Both Southeast Asian and North African experiences of women activists are becoming more and more present as resources and networks from which Sudanese women activists can benefit. This was not the case in the early 1980s and 1990s when networks were almost exclusively active through Europe and the United States of America, partially because funding for women's organisations in Sudan came mainly from these two continents. Currently the networking relation between women's NGOs exists also outside the framework of donor organisation/local partner. VAW would, hence, be localised, to a considerable extent, by including the frame of religion, a South perspective to feminism and an African experience in dealing with the policy issue.

This partnership programme intensified the network relations between the different organisations involved. Prior to the implementation phase of their joint project they organised various activities under the theme of VAW. Violence in Darfur was the centre of these activities, but often the focus was enlarged and the VAW programme included more than the rape cases in Darfur. More importantly in their everyday work these organisations integrated the agenda of VAW and rights as part of the women's NGOs discourses on peacebuilding. In their different advocacy, training, and lobbying activities for the drafting of the new constitution, conflict resolution, women's participation in politics and FGM/C,[14] the discourse on women's rights, and violation of rights become instrumental. This is not to suggest that the inclusion of the language of rights and VAW in the different agendas of the peacebuilding phase is the result of this particular partnership project on VAW. Rather the partnership programme is used here as an example to reflect how translocal networks of women's organisation function, and at the same time how the global development concepts on VAW and the related women's rights agendas are situated in local agendas. Additionally these concepts are also becoming a medium in which to further politicise the (local) agendas of women's NGOs for peacebuilding in Sudan.

Although the partnership project on VAW is not yet under implementation, the networking relations around the agenda of violence are very intensive at local, regional, as well as international levels. Through translocal networks and networking relations between women's NGOs and activists the
(local) perspective and agenda of VAW finds its way to the regional policy
institutions such as the African Union and to international ones like the
World Bank, UN, and the European donor organisations who fund the
peacebuilding phase.

VAW, Peace, and Situating Women's Political Agency:
A Conclusion

To understand how the agenda of VAW is locally situated one has to refer to
two major actors, women's NGOs and the state. Studying the agenda of
VAW in Sudan reveals how global development concepts are negotiated
within the context of political transformation. However, it does not show
that VAW is conceptualised, addressed, or questioned in effective interactive
ways which would reach a wide sector of the different communities involved
to address the social, cultural, political, and economic dimensions of violence at a societal level. There are many reasons for this lack of capacity of
NGOs to tackle gender issues in a socially interactive ways. In Aba Seed's
(2002, 60) opinion, a major problem for women's activism in Sudan is their
approach to women's issues that tends to use fixed categories, definitions, and
frames rather than developing interactive ways and perspectives to deal with
gender questions. In addition she argues that women activists, who work
with the agenda of rights, focus more on opposing and strategising against the
Islamist state. That is to say working under an authoritarian undemocratic
system leads to the weakening of the capacity of the NGOs to address women
and gender questions. Hilhorst and Leeuwen (2005, 99–101) write along the
same lines about women's NGOs in the South of Sudan. They emphasise
that local NGOs' discourses are shaped to provide a basis of identification
with international discourses in the areas of peace, gender, and rights. Consequently, with the international funding available for the peacebuilding
phase many NGOs tend to present themselves and their agendas according
to the interest of the donors. This, argue Hilhorst and Leeuwen, leads to
weak conceptualisation of projects and shallow implementations strategies of
these projects.

The case of the agenda of VAW presented in this paper is not very different. VAW as one of the agendas of the peacebuilding phase is undergoing the
same patterns just discussed. Hence projects on VAW can be described as

lacking the capacity to interact with the majority of Sudanese women. Nevertheless while projects might be weak, VAW as a global development concept is increasingly gaining significance in the local political context of peace and democratisation. The agency of women activists working with VAW agendas is clear if we look at how the discourses on women and human rights are being placed in the local political level and agenda for peace. This, in the long term, helps in transforming the state's institutions and practices and in imposing a more democratic and rights-oriented political logic. Hence, the importance of the discourse on VAW can only be analysed by referring to a wider (local) political level and the relation between women's NGOs and the state.

To illustrate this argument it is worth considering the various stages, strategies, and means through which VAW is situated in the local political agenda. During the 1990s women activists avoided the direct use of the concept of VAW. While the concept provided activists with a global frame and reference through which to work with local and culturally based issues like FGM/C, it was tactically eliminated as a means of presenting the agenda of women's organisation. With such a nonprovocative strategy women's NGOs managed to address gender concerns as women's matters rather than political matters. This, as Bayat (2004, 5) stated in relation to activism in the Middle East and Muslim societies, is a "delicate art of presence in harsh circumstances, the ability to create social spaces within which those individuals who refuse to exit can advance the cause of human rights, equality, and justice, and do so under formidable political conditions."

With the signing of the peace agreement and the deterioration of the situation in Darfur, the political context changed. Human rights became an important component for guiding the transformation process. Thus women's NGOs change their strategy and find a new spot to "step their feet" in local politics. The perspective from which to tackle the agenda of VAW moves from women's matters to political matters, and rape cases in Darfur become the entry point for NGOs in bringing the agenda of VAW to local political discourses. No doubt that the individual agency of women and the way this agency is shaped by the social and political structures are decisive factors in how VAW is currently operating. The cases of the three activists presented in this chapter show that VAW enters the local political agenda as a frame to negotiate the institutional and political rather than the social and everyday life levels. The discourse on VAW targets more the negotiation of institutional politics as well as the oppressive politics and practices of the state. Thus it remains basically at an advocacy level with poor links to the everyday life of different Sudanese women.

Due to the hostility between NGOs working in the area of rights and the state, the need of the former to secure funds, generate political support to stabilise their presence, and their engagement in influencing local development politics these NGOs tend to focus intensively on translocal networking. The translocal networking of women's NGOs is connecting the local agenda of VAW to global ones. Networks of women's NGOs move the agenda of VAW from political matters to global political matters. Through networking, the frame of rights and human rights becomes a reference point in conceptualising the local agenda of women's NGOs. Women's NGOs working with the agenda of VAW are not only keeping the issue of rape in Darfur under political scrutiny. They are also forming a channel through which rights and human rights debates are maintained as a frame to negotiate peace and democratisation.

Accordingly, while VAW agendas might be applied as a strategy to gain funding and secure a career, or as a means of political opposition to the state, it becomes a real political discourse and a means for negotiating peace and transformation. This is one way in which the agency of women's NGOs is situated in the peacebuilding phase despite their lack of capacity to develop an interactive approach with the majority of Sudanese women and their constant preoccupation with the quest for funding.

Notes

1. The Sudanese branch of PANOS Britain, which is an organisation working in the area of violence in general and VAW in particular.

2. He is a former prime minister of Sudan, a key intellectual and political figure in the country and the leader of the Ummah party, one of the biggest and oldest parties in Sudan which represent the political wing of the Mahdia movement that started in 1881. Currently his party is in opposition.

3. Upon the request of the participants of this research and to protect them all, names of persons, places, and organisations are concealed. The stories of these women were also slightly changed, in ways that do not interfere with the significance of the case and the chronology of the life story as told by the women, as an effort to anonymise the persons.

4. The subject of "wife battery" represented a heated discussion, specifically that the implementation of the Islamisation project led to the emergence of religious authorities advocating that wife beating is an admissible practice in Islam. The right of the husband to beat his wife and the conditions under which he is allowed to use this measurement were often the subject, for example, of TV talk shows. Although there are different positions regarding the conditions under which a man is allowed to beat his wife, there is no male religious authority going so far as saying that the practice is prohibited in Islam. Leila represents a pioneer in this regard, as she uses the same approach as religious men, however she reaches a different conclusion; namely that wife battery is prohibited in Islam.

5. See An-Na'im (1997a, 1997b), Hamad (1994), Amnesty International's Sudan Report (1992) for more discussion on this issue.

6. *Thawrat Elengaz* is the name which the Islamists used to describe their regime. It means the salvation revelation.

7. Middle class in this case is defined in relation to white-collar employees of the civil service. It is a social class which is urban-centred and constitutes the educated social elite.

8. Hale (1996) did interview women active in the NIF in 1988 during the short democratic period (1985–1989). This discourse of the Islamist women that Hale referred to developed in the context of political openness and competition where not only Islamists were coopting from leftists, but also the opposite. Hale, in the same book in a chapter titled "The Wing of the Patriarch: The Sudanese Communist Party and the Women's Union" (1996, 151–185), shows how leftist forces in Sudan, while competing with the Islamists, were coopting the language and some of the strategies of the Islamists.

9. My exchange with some leftist women activists showed that there is a high level of acceptance of Leila's activist engagement. One even commented that "if one closes one's eyes and listens to [Leila] one would think that her talk is not coming out of a mouth of an Islamist but a communist who is involved for ages in women's liberation."

10. The Arabic noun *taa`un* and the verb *beneta'un* are often also used to express relations of cooperation between more than one organisation. However some of the activists in a group interview about this subject explained that they intentionally use the term to avoid the "politicised expressions of networks and networking, which will put you in a problem with HAC."

11. Peace and FGM are the main thematic issues of the registered networks of women's organisations; accordingly the networks are registered under names such as "peace and development network," or "the Sudanese network for the eradication of all forms of FGM."

12. It should also be noted here that the presentation of the empirical data for this section is based on reconstructing some events and participatory observations in a way that does not interfere with the essence of the data and the subject. This strategy of data presentation is applied to anonymise persons and organisations and to limit the amount of data for the purpose of this (short) article.

13. The Amanitare network.

14. These are some of the activities organised by the NGOs involved in the partnership project on VAW. Participatory observations of these different activities were part of the research conducted in Sudan.

I V

CONCLUSION

~

CHAPTER NINE

Diversified Development: Women's Agency and the Constitution of Translocal Spaces

Salma A. Nageeb

This final chapter will explore how women's organisations situate their agendas in an institutional sociopolitical context. The processes of restructuring the public sphere were analysed in the first chapter of comparative analysis (chapter 5) by focusing on processes of social interaction and modes of communication which are adopted by women activists to position themselves and their agency in the local context of everyday life. We looked at the act of addressing, advocating, and negotiating a specific development agenda which is necessarily grounded in a specific local context. To take this discussion further, we analyse in the following the processes and strategies through which these agendas become an integral part of development debates and/or plans. Our aim is to show another dimension of the agency of women's NGOs, namely how women activists and NGOs advocate or negotiate a particular development vision in translocal gendered spaces by discussing the translocal agency of women's organisations and activists. This agency of women's organisations is shaped by their engagement with institutions, discourses, and authorities both at local and global levels through which they build discursive arenas that link these two levels. Analysing how translocal gendered spaces are constituted through the agency of women's organisations also entails looking at the relation between women's NGOs, state, international development agents, and discourses.

On the basis of the empirical findings, three different though interlinked processes through which women's organisations constitute translocal gendered spaces can be identified and will be analysed in this chapter. This is accomplished first, by differentiating (local) discourses on Islam, a process which becomes increasingly important as a result of the growing influence of Islamisation movements globally and locally as well as global debates on Islam. Second, these organisations seek to offer an alternative approach to women and gender issues which focuses on the agency rather than the victimisation of women, thus they move away from a vulnerability to a rights approach.[1] Third, while doing so, women's organisations negotiate global concepts of rights which become increasingly differentiated according to the experiences of women's NGOs at local levels. Although these three processes take place at specific local levels and within the context of different types of Islamisation, as the case studies in Sudan, Senegal, and Malaysia have shown, nonetheless they reveal the interconnection (also in the sense of confrontation and comparative interaction) between global politics, discourses, and institutions on the one hand and local norms, systems of meanings, and institutions on the other. This interconnection between the local and the global constitutes a two-way process which is formed through networks and networking relations. It can be regarded to empirically ground the concept of glocalisation (Robertson 1995).

When studying the constitution of translocal gendered spaces, we acknowledge that globalisation made it increasingly difficult to equate social space with physical space (Massey 1994, McDowell 1999, Olesen 2005). This does, however, not mean that the translocal gendered spaces on which our analysis is focused are detached from physical (local) space. Rather, by focusing on the agency of women's organisations and their constant attempts to change (local) development politics and plans we want to analyse the restructuration and transformation of space (Olesen 2005, 420–422). To demonstrate this transformation the links and interactions between local, national, and translocal institutions, discourses, and organisations (empirically demonstrated in chapters 6, 7, and 8) will be traced back as well as the ways they lead to the constitution of translocal gendered spaces.

Differentiating the Local Discourses on Islam

In the first part of this chapter we look at how women's NGOs legitimise their global development agendas in the Muslim societies studied. Here religion plays an important role and it will be shown that discourses on Islam became an integral part of women's NGOs attempts and strategies to influence national development plans and local social authorities. These strategies are nevertheless always accompanied by attempts of women's organisations to change the rationale of development politics. This seems of special importance since in all the three cases studied the so-called vulnerability approach represents the dominant state approach to gender and women's issues.

The case studies have shown that Islamisation processes are experienced differently in the three countries—Sudan, Malaysia, and Senegal—and relate differently to the respective social and state structures. Women's NGOs have to deal with the question of Islamisation either as state projects, as in Malaysia and Sudan, or as the politics of the opposition, through which a part of the society is excluded from the secular national modernisation project, such as in Senegal. Independently of such differences, it can be observed that local discourses on Islam are 'worked at' and addressed by women's NGOs primarily at two levels: at the level of everyday life and at the level of strategy formation. At the level of everyday life, as has been discussed in chapter 5, women activists must deal with the politicisation of religion as part of their social reality which (partially) shapes modes of social interaction and communication. The strategic level of addressing local Islam(isation) discourses on the other hand is related to the question of how development agendas of women's organisations are shaped, situated, and negotiated—through the agency of women's NGOs—within the context of the growing Islamist movements. The following discusses this dimension in particular.

Irrespectively of their concrete agenda—the reform of the family code in Senegal, situating the Violence Against Women (VAW) agendas in Sudan, or negotiating human rights within the framework of the Convention on the Elimination of All Forms of Discrimination against Women (CEDAW) in Malaysia—women activists in all three countries studied are increasingly confronted with the need to ensure the religious legitimacy of their agendas. The various strategies which women's NGOs adopt to give more political weight to their agendas, especially within the context of local discourses on Islam, can be classified according to two major patterns. Activists engage themselves either in advocating or developing a "progressive"[2] interpretation of Islamic sources. The meaning of the term *progressive* refers to the way this term was used in the countries studied. The term implies that a specific interpretation of Islamic sources was chosen which allows women's NGOs to promote or negotiate global development concepts in the respective contexts. In the three cases studied global development concepts are often stereotyped, either by the state or other actors, as Western, foreign, or non-Islamic ideas. Those NGOs who advocate these concepts therefore seek to legitimise these development goals or visions by linking global politics and concepts of moderate Islamic ethics and interpretations of religious sources. Hence they adopt a progressive Islam discourse aimed at legitimizing global development concepts and agendas by emphasising its compatibility with general Islamic ethics. While doing so they seek to compete with Islamisation currents. Or, and this is the second pattern derived from the empirical studies, the women activists advocate Islamisation politics, projects, and Islam reformist discourse and movements (see Loimeier 1997; Salvatore 1997, 2001), arguing that these offer the appropriate frame to address social, gender, and development concerns. This means they work within the frame set by these Islamic movements and politics.

Negotiating Gender within Progressive Islam Discourse

The differentiation of the local discourses on Islam by introducing a progressive Islam discourse can be analysed by considering the case of Senegal. The reform of the family code discussed by Sieveking (chapter 6) demonstrates that the secular government in Senegal opts to link up with the global standards and concepts of women's rights and gender equality. At the same time that the government protects its secular orientation, however, it avoids contentious areas and symbolic confrontations with local religious authorities. As a result, the task to transfer its position concerning the reform of the family code to the local communities is left to women's NGOs. Thus it is women's NGOs and activists who are engaged in debating and promoting the family code and sensitising the population with the need for its reform. They are left with the task of negotiating, confronting, or cooperating with local religious authorities while promoting the code. Within this context an important strategy which women's NGOs adopted while campaigning for the reform is the formation of alliances with translocal progressive Islamic scholars and the development and adoption of a religious and thus Islamic argumentation for gender equality (see chapter 5). The progressive Islam discourse which they have adopted to promote the reform of the code is embedded in the local norms of solidarity, reciprocity, and social security. It differs from the dominant and traditional Sufi one which tends to remain silent or rely on traditional institutions when dealing with women and gender issues. But the progressive Islam discourse used by women's NGOs to campaign for the reform of the family code is also different from the Islamic reform discourse. The Islamic reform discourse relates to global development concepts but more in terms of othering the West, rejecting global gender and rights concepts, and offering instead a global Islamic/ist alternative. In this context the adoption of a progressive Islam discourse enables women activists to address issues such as women's rights or gender equality. Women's NGOs, particularly through the strategic alliance with moderate Islamic scholars, enlarge their space for manoeuvring between the growing Islamist tendencies and the passivity of the state concerning the position of both traditional and reform Islamic movements, especially regarding women and gender issues.

In Senegal therefore the progressive Islam discourse used by women activists aims at enhancing rather than questioning the legitimacy of the state and its development agenda. In Malaysia and Sudan the situation differs since Islamisation processes are led in different ways by the respective governments. Here women's NGOs address local Islam discourses at different levels as the empirical studies in the two countries have shown. They address either the process of Islamisation in general as monopolized by the state which leads, especially in Sudan, increasingly to the control of women. Or they focus on Islam as part of the social structure and social differentiation processes, particularly in relation to ethnicity, as shown especially in the case study in Malaysia.

In Sudan the adoption of the translocal Islam discourse by women's NGOs is embedded and part of the politically critical relationship between women's NGOs and the state and aims to challenge the state's hegemonic politics and power. During the 1990s, the state Islamisation project and practices penetrated all spheres of social and political life leading to the instrumentalisation and control of women. This intensive acculturation process framed the processes of negotiating global development concepts by women activists. Civil actors were constantly obliged to face the question of the relation between their political and development agenda and Islam. Local Islam discourses and in particular the state discourse on Islam had to be negotiated where a global development agenda was at stake. To campaign for reproductive health, eradication of harmful traditional practices, or any other agendas, activists framed their claims by adopting a progressive Sharia interpretation used by activists from the Maghreb countries or even Malaysia. This situation (only slightly) changed after signing the Comprehensive Peace Agreement (CPA).[3] The strategies adopted by women's NGOs to situate their agendas became more explicitly linked to the African context and regional development issues since these issues increasingly play a central role in the peace process and the current phase of peace building. To position their peace agendas women activists adopt a progressive translocal Islam discourse which gives religious legitimacy to the women's NGOs' agendas. At the same time many organisations strategically seek to link up with various regional and African institutions which support a more democratic Sudan. Through these links women's NGOs aim to address the African components of the various Sudanese cultures and regions instead of focusing exclusively on the so called Arab culture which is symbolically linked to Islam. Despite this slight reorientation to the African context, and due to the intensive restructuration process which took place during the 1990s, one major challenge that women's NGOs still face is the question of the religious legitimacy of their agendas. It is through the agency of urban, educated, and translocally connected activists and organisations that a progressive Islam discourse is linked to local politics and agendas of development. Similar to the case of Senegal, alliances with the knowledge authority of progressive Islamic scholars is an important strategy for women's NGOs. It enables these NGOs to address different issues, be it VAW, HIV/AIDS, or structural inequalities, following not only gender but also ethnic, regional, and religious lines. However, unlike in the case of Senegal, where the adoption of a progressive Islam discourse is strategically employed by women activists not only to address the everyday life and community levels but also to support the government development politics, Sudanese activists employ a translocal progressive Islam discourse as a fundamental strategy targeting the enlargement of the space for women's NGOs and their agendas at the political and public levels.

In Malaysia, NGOs working on the issue of Muslim women's rights such as Sisters in Islam (SIS) are contributing to the development of a progressive intellectual interpretation of Islamic sources. This discourse is formulated through the work of an epistemic community of social scientists, academics, and Islamic scholars and researchers who focus on providing well-researched (re)interpretations of Islamic sources to produce an alternative Islamic gender and development vision and to combat the religious interpretations of Islamist movements. This progressive Islam discourse is not only important at the local level to challenge the Islamisation policies adopted by the state, but also at the global level as the case study by Spiegel has shown (chapter 8). Malaysia is viewed by many Muslim countries, including Sudan, as a model of how Islam and modernisation could be successfully combined. Particularly in the area of human and women's rights women's NGOs and activists are referred to by Sudanese activists as examples of how Muslim activists can and should address modern issues. In this sense the progressive intellectual Islam discourse developed and advocated by Malaysian activists in the area of women and human rights is used translocally as a strategy to actively counteract Islamist states and movements.

The process of differentiating local Islam discourses in Malaysia is, hence, embedded in the glocalised life-world of urban, professional women who adopted global development concepts to negotiate the power of an authoritarian state and hegemonic ethnicity and religious-based identity construction. They produced a new form of authority and knowledge in a Muslim feminist academic and professional community whose work and (scientific) production is recognised by NGOs and development agents not only at the regional, but also at the global level. Neither in Senegal nor in Sudan has such an epistemic community or such globally well-linked Muslim feminist organisations yet been developed.

However, in all the three case studies the adoption of a progressive Islam discourse is an important strategy for women's NGOs in facing the growing politicisation of religion while positioning their agendas of development. Yet it is more in the case of Sudan and Malaysia that this process—of developing and advocating progressive Islam discourse by women activists—is a politicised one adopted basically at an advocacy level and embedded in an antagonistic and critical relation between NGOs on the one hand and the state and religious authorities on the other. Thus in both cases these progressive Islam discourses are an important means for enlarging their room for manoeuvre in the respective political arenas. In the case of Senegal, introducing a progressive Islam discourse is less a politicised process since it targets everyday activities and practices and emphasises a general religious ethics of men's and women's duties, rights, and responsibilities as shaped by the local norms and social institutions. Nevertheless, in all three countries and most strongly in Senegal this strategy of actively pursuing and interacting within an Islamic knowledge framework is contested and considered as counterproductive, especially by liberal feminists who often represent pronounced postcolonial and/or regional positions. Thus adopting a progressive Islamic discourse as described above can divide the women's movement and enhance the old cleavages between urban or intellectual and rural or "traditional" women (Badri 2006; Othman 2006; Sow 2003).

Apart from this distinction, however, whether progressive Islam discourses are developed or adopted by women's NGOs at an advocacy political level or are crystallised around societal and everyday institutions and practices, they represent an important instrument through which global development concepts are situated. Simultaneously through these negotiation strategies and through the agency of women's NGOs and activists in the different localities a different and alternative Islamic vision on development and social transformation gets introduced and discussed.

Negotiating Gender within Islamist and Islam Reformist Discourse

There is an important distinction to make within the context of Islamisation processes, between progressive Muslim scholars or Muslim feminists on the one side (see Moghadam 2002), and Islamist and Islam reformist female activists whose views on development and gender are embedded within Islamisation or Islam reformist movements and politics on the other. The latter

generally tackle the question of women and gender from a different perspective, which represents the second pattern of differentiating local Islam discourses. And although they might not use the global development terminologies, their (modern) Islam discourse also aims at providing women with
an alternative vision of how to address so-called modern issues such as rights.
In other words these actors use global Islamist or Islamic discourse as a liber-
ating alternative for women. The empirical research in the three countries
has shown that Islamist and reformist women activists, to different degrees,
constitute their agency and social spaces by reshaping the global Islamist discourse. Their capacity reveals different meanings and dimensions which do
not necessarily correspond to the instrumentalisation and oppression arguments which characterise the mainstream political and academic debates on
gender, Islamisation movements, and the politics of Islamist movements. It
is, as the empirical data shows, much too simple to describe these activists as
merely resisting the secular–liberal orientation of the state as in Senegal or
as simply supporting the Islamisation projects of the governments in Sudan
or Malaysia. The political agency and project of these women who adopt
Islamist/Islamic discourse "can only be understood through the exploration
of their ethical practice" (Mahmood 2005, 35). Activists from Ibadu Rahman in Senegal, Um Elmumineen in Sudan, or the Women's Development
Foundation in Malaysia, for example, represent this type of agency. Their discourses on women's rights and Islam are embedded in a historical and globalised discourse on Islam and Islamic ethics (see Ali 2006). Whereas the discourses might completely reject the global development concepts on the
basis that they are a Western product, they are at the same time important
for the construction of a global Islamic alternative. The politics of these organisations can best be described, as Abu-Lughod (1998, 4) has pointed out
in relation to Islamism, as an "alternative modernity" shaped by discourses
on modernity and Westernisation, which it intends to counter. Or, even as
"multiple modernities" (Eisenstadt 1999; Stauth ed. 1998; Randeria 2002)
shaped by translocal global flows.

On the basis of our research we found that NGOs which work within the
frame of Islamist or reformist politics in all three countries often apply a charity approach accompanied—without conceptual debates—by globalised classical women in/and development approaches.[4] Kaag (2005, 30), in her study
on Islamic NGOs in Chad, argues that this kind of NGO "provides a good
example of alternative ways in which transnational Islam is being shaped."
In the cases of the Islamic women's NGOs that we studied, the charity and
WID approach is taken further into the general idea of "transnational solidarity" (see Mohanty 2003; Tripp 1999) and of the importance of enhancing

the Umma, the worldwide community of Muslims. This takes place either according to the position of these organisations in the local development map, or to their relation and interaction with other types of women's NGOs.

This became relevant particularly after the events of 11 September 2001, when the sense of belonging to the Umma became a significant perspective, especially for approaching local development issues and interaction among different development actors (Sesemann 2005, 10–11). Thus, generally speaking, global development programmes such as income-generation projects or consciousness-raising strategies are implemented parallel with projects for religious education and sensitisation. In Malaysia and Sudan in particular, organisations working with such an approach cooperate closely with the state. However, this so-called mainstream approach is beginning to change due to the competition and comparative interaction between different types of women's NGOs and their agencies, as the empirical data presented in the previous chapters has shown. The findings have revealed that many of the organisations which work within the frame of Islamisation and reform movements are increasingly trying to capacitate women in gaining their own position in the economy and society by adopting the global concept of empowerment.[5] Abu-Lughod (2002, 428) in her study on the marriage of feminism and Islamism in Egypt focused on the relationship between "those who seek to locate women's emancipation, variously defined, at the heart of development of nation and society and those who try to dislocate such a project as alien [and] Western imported." She argued that although these types of activism conceive of themselves as oppositional "[w]hat a comparison between their output on women suggests, however, is that there are surprising areas of overlap, even as they define their projects quite differently vis-à-vis modernity and the West" (2002, 433) (see Adamu 2006).

In Senegal, organisations working with a reformist orientation came to the fore only after the breakdown of the groundnut economy and the ongoing economic crisis which seriously affected the long-standing relation between the state and the Sufi orders. The crisis and the changes in the socioreligious structures and relations opened the door for an alternative Islamic discourse advocated mainly by Islamic reform movements who are critical of the state's secular orientation. Hence in Senegal—unlike the cases of Sudan and Malaysia—the Islam reformist discourse on development is an oppositional discourse that operates more at the margin of development institutions.

To summarize, the analysis of the findings suggests that studying processes of how different groups negotiate global development concepts allows one to understand how (different) Islam discourses relate to local politics. The process of differentiating Islam discourses is largely structured by the relation between women's NGOs, the state, and the international development community. On the basis of these relations and the interfaces between these actors in a particular sociopolitical context, a specific Islam discourse is (instrumentally and/or strategically) adopted by women activists to situate their development agendas. Translocal progressive Islam discourses are used largely as a political strategy to challenge the hegemonic power of the Islamist state in Sudan and Malaysia. In the case of Sudan these organisations depend almost entirely on the financial support of international donors (with the exception of Islamic organisations whose funding comes also from the state as well as translocal Islamic organisations such as Dawa). In the case of Malaysia this is not accepted by the government, however, there is some support of academic activities and transnational exchange between women's organisations by international associations. In both cases the support of the international development agents—whether political or/and financial—is an important means in reinforcing the process of democratisation and weakening the state's power and authoritarian style of politics. In Senegal on the other hand the adoption of a progressive Islam discourse is a means to support the cooperation between the secular orientation of the state and the politics of international development agents and donors.

The advocacy of Islamist or reformist Islam discourses by some women's NGOs is an important means in Malaysia as well as in Sudan for transferring the state politics of Islamisation to the everyday life and societal level. On the contrary in Senegal, the reformist discourse is a means to negotiate and delegitimise the state's secular politics. On the basis of our empirical research and analysis we argue that Islam—to different degrees—is increasingly at the centre of negotiating and legitimising a specific vision on development. At the same time the increasing role of Islam in shaping local development politics and agendas does not necessarily lead to the marginalisation of global development concepts such as women and human rights, gender equality, or combating VAW. On the contrary, these groups that we studied redefine, (re)conceptualise, and contextualise global development concepts, partially, at least, through their confrontation with the specific Islamic norms, institutions, or discourses which characterise the specific social and political context at hand. To take this discussion further and to focus on how global development concepts are negotiated and reshaped, our discussion in the next section will focus on another related dimension. The analysis will be centred on how the agendas of women's organisations move the rationale of development from the victimisation and vulnerability of women to concepts of rights. Again, the relations between NGOs, the state, and development agents which are embedded in a specific sociopolitical and religious context are the major focus of the discussion. It will be shown that NGOs position their agendas by introducing and advocating a *rights* instead of the *vulnerability* perspective. By doing so global concepts of rights become subject to re-contextualisation and redefinition according to the local context in which they operate.

Moving from the Notion of Vulnerability to Rights

The analysis so far has shown that many women's organisations in the three countries studied adopt an Islamic framework of a holistic society and the related idea of bringing the victimised or vulnerable women back into the society. In Malaysia and Sudan such an approach characterises the agendas of Islamic organisations whose work is in line with state politics. In Senegal the vulnerability approach is manifested in the secular development politics and conventional Women in Development discourses of the state and women's NGOs supporting the state's agenda. The conceptually very problematic assumption behind the *vulnerability* or *unfortunate women* approach is that it does not address the social foundation of economic problems, nor are the gender relations and social inequalities leading to such vulnerabilities analysed.

However, the case studies have also displayed that in Malaysia and Sudan NGOs which advocate policy and development perspectives not coinciding with those of the state often work from the (global) rights perspective (see Ali 2006; Elson 2002; Molyneux, Razavi 2002). The global rights perspective embodies political potential which might challenge the state's development perspectives and their influence and power, especially in response to state attempts both to control and monopolise classical development fields. In Malaysia the major motivation for this is to achieve a quantitative growth-oriented development goal. In Sudan the state—particularly before the signing of the CPA in 2005—occupied the development field in order not to give any space for political opposition against the Islamisation project. To a lesser degree this can also be observed in Malaysia. These political situations point to the fact that in both countries women's NGOs are mostly found in urban areas whereas rural development projects and activities are monopolised by the state. These women's organisations work with a rights perspective whereas the state generally adopts a vulnerability approach. Additionally, women's NGOs are often translocally oriented due to the limited spaces, whereas in Senegal, on the contrary, women's NGOs are very active in rural or classical development issues.

Advocacy on the Political and Public Levels

Despite the monopolization of development discourses and strategies by the state in Malaysia as well as in Sudan, many of the women's activists and NGOs challenge the state's development activities by working with and in-stitutionalising the notion of rights in local development practices. The rights perspective critically addresses various issues such as gender relations at the social and political levels, ethnic, regional, religious and economic in-equalities, and marginalisation. By doing so women's NGOs create a space for negotiating their agenda despite the restrictive contexts. These spaces are constituted by elaborating a perspective to women and gender issues differ-ent from that of the state and other local institutions.

To discuss these issues in more detail it is worth considering the case of Malaysia. The example of the CEDAW process, which Spiegel (chapter 4) discussed, shows how women activists in Malaysia advocate and diversify the concept of rights, thereby challenging the strong developmentalist state which adheres to victimisation as an approach to address gender issues. Through strong networking between women's NGOs, activists aim to chal-lenge the culturalist undertone which dominates the state's approach to CEDAW and which follows a frame of claiming differences of traditions and customs. They seek to replace it with the language and perspective of rights. Interesting to note is that at a societal level and at the level of programme implementation these activists strategically avoid the use of a "strong lan-guage of rights," whereas at a political and advocacy level they reverse this strategy and stick to the "strong language of rights" in order to weaken the state's position.

In the case of Sudan and within the context of the peacebuilding processes, women activists who have taken up global development concepts are clearly shifting their strategy by adopting a more politicised rights approach. The ex-ample of the agenda of VAW, discussed in chapter 7, shows how women ac-tivists attempt to move their perspectives from depoliticised "soft" frames of reproductive health or eradication of harmful traditional practices to ad-dressing VAW through the more politicised frame of peace and democratisa-tion. Like in the case of Malaysia, networking among women's NGOs in Su-dan, although not in an institutionalised manner as in Malaysia or Senegal, plays a significant role in shifting the approaches of women's NGOs from vulnerability and victimisation to rights concepts. Worth noting here is the difference between the nature of the agenda of VAW in Sudan and Malaysia. In Malaysia VAW is used by women's NGOs as a less political agenda and a "soft" issue, which would not be contested by the state in contrast to eco-nomic issues which directly touch its developmentalist approach. In Sudan

in contrast by openly adopting the agenda of VAW women's NGOs explicitly relate their agendas to politically heated issues related to regional conflict, peacebuilding, and the question of marginalisation and inequalities.
Nevertheless this politicised agenda of VAW—and the rights perspective
embedded in it—is still characterised by the strong adoption of a generalised
global rights and VAW frame and a weak contextualisation of this agenda according to the different social, ethnic, and cultural settings in Sudan. It is the
financial dependency of Sudanese NGOs which adopt the agenda of VAW of
international development donors that plays a decisive role in shaping the
quality of the rights approach to women, gender, and development issues in
general and the VAW agenda in particular. As a result of this financial dependency there is strong proximity between the VAW discourse of Sudanese
women's NGOs and that of international development agents. In addition,
the weak presence of these women's organisations at the everyday and community levels, due to the control practiced by the state over these organisations, leads to a shallow implementation of the rights approach. As a result
the rights approach of women's NGOs remains basically a general political
frame which is not yet fully diversified and translated into an interactive approach to tackle women and gender issues.

In Senegal the state has a secular orientation, as discussed already, and
a development agenda which is strongly influenced by the policy of the
Western donors. This implies that the state is more open, compared to
Malaysia and Sudan, to the rights approach. However, as Sieveking has
shown in chapter 6, state policy is still dominated by populist approaches
to women and gender issues, vigorously using vulnerability and victimisation when dealing with women and gender concerns and issues. In Senegal
it is an epistemic community of academicians, sociologists, and other researchers who openly criticise the vulnerability perspective of the state and
women's NGOs. A study conducted by sociologists, feminist activists, and
historians openly criticising a publication by the Ministry of the Family
(République du Sénégal 1993) and funded by different international donors
with the title "Senegalese women by the year 2015" is an example. The
critical study aims at moving the national debate on gender towards questioning the mechanism of subordination and vulnerability instead of conceptualising development plans on the basis of a culturalist approach to social inequalities.

The findings from Senegal, Sudan, and Malaysia suggest that the confrontation between the vulnerability approach adopted by the state and the
rights perspectives of mostly professional urban activists in all three countries
takes place explicitly at the political advocacy level.

Everyday and Community Levels

Nevertheless the case studies also show how the less politicised process of advocating women's rights at the everyday and community levels takes place. This process embodies significant transformative potentials (see Kabeer 1994) which relate to the specific context and social settings under focus.

Particularly in Senegal, due to the affirmative relations between women's NGOs and the state, the former play a leading role in implementing national development policies. The example of the discussion of the family code in Madina demonstrates that global concepts of rights are subject to a constant process of recontextualisation, as Sieveking in chapter 6 has analysed. Thus the example shows that the translation of the global concepts of rights not only takes place at the national level by professional and urban activists, but also at the regional and local levels. But the advocacy and reconceptualisation of rights at these levels addresses the issue of entitlement to rights which corresponds to local norms, institutions, and a logic of solidarity, exchange, reciprocity, and social security. Hence local actors transform global concepts of rights into a concept of rights of entitlement which does not necessarily challenge the local social, religious, ethnic, and gender structures (and inequalities). Rather this rights perspective works within the existing social hierarchies and institutions. At a first glance it seems that this local(ized) perspective to rights does not lead to the transformation of the existing social institutions and structures. It is nevertheless important to emphasise that the transformative potential of the local rights perspective must be understood within the logic of the everyday practices of women in these communities and not on the basis of international standards of rights which are predominantly perceived by local communities as Western feminist agendas that do not correspond with local norms.

The same can be observed in Sudan and Malaysia especially when analysing the organisations which work with the concepts of rights at everyday and community levels, despite the restrictions mentioned above. These organisations adopt similar strategies as observed in Senegal. Their approaches focus as well on advocating specific rights to which certain groups are entitled on the basis of their social positions and identities. This strategy is very popular especially in the case of organisations which have adopted an Islamic perspective to women and development issues. Such organisations focus on "educating disadvantaged and unfortunate women" by advocating the rights these women have according to Islam and which might help them improve their situation. They contextualise rights and link them to the existing Islamic frame of social interaction and solidarity. While doing so these organisations, through their programmes and philosophy, affirm local norms and work within the existing social institutions rather than confronting them. Since these organisations cooperate with the respective state authorities, the contextualisation of rights in these cases is a process that aims first of all at finding a local rights perspective that is not labelled Western to solve women's problems without losing their social or religious identity.

In Malaysia some organisations which are not necessarily Islamic adopt similar strategies. They depoliticise their rights perspective by avoiding issues which are under the monopoly of the developmentalist state. Hence, as Spiegel has argued in chapter 7, VAW is one such depoliticised approach to rights, a soft issue which focuses on everyday practices and social problems rather than on development issues taken up by the state. In this case global rights are localised by distancing these rights from areas which are under the strong control of the developmentalist state such as economic rights.

The analysis so far has shown that the processes of contextualising rights and embedding them in the everyday life and social structures of local communities are ambivalent. The ambivalence of these processes is related to two dimensions. First, these processes can lead to the reproduction of the dominant social, gender, and religious orders in the family and economy. Second, despite the reproduction of the dominant social gender order women activists and NGOs who adopt these contextualised rights perspectives develop a rather subversive discourse on economic and social independency on an everyday life basis. Female subjectivities are constructed in collective processes of reflection, learning, and consciousness raising, where general (Islamic) social ethics are adopted instrumentally by women.

The process of adopting and contextualising global concepts of rights by women's NGOs is shaped in a certain sense by the relation of the organisations to the respective state. As the analysis has shown, this relation can either be confrontational or cooperative. Accordingly these processes manifest themselves at an advocacy or everyday and community level. But regardless of whether a politicised or a more depoliticised rights approach is chosen, transformative potentials are embedded in the perspective of rights in general, independently of the differences discussed above. At the local level women activists contribute to the (re)shaping of local development practices by gradually replacing the perspective of vulnerability with that of rights and hence from a victimisation to an agency approach for development, even when an Islamic frame of reference is applied.

The analysis so far has shown that the rights perspective has gained tremendous importance in all three countries studied and, interestingly, independently of the general orientation of the organisations studied. In the following it will be discussed how the global concepts, agendas, and discourses on women's rights are restructured and diversified. It is especially in the global arenas where various actors interact and bring their different experiences of different local settings to negotiate global development concepts.

Negotiating Global Rights

The previous section has shown that at the national as well as local level women's NGOs create spaces for their different agendas by moving from the perspective of victimisation and vulnerability to that of rights. While doing so and through the agency of the various actors involved, global rights concepts become localised and contextualised and local development agendas gradually become reshaped. Our discussion in this section aims at studying another dimension of the process of negotiating global concepts of rights. The special focus will be on the translocal dimension of the process of negotiating women's rights. The field results can be theorised and summarized as follows: While the interface between women's NGOs and the state is an important aspect for the understanding of the process of localising global notions of rights, translocal networking relations of women's NGOs contribute to the reshaping of global notions of rights according to the experiences made at the local level.

The relationship between international development agents, states, and women's NGOs structures—although differently as the case studies have revealed—the process of translocal networking between women's NGOs (see Mohanty 2003; Parpart, Marchand 1999). In Malaysia international development agents and donors are not as important for women's NGOs as in Sudan and Senegal. In these two countries they are of critical significance since they finance the work of these organisations. In Malaysia women's organisations mainly raise funds locally and through their own academic and other professional activities. The relation between Malaysian women's NGOs and international development agents is characterised as a form of networking, providing political support through this global arena of interaction, and as a frame of reference. The case of Sudan is different where women's NGOs depend (financially and thus for their very existence) on international development agents and donors as local and state resources and financial support are almost not available for non-Islamic women's NGOs. This networking between women's NGOs and international development agents has two very important consequences. First, through networking women's NGOs strengthen their financial position to be able to operate vis-à-vis the state which tries to control the work of NGOs and to limit their space of action.

Secondly, through networking with international organisations, as the example of VAW shows, local networks of women's organisations come into existence and subsequently become stabilised or supported. Therefore, as discussed in chapter 8, translocal networking can be observed, especially in Sudan, more often than local networking between women's organisations. In Senegal as well, NGOs depend on the financial support of the international development agents, but the case is slightly different. Here NGOs and the state cooperate to implement development projects that coincide with the agendas of international development agents. In addition networking between women's NGOs at a local level is embedded in the local structures where various forms of community and religious-based organisations exist, and functions as part of the social fabric. Accordingly, compared to Sudan where translocal networking is also a means to create local networks of organisations, in Senegal the local structures and social organisations support processes of networking among women's NGOs. Besides these networks state-initiated structures of women's groups do exist which still act as representatives in the public sphere, capturing the activities locally. Thus translocal networking occurs but is in this respect not so important.

Yet in all the three contexts studied translocal networking processes, as demonstrated in chapters 6, 7, and 8, reveal the interaction between local and global forces and agencies of development regardless of whether translocal networking takes place among women's organisations or between these organisations and international development agents, or whether it is of political or financial importance. Thus translocal networking between women organisations indeed represents an effective channel for influencing the local politics of development. This is even more so in cases where the governments control or try to limit the involvement of civil activists in local politics. Thus interactions among women's NGOs and between women's NGOs and international development agents in global arenas such as conferences, workshops, and meetings becomes a significant means to capacitate these organisations and for them to form their development agendas and strategies for advocating them. In these global arenas development concepts such as women's rights do not stand only as a static frame of reference. Rather, through the social interactions which take place at this level women activists redefine and differentiate these global development concepts and relate them not only to gendered sets of social stratification but also to ethnic, religious, and regional lines and economic (in)equalities.

Women's rights concepts and discourses are developed, as has been shown in the second part of the volume, in translocal spaces and through translocal networking relations. These spaces, such as Beijing and Beijing+10 and the regional conferences for the preparation of such events, host various types of women organisations and activism (see e.g., Lachenmann 1998a; Molineux, Razavi 2002; Wichterich 2000). The organisations vary according to the development agenda they advocate, their relation to the state, Islam and Islamisation processes, regional identities, and development approaches just to name some aspects. Global development concepts are discussed by operationalising differences and experiences made at the local levels in these translocal spaces. As the example of the Asia–Pacific NGO Forum on the Beijing Platform for Action +10, discussed by Spiegel in chapter 6, has shown, the collective identity of sisterhood is shaped by bringing in and discussing the local experiences to reach a global understanding or frame for women's agendas. The example of translocal networking for the agenda of VAW in Sudan speaks to this effect as well. The process of networking at local, regional, and international levels implies various forms of othering and interaction between women activists who might have a common agenda but different local experiences. Before reaching a common plan or goal as a collective product that speaks for a global concern, local experiences and interests are highlighted, connected, and pushed forward to shape what will finally appear as a global concept or vision. In this sense global development concepts become more differentiated by allowing the local experiences to shape these concepts. The global discourses on rights thus address a range of issues that include, for instance, working, disabled, displaced, and Muslim women's rights, the rights of women in conflict and war zones, girls' rights, and so forth. Hence the variation of women's experiences, identities, and needs at the local levels increasingly become a source for conceptualising global discourses on rights. Diversity becomes a key concept in debating these issues through translocal relations and networks in the age of globalisation.

Interestingly not only at the local level but increasingly also at the translocal level Islam represents an important frontier for negotiating rights and identities. In translocal spaces and while negotiating the global development concepts and visions, women exchange strategies and discuss how to address the issue of the growing influence of Islamist movements globally, regionally, and locally. This aspect in particular was always highlighted by women activists interviewed in the countries studied as an important strategic dimension of translocal networking. Thus one very important dimension of the translocal gendered spaces—constituted by negotiating rights—is their relation to discourses on Islam and the West. Whereas dichotomies have been shown to have emerged at the Beijing conference on women in 1995 (Lachenmann 1998a), at the follow-up international conferences after Beijing women activists contributed to the transcendence of global dichotomies and to the differentiation of the Islam discourse at the global level. Two discourses evolved in the translocal space; one on difference and the other one on sisterhood with a pluralisation of identity politics and a fragmentation of women's movements on national but also transnational levels (Wichterich 2000). As discussed through the example of the Asia–Pacific NGO Forum, the various local experiences and perspectives of Muslim women concerning religion were used to introduce a new discursive order. This discursive order challenges the homogenisation of the notion of Muslim identity, the equation of Islam with fundamentalism, and the limitation of Muslim women's possible range of identities to only a religious one.

By deconstructing the global discourse on Islam, women activists aim at creating a common ground for addressing Muslim women's rights. However, there is an ambiguous dimension to the social interactions that take place through translocal networking. The interactions between Muslim women in translocal spaces include othering processes that shape the perception of the self, especially the perception of women activists, their "Islam," local situations, and agendas. The example of Raina from Malaysia, introduced by Spiegel in chapter 6, who compares the situation of Muslim women in Malaysia with that of other women from Tanzania and Lebanon illustrates that through translocal networks Muslim societies get assessed on the basis of their relation to and intensity of incorporation of global development concepts in local development visions. Furthermore the level of economic development also plays a significant role in this process of assessment and differentiation. Many Islamist women activists are engaged in similar processes. Such an example was revealed in 2004 at an international meeting of the Muslim Women International Board, an Islamist women's NGO whose head office is in Khartoum. The meeting was organised, as explained by one of the activists, to "bring Muslim women together and to unify their efforts to improve the status of Muslims in the world." The social interaction between the participants from different countries was strongly shaped by a comparative interaction. In this case Muslim societies were differentiated and hierarchies drawn up according to their relation to global Islamisation movements. When making these judgements, categories like "Islam" and "traditional Islam," "traditional Muslims," "Westernised Muslims," "ignorant Muslims," and even "lazy Muslims" were often used during the conference to emphasise diversity. From these debates conclusions were drawn for conceptualising global agendas for Muslim women. This, interestingly, shows that similar global practices can be observed for women involved in the progressive Islam discourse and women involved in the Islamist reformist discourse. In translocal spaces women activists definitely deconstruct the global discourse on "The Islam" in order to build collectively common global agendas for women. But the role of social actors is ambiguous. The ambiguity of the actors in the cases cited above shows that shaping or developing a common agenda implies othering processes and leads to the discursive hierarchisation of Muslim societies.

Despite the ambiguity, however, translocal networking and the negotiation of global rights concepts contribute to the constitution of a (also local) public sphere and the formation of political dissent in all the countries studied. The transformative potential of these public spheres which women's NGOs constitute through translocal networking is based on the possibility to link up (diversified) global rights concepts to broader societal issues such as democratisation, sustainable development, religious pluralism, and peace building. The practice as well as the strategy of reconceptualising global rights concepts thus goes beyond processes of othering which take place among women's NGOs and activists in global arenas. Reconceptualising rights means "bringing these concepts home" by embodying them in local systems of meaning and local logics of social practices and institutions. Simultaneously at the global level, local systems of meanings become an integral part of the definition of (diversified) global rights concepts. This can be seen in global events and by documents elaborated through critical interaction in a transnational platform mainly provided by UN institutions and their NGO connections. Here women academics and activists are coming together and forming what could be called a "cosmopolitan epistemic community" as the Beijing +5 and the Beijing+10 process have shown (see Molyneux, Razavi 2005; Women Watch).

Constituting Social Spaces: Concluding Remarks

Our research on negotiating development focused on analysing social relations and processes which take place in the public sphere and which seek to situate a particular development agenda. While negotiating development, women's NGOs are engaged in the process of differentiating the local discourses on Islam. The strategies which they adopt, be they advocating progressive translocal Islam discourses or redefining Islamist politics and discourses to include women's interests, lead to (further) differentiation of local Islam discourses. We argue that global Islamisation currents and movements not only lead to the intensification of the politicisation of religion in local politics. Rather, the presence of these movements in local politics makes the question of the relationship between Islam and a specific vision and agenda of development more heated and causes Islam discourses to become more differentiated.

Women activists in Sudan and Malaysia and to a lesser degree in Senegal are caught between nondemocratic authoritarian regimes and Islamist-inspired opposition movements, both of which tend to impose social and political control on people in the name of religion or national identity. Simultaneously, to different degrees, but specifically in the cases of Sudan and Malaysia, the respective governments and societies which we studied tend to question all kinds of foreign interventions and interests in the name of protecting national and religious identities. Under these conditions and specifically in the cases where the state adopts Islamisation politics, many women activists choose to be vocal despite the opposition and control they face, specifically from their governments. Bayat, while focusing on the Middle East in general and the Iranian case in particular, refers to such situations where individuals or groups choose to assert their public presence and thereby advance the causes of human rights or social justice under difficult political conditions as "the delicate art of presence" (Bayat 2004, 4–5). However, Bayat stresses the difference between "active citizenship" on the one side, which refers to "how lay citizens, within their ordinary practices of everyday and through the art of presence or active citizenry, may recondition the established political elite and refashion state institutions in their habitus," and activism on the other. Activism, he argues, is "the extra-ordinary practice to produce social change, is the stuff of activists who may energize collective sentiments when the opportunity allows." What is crucial for democratisation is "a sustained presence of individuals, groups and movements in every available social space, whether institutional or informal, in which it asserts its rights and fulfils its responsibilities" (Bayat 2004, 4–5). Considering our empirical cases, it is not only the politically planned projects, distinct agendas, and arduous strategies of women's groups and movements which might lead to democratisation and social transformation. Equally importantly, social transformation is the product of the presence of these groups and activists and their issues such as social and gender rights and justice in these societies despite the fact that their agendas as well as their practices are often controlled. Women's groups' advocacy on the political and public level as well as on an everyday and community level reveals their constant attempts to sustain their presence and negotiate or negate social and political control. This leads to the transformation of the very space they occupy. It is precisely in these spaces, which women's groups occupy and consequently transform, that alternative Islam discourses and practices are produced. Differentiating local Islam discourses is often an unintended outcome of the everyday practices, strategies, and social interactions of women activists who attempt to include gender and social rights, CEDAW, VAW, or the reform of the family code as integral agendas of local processes of democratisation. Hence the unintended processes of differentiating local Islam discourses are as significant as the distinct and politically planned agendas of women's NGOs for understanding how social transformation and democratisation occur.

Within this context global rights are increasingly negotiated and shaped by different processes such as the refusal of the vulnerability perspective of the state or other actors or the introduction of a progressive Islam discourse on rights at the local level. While negotiating and localising global concepts of rights, women contribute to the further politicisation of the public sphere. Agendas of women's organisations are no longer merely "women's things" or "soft issues." In particular, the adoption of the rights approach gives the agency of women's NGOs more political weight and further politicises their agendas, as we have shown in the previous chapters. Women and gender issues are thus moving from the "soft" areas of charity and social welfare to the "hard" areas of political restructuration, democratisation, and human rights. While advocating the rights agendas, women's activists represent a "transnational public" which is "crucially defined by their engagement with authorities at national and international levels" (Olesen 2005, 422–425). What is of special importance in the contexts studied are not only the forms of relations between these two levels for understanding social change and transformation, but—as Olesen also claims—to identify and study how these relations and the involved individuals and groups construct social (gendered) spaces (see also Salvatore 1997, 2001, and debates in Spiegel rapp. 2005). Social spaces, as our examples show, are not detached from physical spaces. They are rooted in specific places, people, and in social interactions between these people (see Harcourt, Escobar 2002). Yet what is significant and must be emphasised is that in the age of globalisation the transformation of space is very much shaped by a (new) way of linking the local with the global. In the case of our research, women's groups constitute translocal gendered spaces through the act of simultaneously addressing local social and state authorities and global development agendas, combining global rights perspectives with local systems of meaning, and consequently create a translocal discursive arena which seeks to influence and reshape local politics.

Our research and analysis demonstrated a two-way connection between global and local discourses and organisations. We were able to study this connection by analysing the constitution of translocal spaces, the agency of women's organisations and activists, as well as networking relations. Through networking—both at the level of organisations and ideas—translocal gendered spaces are constituted by women's organisations. At the local level these spaces are shaped by constantly interlinking global politics, discourses, and concepts of development with local structures and institutions. In global arenas othering processes as well as comparative and social interaction between women's activists lead to the production of difference. But since we aimed at going beyond dichotomies and differences we looked instead at how these processes shape women's (translocal) agency. In global arenas women's organisations oppose the homogenisation of identities and religious discourses. In doing so, they reshape the global discursive order through validating the experiences made by women's NGOs at local levels. As argued by Mahmood (2005, 18), agency is not to be viewed as simply a "synonym of resistance to relations of domination, but as a capacity for action that specific relations of subordination create and enable."

Thus the multidimensional methodology chosen to approach the question of women's agency and the constitution of translocal gendered spaces pushed us to consider the various power dynamics and relations between different actors and levels (societal, institutional, local, and global) which shape the agency of women's activists. The translocal agency of women's activists is, hence, embedded in multidimensional unequal power relations as shown. These unequal power relations and the resulting diversified experiences and perspectives of women's NGOs and activists are a central element for understanding how global women's rights concepts and agendas are shaped. Thus studying and analysing how women's translocal agency is constituted allowed us to understand how global development concepts are negotiated. Simultaneously, adopting the constitution of translocal space as a research approach offered us a frame to apprehend those connections and relations between different levels and structures which are tied to a certain locality but, at the same time, surpass the limits of that locality. In this way our research findings contributed to addressing "processes of entanglement" which move beyond Islam/West dichotomies (Abu-Lughod 1998, 14).[6] It also contributes to the analysis of the agency of women in Muslim societies as a capacity for action demonstrated in the multiple and diversified acts of negotiating identity, development, social and political justice, traditional and religious institutions, women's rights, and hence the contradictory outcomes of processes of globalisation.

Notes

1. When used as a policy approach we consider the concept of vulnerability, a term introduced globally within the fight against poverty, as being oriented mainly towards the individual situation. This approach could be subsumed under the old deficit approaches, which implies that neither their own life-world, capacities, and strategies of the people as actors, nor on the structural and institutional context and dynamics of their position in society and economy

including securing of livelihoods and entitlements, are looked at. A rights' approach on the other hand goes beyond structural policy towards a vision of equality and justice.

2. Islamic scholars who support the adoption of global agendas and concepts of development—locally known as progressive—are generally in favour of social transformation processes which do not isolate Muslim societies from the wider global context and global changes. Hence these "progressive" Islam discourses are adopted by NGOs to face the growing Islamisation processes locally as well as globally.

3. The agreement was signed between the government of Sudan and the Sudanese People Liberation Army/Movement (SPLA/M) in January 2004. The explosion of the situation in Darfur, a second global concern, changed the situation further (see Nageeb chapter 8).

4. A charity approach in social policy refers to "helping" needy people by motifs intrinsic in one's own moral obligation and stands in contrast to approaches focusing on solidarity, agency, or capacity building with the aim to enable people to cope with the situation on a sustainable basis. The classical Women in Development approach often has proven too narrow focusing exclusively on women and their integration in development processes without taking into account gender relations and gendered institutions in society and policies as implicit in a gender approach of empowerment.

5. The most vivid case in this regard is Sudan, where the empowerment approach, translated in the Arabic term *Tamkieen* is adopted by Islamist women activists as a (political) slogan for their agendas of (Islamic oriented) development and social transformation. The most powerful organisations are directed and founded by wives of prominent political leaders including the First Lady who is the head of at least one of these organisations in addition to her honorary membership in some others.

6. See also Randeria 2002 on "entangled histories of uneven modernities."

~

Bibliography

Aba Seed, Nagat Elias. 2001. "Sudanese Women and the Missing Role of Civil Society Organisations" in *Sudanese Women: Liberation and Creativity. Sudanese Writings*. no. 15, March. Khartoum: Centre for Sudanese Studies, pp. 46–63 (in Arabic)

Abaza, Mona. 1998a. "The Sociology of Progressive Islam between the Middle East and Southeast Asia" in *Islam–Motor or Challenge for Modernity. Yearbook of Sociology of Islam Vol. 1* edited by Georg Stauth. Hamburg: LIT, pp. 129–152

———. 1998b. "Images on Gender and Islam. The Middle East and Malaysia, Affinities, Borrowings and Exchanges" in *Orient*, vol. 39, no. 2, pp. 271–284

———. 2002. *Debates on Islam and Knowledge in Malaysia and Egypt. Shifting Worlds*. London: Routledge

———. 2004. "Brave New Mall" in *Al-Ahram Weekly Online*, 16–22 September 2004, no. 708, http://weekly.ahram.org.eg/2004/708/feature.htm

Abu-Lughod, Lila. 1998. *Remaking Women: Feminism and Modernity in the Middle East*. Princeton: Princeton University Press

———. 2002. "The Marriage of Feminism and Islamism in Egypt: Selective Reproduction as a Dynamic of Postcolonial Cultural Politics" in *Anthropology of Globalisation: A Reader* edited by Jonathan Xavier Inda and Renato Rosaldo. Oxford: Blackwell Publishing, pp. 181–195

Adamu, Fatima. 2006. "Women's Struggle and the Politics of Difference in Nigeria" *gender politik online*. FU Berlin http://web.fu-berlin.de/gpo/pdf/tagungen/fatima_l_adamu.pdf.

Adjamagbo, Agnès, Philippe Antoine, and Fatou B. Dial. 2004. "Le dilemme des Dakaroises: entre travailer et 'bien travailler.'" in *Gouverner le Sénégal. Entre ajustement structurel et le développement durable* edited by Momar-Coumba Diop. Paris: Karthala, pp. 247–272

Ahmadi, Hala. 2003. *Globalisation, Islamism and Gender: Women's Political Organisations in the Sudan*. Dissertation. Nijmegen: Catholic University of Nijmegen

Ahmed, Leila. 1992. *Women and Gender in Islam: Historic Roots of a Modern Debate*. Yale: Yale University Press

Al-Azmeh, Aziz. 1993. *Islams and Modernities*. London: Verso

Albrow, Martin, and Elizabeth King, eds. 1990. *Globalization, Knowledge and Society: Readings from International Sociology*. London: Sage

Ali, Shaheen S. 2006. "Women's Rights, CEDAW, and International Human Rights Debates: Toward Empowerment?" in *Gender and Empowerment in a Local Global World* edited by Shirin Rai, Jane L. Parpart, and Kathleen Staudt. London: Routledge, pp. 61–78

An-Na'im, Abdullahi A. 1997a. "Islam and Human Rights in Sahelian Africa" in *African Islam and Islam in Africa, Encounters between Sufi and Islamists* edited by Eva E. Rosander and David Westerlund. London: Hurst, pp. 79–94

———. 1997b. *The Politics of Islamization in African. Constitutional and Legal Implications*. Paper presented for the Centre for African Studies, University of Cape Town

Anwar, Zainah. 2004. "Islamisation and Its Impact on Laws and the Law Making Process in Malaysia" in *Warning Signs of Fundamentalism* edited by Ayesha Imam, Jenny Morgan, and Nira Yuval-Davis. Nottingham: Women Living under Muslim Laws, pp. 71–78

Appadurai, Arjun. 2000. "Grassroots Globalisation and the Research Imagination" in *Public Culture*, vol. 12, no. 1, pp. 1–20

Ardener, Shirley. 1964. "The Comparative Study of Rotating Credit Associations" in *Journal of the Royal Anthropological Institute*, vol. 94, no. 2, pp. 201–229

Ardener, Shirley, and Sandra Burman, eds. 1995. *Money Go-Rounds: The Importance of Rotative Savings and Credit Associations for Women*. Oxford: Berg Publications

Augis, Erin J. 2003. *Dakar's Sunnite Women: The Politics of Person*. Dissertation submitted to the Faculty of the Social Sciences, Department of Sociology, University of Chicago, Ann Arbor: ProQuest Information and Learning Company (UMI Microform 3070154)

Badri, Lamya. 2005. *Development through Networking: Global Discourses and Local Agenda. Women Negotiating Political Space in Sudan*. Paper presented at the workshop "Negotiating Development: Translocal Gendered Spaces in Muslim Societies," 13–15 of October 2005 in Bielefeld. http://www.uni-bielefeld.de/tdrc/pdf/badri.pdf

———. 2006. "Feminist Perspectives in Sudan" in *gender politik online*. FU Berlin http://web.fu-berlin.de/gpo/pdf/tagungen/balghis_badri.pdf

Balchin, Cassandra. 2002. "The Network 'Women Living Under Muslim Laws': Strengthening Local Struggles through Cross-Boundary Networking" in *Development*, vol. 45, no. 1, pp. 126–131

———. 2007. "Women Living Under Muslim Laws. The Challenges Facing a Transnational Gender Network in post-11 September Context" in *International Feminist Journal of Politics*, vol. 6, no. 4 December, pp. 679–683

Barlas, Asma. 2002. *"Believing Women" in Islam: Unreading Patriarchal Interpretations of the Qur'an*. Austin: University of Texas Press

Bayat, Asef. 2004. "The Art of Presence" in *ISIM Review 14*, June, pp. 4–5

———. 2005. "What Is Post-Islamism?" in *ISIM Review 16*, Autumn, pp. 4–5

Beck, Kurt. 1998. "Kordofan Invaded, Peripheral Incorporation and Social Transformation" in *Islamic Africa: Social, Economic and Political Studies of the Middle East and Asia* edited by Reinhard Schulze. vol. 63, pp. 245–295

Bell, Diane, Pat Caplan, and Wazir Jahan Karim, eds. 1993. *Gendered Fields: Women, Men and Ethnography*. London, New York: Routledge

Berger, Peter L., and Thomas Luckmann. 1966. *The Social Construction of Reality: A Treatise in the Sociology of Knowledge*. Garden City N.Y.: Doubleday

Berg-Schlosser, Dirk. 2000. "Mehrebenen-Analysen" in *Armut und Demokratie. Politische Partizipation und Interessenorganisationen der städtischen Armen in Afrika und Lateinamerika* edited by Dirk Berg-Schlosser and Norbert Kersting. Frankfurt M./New York: Campus, pp. 251–270

Bernard, H. Russel, ed. 2000. *Handbook of Methods in Cultural Anthropology*, Walnut Creek: Altamira Press

Bilal, Abdelrahim. 2004. *Social Problems and Civil Society in Sudan.* Khartoum: Dar Azza (in Arabic)

Burawoy, Michael et al. 2000. "Preface" in *Global ethnography. Forces, connections, and imaginations in a postmodern world* edited by Michael Burawoy et al. Berkeley: University of California Press, pp. ix–xv

———. 2000b. "Grounding Globalization" in *Global Ethnography. Forces, Connections, and Imaginations in a Postmodern World* edited by Michael Burawoy et al. Berkeley: University of California Press, pp. 337–350

Burawoy, Michael et al., eds. 2000. *Global Ethnography: Forces, Connections, and Imaginations in a Postmodern World.* Berkeley: University of California Press

Cagatay, Nilüfer, Diane Elson, and Caren Grown. 1995. "Introduction" in *Gender, Adjustment and Macroeconomics. Special Issue in World Development* edited by Nilüfer Cagatay, Diane Elson, and Caren Grown. vol. 23, no. 11, pp. 1827–1836

Camroux, David. 1996. "State Responses to Islamic Resurgence in Malaysia. Accommodation, Co-option, and Confrontation" in *Asian Survey*, vol. XXXVI, no. 9, September, pp. 852–868

Cantone, Cléo. 2005. "'Radicalisme' au féminin? Les filles voilées et l'appropriation de l'espace dans les mosquées à Dakar" in *L'Islam politique au sud du Sahara. Identités, discours et enjeux* edited by Muriel Gomez-Perez. Paris: Karthala, pp. 119–130

Case, William F. 2002. "The New Malaysian Nationalism: Infirm Beginnings, Crashing Finale" in *Asian Ethnicity*, vol. 1, no. 2, pp. 131–147

Centre Africain de l'Entrepreneuriat Féminin. 2001. *Muslim Women and Development. Action Research Project. Synthesis report, Annex 5, Senegal.* Amsterdam: KIT Gender, and Women and Development Division/Ministry of Foreign Affairs, http://www.kit.nl/specials/assets/images/Muslimwomen-synthesis-Senegal.pdf, (download 17 August 2006)

Chernoff, John M. 1979. *African Rhythm and African Sensibility: Aesthetics and Social Action in African Musical Idioms.* Chicago: University of Chicago Press

Chua, Beng H. 2000. *Consumption in Asia.* London: Routledge

Coalition on Women's Rights in Islam. 2002. *Hudud in Terengganu—A Law to Protect Rapists*, http://www.muslimtents.com/sistersinislam/letterstoeditors/090502.htm

Creevey, Lucy. 1996. "Islam, Women and the Role of the State in Senegal" in *Journal of Religion in Africa*, vol. 26, no. 3, pp. 268–307

———. 2006. "Senegal: Contending with Religious Constraints" in *Women in African Parliaments* edited by Gretchen Bauer and Hannah E. Britton. Boulder, London: Lynne Rienner Publishers, pp. 151–169

Crouch, Harold. 1993. "Malaysia: Neither Authoritarian nor Democratic" in *Southeast Asia in the 1990s: Authoritarianism, Democracy and Capitalism* edited by K. Hewison and Garry Rodan. Sydney: Allan and Unwin

———. 2005. "Industrialization and Political Change" in *Transformation with Industrialization in Peninsular Malaysia* edited by Harold Brookfield. Kuala Lumpur: Oxford University Press, pp. 14–34

Cruise O'Brien, Donald B. 1992. "Le contrat social sénégalais à l'épreuve" in *Politique africaine*, vol. 45, no. Sénégal: La démocratie à l'épreuve, pp. 9–20
———. 2003. *Symbolic Confrontations. Muslims Imagining the State in Africa*. London: Hurst & Co.
Dannecker, Petra. 2002. *Between Conformity and Resistance. Women Garment Workers in Bangladesh*. Dhaka: Dhaka University Press
———. 2004. "Bangladeschische Migrantinnen im Spannungsfeld zwischen Globalisierung, Ausgrenzung und nationaler Identität" in *Peripherie*, vol. 24, no. 95, pp. 341–360
———. 2005. "Bangladeshi Migrant Workers in Malaysia: The Construction of the 'Others' in a Multi-Ethnic Context" in *Asian Journal of Social Science*, vol. 33, no. 2, pp. 246–267
Dannecker, Petra, and Anna Spiegel. 2006. "'Let's Not Rock the Boat.' Frauenorganisationen und Demokratisierung in Malaysia" in *International Quarterly for Asian Studies*, vol. 37, no. 3–4, pp. 297–319
Davids, Tine, and Francien van Driel. 2005. "Changing Perspectives" in *The Gender Question in Globalization. Changing Perspectives and Practices* edited by Tine Davids and Francien van Driel. Aldershot: Ashgate, pp 3–24
Denzin, Norman K. and Yvonna S. Lincoln, eds. 1994. *Handbook of Qualitative Eesearch*. London: Sage
Diaw, Aminata. 2004. "Les femmes à l'épreuve du politique: permanences et changements" in *Gouverner le Sénégal. Entre ajustement structurel et le développement durable* edited by Momar-Coumba Diop. Paris: Karthala, pp. 229–245
Diop, Momar-Coumba, ed. 2004. *Gouverner le Sénégal. Entre ajustement structurel et le développement durable*. Paris: Karthala
Douglas, Mary. 1970. *Natural Symbols*. London: Routledge
Economic Planning Unit. 2006. *Eighth Malaysia Plan (2001–2005)*. Putra Jaya: Economic Planning Unit, Prime Minister's Department, Malaysia
Eisenstadt, Shmuel N. 1999. "Multiple Modernities in the Age of Globalization" in *Grenzenlose Gesellschaft?* edited by Claudia Honegger, Stefan Hradil, and Franz Traxler. Opladen: Leske+Buderich, pp. 37–50
El-Affandi, Abdelwahab. 1991. *Turabi's Revolution: Islam and Power in Sudan*. London: Gray Seal Books
Elbatahani, Atta. 2004. "Women and Transitional Periods" in *Challenges Facing Sudanese Women: A Conceptual and Analytical Frame*, Publications of the Gender Centre: 3/2004, Khartoum: Gender Centre (in Arabic)
Elson, Diane. 2002. "Gender Justice, Human Rights, and Neo-liberal Economic Policies" in *Gender Justice, Development, and Rights* edited by Maxine Molyneux and Shahra Razavi. Oxford: Oxford University Press, pp. 78–114
Elwert, Georg. 2003. *Feldforschung. Orientierungswissen und kreuzperspektivische Analyse*. Sozialanthropologische Abeitspapiere, H. 96, FU Berlin Institute for Ethnology, Berlin: Schiler
Escobar, Arturo. 1995. *Encountering Development*. Princeton: Princeton University Press
Evers, Hans-Dieter. 1997. "The Symbolic Universe of UKM: A Semiotic Analysis of the National University of Malaysia" in *Sojourn*, vol. 12, no. 1, pp. 46–63
Evers, Hans-Dieter, and Solvay Gerke. 1999. *Globale Märkte und symbolischer Konsum: Visionen und Modernität in Südostasien*, Working Paper No. 314, Sociology of Development Research Centre, Faculty of Sociology, University of Bielefeld. http://www.uni-bielefeld.de/tdrc/publications/working_papers/WP314.PDF

Ezello, Joy. 2006. "Feminism and Islamic Fundamentalism: Some Perspectives from Nigeria and beyond" in *Signs. Journal of Women in Culture and Society*, vol. 32, no. 1, pp. 40–47

Featherstone, Mike. 1991. *Consumer Culture and Postmodernism*. London, Newbury Park, New Delhi: Sage

Featherstone, Mike, Scott Lash, and Roland Robertson, eds. 1995. *Global Modernities*. London, Thousand Oaks, New Delhi: Sage

Fischer-Rosenthal, Wolfram and Gabriele Rosenthal. 1997: "Narrationsanalyse biographischer Selbstpräsentationen" in *Sozialwissenschaftliche Hermeneutik* edited by Ronald Hitzler and Anne Honer. Opladen: Westdeutscher Verlag, pp. 133–164

Flick, Uwe, Ernst von Kardoff, and Ines Steinke, eds. 2004. *A Companion to Qualitative Research*. London: Sage

Gerke, Solvay. 1999. "Globale Märkte und symbolischer Konsum. Visionen von Modernität in Südostasien" in *Spiel ohne Grenzen. Ambivalenzen der Globalisierung* edited by Claudia Rademacher. Opladen: Westdeutscher Verlag, pp. 35–54

Giddens, Anthony. 1979. *Central Problems in Social Theory. Action Structure and Contradiction in Social Analysis*. Berkeley: University of California Press

Gittler, Alice Mastrangelo. 1999. "Mapping Women's Global Communications and Networking" in *Women@Internet. Creating New Cultures in Cyberspace* edited by Wendy Hartcourt. London: Zed Books, pp. 91–101

Golde, Peggy. 1986. *Women in the Field: Anthropological Experiences*. Berkeley: University of California Press

Grosz-Ngaté, Maria, and Omari H. Kolole, eds. 1997. *Gendered Encounters: Challenging Cultural Boundaries and Social Hierarchies in Africa*. New York, London: Routledge

Guèye, Cheikh. 2002. *Touba: la capitale des mourides*. Dakar, Paris: enda, Karthala

Gupta, Akhil, and James Ferguson, eds. 1997. *Culture, Power, Place: Explorations in Cultural Anthropology*. Durham, London: Duke University Press

Habermas, Juergen. 1989 (1962). *The Structural Transformation of the Public Sphere*. Cambridge MA: MIT Press

———. 1992. "Further Reflections on the Public Sphere" in *Habermas and the Public Sphere* edited by Craig Calhoun, Cambridge MA: MIT Press

Hale, Sondra. 1996. *Gender Politics in Sudan, Islamism, Socialism and the State*. Boulder: Westview

Hamad, Abdelhadi Al-Zubair. 1994. "Sudan" in *Academic Freedom 3: Education and Human Rights* edited by John Daniel et al. London: Zed Books, pp. 68–88

Hannerz, Ulf. 2000. "Transnational Research" in *Handbook of Methods in Cultural Anthropology* edited by H. Russel Bernard. Walnut Creek: Altamira Press, pp. 235–256

Harcourt, Wendy, ed. 1999. *Women@Internet. Creating New Cultures in Cyberspace*. London, New York: Zed Books

———. 2002. "Editorial: Social Justice at the Crossroads" in *Development. Thematic Issue: Place, Politics and Justice: Women Negotiating Globalization* edited by Wendy Harcourt. vol. 45, no. 1, pp. 5–6

Harcourt, Wendy, and Arturo Escobar. 2002. "Lead Article. Women and the Politics of Place" in *Development. Thematic Issue: Place, Politics and Justice: Women Negotiating Globalization* edited by Wendy Harcourt. vol. 45, no. 1, pp. 7–13

Harcourt, Wendy, Lila Rabinovich, and Fatma Aloo. 2002. "Women's Networking and Alliance Building: The Politics of Organizing in and around Place" in *Development. Thematic*

Issue: Place, Politics and Justice: Women Negotiating Globalization edited by Wendy Harcourt. vol. 45, no. 1, pp. 42–47

Harders, Cilja. 2000. "Dimensionen des Netzwerkansatzes: Einführende theoretische Überlegungen" in *Islamische Welt als Netzwerk. Möglichkeiten und Grenzen des Netzwerkansatzes im islamischen Kontext* edited by Roman Loimeier. Würzburg: Ercon, pp. 17–52

Heath, Deborah. 1994. "The Politics of Appropriateness and Appropriation: Recontextualizing Women's Dance in Urban Senegal" in *American Ethnologist*, vol. 21, no. 1, pp. 88–103

Hess, Sabine. 2001. "Transnationale Überlebensstrategien von Frauen – Geschlecht und neuere Konzepte der Transkulturalität" in *Die andere Hälfte der Globalisierung. Menschenrechte, Ökonomie und Medialität aus feministischer Sicht* edited by Steffi Hobuss, Christina Schües and Nina Zimnik. Frankfurt, New York: Campus, pp. 197–225

Hilhorst, Dorothea and Mathijs van Leeuwen. 2005. "Global Peacebuilder and Local Conflict. The Feminization of Peace in Sudan" in *The Gender Question in Globalization. Changing Perspectives and Practices* edited by Tine Davids and Francien van Driel. Aldershot: Ashgate, pp. 93–108

Hobart, Mark. 1993. *An Anthropological Critique of Development. The Growth of Ignorance.* London, New York: Routledge

Hobuss, Steffi, Christina Schües, and Nina Zimnik, eds. 2001. *Die andere Hälfte der Globalisierung. Menschenrechte, Ökonomie und Medialität aus feministischer Sicht.* Frankfurt, New York: Campus

Holthaus, Ines, and Ruth Klingebiel. 2000. "Vereinte Nationen—Sprungbrett oder Stolperstein auf dem langen Marsch zur Durchsetzung von Frauenrechten" in *Globalisierung aus Frauensicht. Bilanzen und Visionen* edited by Ruth Klingebiel and Shalini Randeria. Bonn: Dietz, pp. 34–65

Ibrahim, Haider. 2001. *Civil and Traditional Society in Sudan.* Cairo: The Centre for Sudanese Studies (in Arabic)

———. 2003. "Introduction" in *The Renewal of the Religious Discourse. Sudanese Writings.* no. 25 edited by Hider Ibrahim. Khartoum: Centre for Sudanese Studies, pp. 3–12 (in Arabic)

Inda, Jonathan Xavier, and Renato Rosaldo, eds. 2002. *Anthropology of Globalization.* Malden, Mass., Oxford: Blackwell

Janson, Marloes. 2005. "Roaming about for God's Sake: The Upsurge of the Tabigh Jamaat in the Gambia" in *Journal of Religion in Africa*, vol. 35, no. 4, pp. 450–481

Jomo K.S., and Chris Edwards 1993. "Malaysian Industrialisation in Historical Perspective" in *Industrialising Malaysia. Policy, Performance, Prospects* edited by Jomo K.S. London, New York: Routledge, pp. 14–39

Kaag, Mayke. 2005. "Islamic NGOs in Chad" in *ISIM Review* 16, Autumn 2005, pp. 30

Kabeer, Naila. 1994. *Reversed Realities: Gender Hierarchies in Development Thought.* London, New York: Verso

Kaelble, Hartmut, and Jürgen Schriewer, eds. 2003. *Vergleich und Transfer. Komparatistik in den Sozial-, Geschichts- und Kulturwissenschaften.* Frankfurt/M.: Campus

Kahn, Joel S. 1995. "The Middle Class as a Field of Ethnological Study" in *Critical Perspectives: Essays in Honour of Syed Husin Ali* edited by Ikmal Said and Zahin Emby. Kuala Lumpur: Malaysian Social Science Association

Kandiyoti, Deniz. 1991. "Introduction" in: *Women, Islam and the State* edited by Deniz Kandiyoti. Philadelphia: Temple, pp. 1–21

Kaschuba, Wolfgang. 2003. "Anmerkungen zum Gesellschaftsvergleich aus ethnologischer Perspektive" in *Vergleich und Transfer. Komparatistik in den Sozial-, Geschichts- und Kulturwis-*

senschaften edited by Hartmut Kaelble and Jürgen Schriewer, Frankfurt/M.: Campus, pp. 341–350

Kheng, Cheah Bonn. 2002. *Malaysia. The Making of a Nation*. Singapore: Institute for South Asian Studies

Klein-Hessling, Ruth. 1999. *Zivilgesellschaft, Frauenorganisationen und Netzwerke*. Working Paper No. 320, Sociology of Development Research Centre, Faculty of Sociology, University of Bielefeld. http://www.uni-bielefeld.de/tdrc/publications/working_papers/wp320.pdf

Knoblauch, Hubert. 2001. "Communication, Contexts and Culture. A Communicative Constructivist Approach to Intercultural Communication" in *Culture in Communication. Analyses of Intercultural Situations* edited by Aldo Di Luzio, Susanne Günthner, and Franca Orletti. Amsterdam: John Benjamins, pp. 3–33

Laaser, Mirjam. 2005. *Geschäftsfrauen im urbanen Afrika: Zwischen Pflichten, Verflechtungen und Handlungsspielräumen in Nairobi*. Unpublished dissertation. Accepted in January 2006 at the Faculty of Sociology, Faculty of Sociology, University of Bielefeld

Lachenmann, Gudrun. 1993. "Civil Society and Social Movements in Africa: The Case of the Peasant Movement in Senegal" in *The European Journal of Development Research*, vol. 5, no. 2, pp. 68–100

———. 1996. *Weltfrauenkonferenz und Forum der Nichtregierungsorganisationen in Peking—internationale Frauenbewegungen als Vorreiterinnen einer globalen Zivilgesellschaft?* Working Paper No. 251, Sociology of Development Research Centre, Faculty of Sociology, University of Bielefeld. http://www.uni-bielefeld.de/tdrc/publications/working_papers/Wp251.pdf

———. 1997a. "Informal Social Security in Africa from a Gender Perspective" in *Searching for Security: Women's Responses to Economic Transformations* edited by Isa Baud and Ines Smyth. London, New York: Routledge, pp. 45–66

———. 1997b. "Intervention, Interaktion und Partizipation - zu einigen Methodenfragen der empirischen Entwicklungsforschung" in *Entwicklung: Theorie - Empirie - Strategie - Institution* edited by Manfred Schulz. Münster: LIT, pp. 99–114

———. 1998a. "Frauenbewegungen als gesellschaftliche Kraft des Wandels. Beispiele aus Afrika" in *Lokal bewegen - global verhandeln. Internationale Politik und Geschlecht* edited by Uta Ruppert. Frankfurt, New York: Campus, pp. 208–233

———. 1998b. *Constructs of Social Security. Modernity and Tradition in West Africa*. Working Paper No. 304, Sociology of Development Research Centre, Faculty of Sociology, University of Bielefeld. http://www.uni-bielefeld.de/tdrc/publications/working_papers/WP304.PDF

———. 1998c. "Strukturanpassung aus Frauensicht: Entwicklungskonzepte und Transformationsprozesse" in *Globalisierung aus Frauensicht. Bilanzen und Visionen* edited by Ruth Klingebiel and Shalini Randeria. Bonn: J.H.W. Dietz, pp. 294–319

———. 2001. "Transformation der Frauenökonomie und Dimensionen der Einbettung in Afrika" in *Die geschlechtsspezifische Einbettung der Ökonomie. Empirische Untersuchungen über Entwicklungs- und Transformationsprozesse* edited by Gudrun Lachenmann and Petra Dannecker. Münster: LIT, pp. 83–110

———. 2002. *Debating Gender Differences and Identities in Muslim Countries: Comparative Perspectives from Africa South of the Sahara*. Paper presented at the workshop: Debating Gender Differences and Identities in Muslim Countries. Ahfad - Humboldt - Link Programme, Berlin

———. 2004a. "Dezentralisierung und lokale Bewegungen - Strukturierung der Gesellschaft und Genderperspektive in Westafrika" in *Sozialwissenschaftliche Perspektiven auf Afrika - Festschrift für Manfred Schulz* edited by Volker Lühr, Arne Kohls, and Daniel Kumitz. Münster: LIT, pp. 54–81

———. 2004b. "Researching Local Knowledge for Development: Current Issues" in *Lokales Wissen—Sozialwissenschaftliche Perspektiven* edited by Nikolaus Schareika and Thomas Bierschenk. Münster: LIT, pp. 123–148

———. 2004c. "Weibliche Räume in muslimischen Gesellschaften Westafrikas" in *Peripherie*. vol. 24, no. 95, pp. 322–340

———. 2005. *Introduction: Methodology and Comparison—Embedding the Research Project*. Paper presented at the workshop "Negotiating Development: Translocal Gendered Spaces in Muslim Societies," 13–15 of October 2005 in Bielefeld. http://www.uni-bielefeld.de/tdrc/pdf/lachenmann.pdf

———. 2006. *Decentralisation and Civil Society: Negotiating Local Development in West Africa*, Working Paper No. 358, Sociology of Development Research Centre, Faculty of Sociology, University of Bielefeld. http://www.uni-bielefeld.de/tdrc/publications/working_papers/WP358.pdf

Lachenmann, Gudrun, and Petra Dannecker. 2002. *Negotiating Development: Trans-local Gendered Spaces in Muslim Societies. Proposal to the Volkswagen Stiftung*. Sociology of Development Research Centre, Faculty of Sociology, University of Bielefeld, www.uni-bielefeld.de/tdrc

Lachenmann, Gudrun, Frauke Bleibaum, Judith Ehlert, Lalla El Oumrany, Daniel Krenz-Dewe, Franklin Odoemenam, Yulika Ogawa-Müller, Sascha Vennemann, and Bertrand Zohy. 2005. *Dezentralisierung, Zivilgesellschaft, Entwicklung. Lehrforschung Westafrika/Mittelamerika*. Working Paper No. 352, Transnationalization and Development Research Centre, Faculty of Sociology, University of Bielefeld. http://www.uni-bielefeld.de/tdrc/publications/working_papers/Wp352.pdf

———. 2006. *Décentralisation, société civile, développement au Sénégal, Projet de recherche d'étudiant(e)s 2004/2005: Rapport d'étude de terrain*. Working Paper No. 357, Transnationalization and Development Research Centre, Faculty of Sociology, University of Bielefeld http://www.uni-bielefeld.de/tdrc/publications/working_papers/WP357.pdf

Lang, Andrea Marianne. 2005. *Das Ineinanderwirken von Aushandlungen in und zwischen sozialen Räumen: Forschung auf der Meso-Ebene. Eine Methodikreflektion*. Working Paper No. 349, Sociology of Development Research Centre, Faculty of Sociology, University of Bielefeld. http://www.uni-bielefeld.de/tdrc/publications/working_papers/Wp349.pdf

Lelart, Michel. 2002. *L'évolution de la finance informelle et ses conséquences sur l'évolution des systèmes financiers, pratiques financieres decentralisées et recompension des systèmes financiers Africains*. Reseau Entrepreneuriat, Agence Universitaire de la Francophonie, Cotonou 16–18 avril 2002 (http://halshs.ccsd.cnrs.fr/docs/00/06/42/71/PDF/lelart_pratiques_Cotonou_2002.pdf)

Lenz, Ilse, ed. 2002. *Gender, Identities and Networks*. Opladen: Leske + Budrich

Lim Teck Ghee. 1995. "Nongovernmental Organisations in Malaysia and Regional Networking" in *Emerging Civil Society in the Asia Pacific Community* edited by Tadeshi Yamamoto. Tokyo: Japan Center for International Exchange, pp. 165–182

Loimeier, Roman. 1994. "Religiös-ökonomische Netzwerke in Senegal - Das Beispiel der muridischen Expansion in Dakar" in *Afrika Spektrum*, vol. 29, no. 1, pp. 99–111

———. 1995. "Säkularer Staat und Islam: Das Beispiel Senegal" in *Macht der Identität—Identität der Macht, Politische Prozesse und kultureller Wandel in Afrika* edited by Heidi Willer, Till Förster, and Claudia Ortner-Buchberger. Münster: LIT, pp 193–207

———. 1997. "Islamic Reform and Political Change: The Example of Abubakar Gumi and the Yan Izala Movement in Northern Nigeria" in *African Islam and Islam in Africa, Encounters between Sufis and Islamists* edited by Eva E. Rosander and David Westerlund. London: Hurst and Co., pp. 286–307

———. 2000a. "L'Islam ne se vend plus: The Islamic Reform Movement and the State in Senegal" in *Journal of Religion in Africa*, vol. 30, no. 2, pp. 168–190

———, ed. 2000b. *Islamische Welt als Netzwerk. Möglichkeiten und Grenzen des Netzwerkansatzes im islamischen Kontext*. Würzburg: Ercon

———. 2006. "'Political Islam' in Contemporary Senegal" in *Politischer Islam in Westafrika. Eine Bestandsaufnahme* edited by Michael Bröning and Holger Weiss. Berlin: LIT, pp. 189–214

Long, Norman. 1992. "Introducion: From Paradigm Lost to Paradigm Regained" and " Conclusion" in *Battlefields of Knowledge: The Interlocking of Theory and Practice in Social Research and Development* edited by Norman Long and Anne Long. London: Routledge, 3–5, pp. 268–277

———. 1996. "Globalisation and Localisation: New Challenges to Rural Research" in *The Future of Anthropological Knowledge* edited by Henrietta L. Moore. London, New York: Routledge, pp. 37–59

———. 2000. "Exploring Local/Global Transformations. A View from Anthropology" in *Anthropology, Development and Modernities. Exploring Discourses, Counter-tendencies and Violence* edited by Alberto Arce and Norman Long. London, New York: Routledge, pp. 184–222

———. 2001. *Development Sociology: Actor Perspectives*. London: Routledge

Lowrie, Arthur, ed. 1993. "Islam, Democracy, the State and the West: A Round Table with Dr. Hassan Turabi" in *World and Islam Studies Enterprises*, Monograph Series No. 1, Tampa, Florida

Mahmood, Saba. 2005. *Politics of Piety. The Islamic Revival and the Feminist Subject*. Princeton, Oxford: Princeton University Press

Marchand, Marianne H., and Anne Sisson Runyan, eds. 2000. *Gender and Global Restructuring. Sightings, Sites and Resistances*. London, New York: Routledge

Marcus, George E. 1998. *Ethnography through Thick and Thin*. Princeton, NJ: Princeton University Press

Massey, Doreen. 1994. *Space, Place, Gender*. Cambridge: Polity Press

Mbilinyi, Marjorie. 1992. "Research Methodologies in Gender Issues" in *Gender in Southern Africa. Conceptual and Theoretical Issues* edited by Ruth Meena. Harare: Sapes Books, pp. 31–70

Mbow, Penda. 1997. "Les femmes, l'Islam et les associations religieuses au Sénégal" in *Transforming Female Identities. Women's Organizational Forms in West Africa* edited by Eva E. Rosander. Uppsala: Nordiska Afrikainstitutet, pp. 148–159

McCann, Carole R., and Seung-Kyung Kim, eds. 2003. *Feminist Theory Reader. Local and Global Perspectives*. New York, London: Routledge

McDowell, Linda. 1999. *Gender, Identity and Place: Understanding Feminist Geographies*. Minneapolis: University of Minnesota Press

Mernissi, Fatima. 1992. *Islam and Democracy: Fear of the Modern World*. Cambridge: Perseus Publishing

———. 1996. *Women's Rebellion and Islamic Memory*. London: Zed Books

Ministry of Women and Family Development. 2004. *Report to the UN Committee for the Convention on the Elimination of all Forms of Discrimination against Women (CEDAW). First and Second Report*. Kuala Lumpur: Ministry for Women and Family Development

Mir-Hosseini, Ziba. 1996. "Stretching the Limits: A Feminist Reading of the Shari'ah in post-Khomeini Iran" in *Islam and Feminism: Legal and Literary Perspectives* edited by Mai Yamani. London: Ithaca Press, pp. 285–320

Moghadam, Valentine M. 2002. "Islamic Feminism and Its Discontents: Towards a Resolution of the Debate" in *Gender, Politics and Islam* edited by Therese Saliba, Carolyn Allen, and Judith A. Howard. New Delhi: Orient Longman Press, pp. 15–52

Mohamad, Maznah. 2002a. "At the Centre and at the Periphery. The Contributions of Women's Movement to Democratization" in *Democracy in Malaysia. Discourses and Practices* edited by Francis Loh Kok Wah and Khoo Boo Teik. Richmond: Curzon, pp. 216–240

———. 2002b. "The Politics of Gender, Ethnicity, and Democratization in Malaysia: Shifting Interests and Identities" in *Gender Justice, Development, and Rights* edited by Maxine Molyneux and Shahra Razavi. Oxford: Oxford University Press, pp. 347–383

Mohanty, Chandra T. 2003. *Feminism Without Borders: Decolonizing Theory, Practicing Solidarity*. Durham, London: Duke University Press

Molyneux, Maxine, and Shahra Razavi. 2002. "Introduction" in *Gender Justice, Development, and Rights* edited by Maxine Molyneux and Shahra Razavi. Oxford: Oxford University Press, pp. 1–44

———. 2005. "Beijing Plus Ten: An Ambivalent Record on Gender Justice" in *Development and Change*. vol. 36, no. 6, pp. 983–1010

Momsen, Janet Henshall. 2004. *Gender and Development*. London, New York: Routledge

Moore, Henrietta L. 1996. "The Changing Nature of Anthropological Knowledge. An Introduction" in *The Future of Anthropological Knowledge* edited by Henrietta L. Moore. London, New York: Routledge, pp. 1–15

Müller, Christine. 2003. "Knowledge Between Globalisation and Localisation: The Dynamics of Female Spaces in Ghana" in *Current Sociology*, vol. 51, no. 3–4, pp. 329–346

———. 2005. *Local Knowledge and Gender in Ghana*. Bielefeld: transcript

Murat, Nora. 2004. "Sisters in Islam: Advocacy for Change within the Religious Framework" in *Warning Signs of Fundamentalism* edited by Ayesha Imam, Jenny Morgan, and Nira Yuval-Davis. Nottingham: Women Living Under Muslim Laws, pp. 141–145

Nagata, Judith. 1994. "How to Be Islamic without Being an Islamic State: Contested Models of Development in Malaysia" in *Islam, Globalization and Postmodernity*, edited by Akbar S. Ahmed and Hastings Donnan. London, New York: Routledge, pp. 63–90

———. 1997. "Ethnonationalism versus Religious Transnationalism: Nation-Building and Islam in Malaysia" in *The Muslim World*, vol. 87, no. 2, pp. 129–150

Nageeb, Salma A. 2004. *New Spaces and Old Frontiers: Women, Social Space, and Islamization in Sudan*. Lanham: Lexington Books

———. 2005a. *Negotiating Development: Trans-local Gendered Spaces in Muslim Societies. A Methodology Paper*. Working Paper No. 354, Sociology of Development Research Centre, Faculty of Sociology, University of Bielefeld. http://www.uni-bielefeld.de/tdrc/publications/working_papers/Wp354.pdf

———. 2005b. *Empirical Findings from Sudan: Development Issues and Actors*. Paper presented at the workshop "Negotiating Development: Translocal Gendered Spaces in Muslim Societies," 13–15 of October 2005 in Bielefeld. http://www.uni-bielefeld.de/tdrc/pdf/nageeb_1.pdf

———. 2005c. *Negotiating Development in Trans-local Gendered Spaces: Preliminary Results*. Paper presented at the workshop "Negotiating Development: Translocal Gendered Spaces in Muslim Societies," 13–15 of October 2005 in Bielefeld. http://www.uni-bielefeld.de/tdrc/pdf/nageeb_2.pdf

———. 2007. "Appropriating the Mosque: Women's Religious Groups in Khartoum" in *Afrika Spectrum*, vol. 42, no. 1, pp. 5–27

Nageeb, Salma A., Nadine Sieveking, and Anna Spiegel. 2005a. *Engendering Development in Muslim Societies: Actors, Discourses and Networks in Malaysia, Senegal and Sudan*. Working Paper No. 353, Sociology of Development Research Centre, Faculty of Sociology, University of Bielefeld. http://www.uni-bielefeld.de/tdrc/publications/working_papers/Wp353.pdf

———. 2005b. *Negotiating Development: Trans-local Gendered Spaces in Muslim Societies*. Report on Workshop 13–15 October 2005. Working Paper No. 355, Sociology of Development Research Centre, Faculty of Sociology, University of Bielefeld. http://www.uni-bielefeld.de/tdrc/publications/working_papers/Wp355.pdf

NGO Shadow Report Group. 2004. *Shadow Report on the Initial and Second Periodic Report of the Government of Malaysia. Reviewing Government Implementation of the Convention on the Elimination of All Forms of Discrimination against Women (CEDAW)*. Kuala Lumpur: National Council for Women's Organisations

Niblock, Tim. 1989. *Class and Power in Sudan. The Dynamics of Sudanese Politics 1898–1985*. New York: State University of New York Press

Olesen, Thomas. 2005. "Transnational Publics: New Spaces of Social Movement Activism and Problems of Global Long-Sightedness" in *Current Sociology*. vol. 53, no. 3, pp. 419–440

Othman, Norani. 1998. "Islamization and Modernization in Malaysia. Competing Cultural Reassertions and Women's Identity in a Changing Society" in *Women, Ethnicity and Nationalism: The Politics of Transition* edited by Rick Wilford and Robert L. Millner. London: Routledge, pp. 170–192

———. 2003. "Islamization and Democratization in Malaysia in Regional and Global Contexts" in *Challenging Authoritarianism in Southeast Asia* edited by Ariel Heryanto and Sumit K. Mandal. New York and London: Routledge, pp. 117–144

———. 2005. "Introduction: Muslim Women and the Challenge of Political Islam and Islamic Extremism" in *Muslim Women and the Challenge of Islamic Extremism* edited by Norani Othman, Petaling Jaya: Sisters in Islam, pp. 1–10

Oya, Carlos. 2006. "From State Dirigisme to Liberalisation in Senegal: Four Decades of Agricultural Policy Shifts and Continuities" in *The European Journal of Development Research*, vol. 18, no. 2, pp. 203–227

Parpart, Jane L. and Marianne H. Marchand. 1999. "Exploding the Canon: An Introduction/Conclusion" in *Feminism/Postmodernism/Development* edited by Marianne H. Marchand and Jane L. Parpart. London and New York: Routledge, pp. 1–22

Perlez, Jane. 2006. "Within Islam's Embrace, a Voice for Malaysia's Women" in *New York Times*, February 19

Pfaff-Czarnecka, Joanna. 2007. "Menschenrechte und kulturelle Positionierungen in asiatischen Frauennetzwerken. Zur Diffusion den Menschenrechtsdiskurses in der reflexiven Moderne" in *Transkulturelle Genderforschung. Ein Studienbuch zum Verhältnis von Kultur und Geschlecht* edited by Michiko Mae and Britta Saal. Wiesbaden: Verlag für Sozialwissenschaft, pp. 271–302

Pieterse, Jan Nederveen. 2001. *Development Theory: Deconstruction, Reconstruction*. London: Sage

Randeria, Shalini. 2002. "Entangled Histories of Uneven Modernities: Civil Society, Caste Solidarities and Legal Pluralism in Post-colonial India" in *Unraveling Ties: From Social Cohesion to New Practices of Connectedness* edited by Yehuda Elkana, Ivan Krastev, Elísio Macamo and Shalini Randeria. Frankfurt, New York: Campus, pp. 285–311

Renders, Marleen. 2002. "An Ambiguous Adventure: Muslim Organisations and the Discourse of 'Development' in Senegal" in *Journal of Religion in Africa*, vol. 32, 1, pp. 61–82

République du Sénégal 1993. *Senegalese Women By the Year 2015*. Abridged version (coordinated by Fatou Sow and Mamadou Diouf). Dakar: Ministère de la Femme de l'Enfant et de la Famille, Population Council

———. 2002. *Document de Stratégie de Réduction de la Pauvreté*. Dakar

———. 2004. *Rapport du Senegal - CEDEF/CEDAW. 1994–1998/1998–2001* (version 31.08.2004). Dakar: Ministère de la Famille, du Développement Social et de la Solidarité Nationale

———. 2005a. *Stratégie Nationale pour l'Égalité et l'Équité de Genre au Sénégal: SNEEG 2015*. Dakar: Fond des Nations Unies pour la Population (UNFPA/Sénégal)

———. 2005b. *Argumentaire Religieux Musulman sur l'Équité de Genre par Dr. Abdoul Aziz Kébé (Islamologue, Expert en Population et Développement)*. Dakar: Ministère de la Famille, du Développement Social et de la Solidarité Nationale; Fond des Nations Unies pour la Population (UNFPA/ Sénégal)

Réseau Siggil Jigeen. 2005. "Révision du Code de la famille. Les féministes au front" in *Kaddu Jigeen ni. La Voix des Femmes*, no. 7, April

Robertson, Roland. 1995. "Glocalization: Time-Space and Homogeneity-Heterogeneity" in *Global Modernities* edited by Mike Featherstone, Scott Lash, and Roland Robertson. London, Thousand Oaks, New Delhi: Sage, pp. 25–44

Salvatore, Armando. 1997. *Islam and the Political Discourse of Modernity*. Reading: Ithaca Press

———. 2001. "The Problem of the Ingraining of Civilization Traditions into Social Governance" in *Muslim Traditions and Modern Techniques of Power. Yearbook of the Sociology of Islam Vol. 3* edited by Armando Salvatore. Münster: LIT, pp. 9–42

Sarr, Fatou. 1998. *L'Entrepreneuriat féminin au Sénégal. La transformation des rapports de pouvoir*. Paris, Montréal: L'Harmattan

Schlee, Günther. 1985. "Mobile Forschung bei mehreren Ethnien. Kamelnomaden Nordkenias" in *Feldforschungen. Berichte zur Einführung in Probleme und Methoden* edited by Hans Fischer. Berlin: Reimer, pp. 203–218

Schultz, Ulrike. 2007. "Autonomy or Security: The Negotiation of Family Norms in Sudanese Families" in *Afrika Spectrum*, vol. 2, pp. 167–194

Schulz, Dorothea E. 2007. "Gender-Entwürfe und islamische Erneuerungsbewegungen im Kontext translokaler institutioneller Vernetzungen: Beispiele aus Afrika" in *Transkulturelle Genderforschung. Ein Studienbuch zum Verhältnis von Kultur und Geschlecht* edited by Michiko Mae and Britta Saal. Wiesbaden: Verlag für Sozialwissenschaft, pp. 177–206

Secor, Anna J. 2002. "The Veil and Urban Space in Istanbul: Women's Dress, Mobility and Islamic Knowledge" in *Gender, Place and Culture*, vol. 9, no. 1, pp. 5–22

Sesemann, Ruediger. 2005. *East African Muslims After 9/11*. Bayreuth African Studies Working Paper No. 3. University of Bayreuth

Shuib, Rashidah. 2005. *Debating Development, Women's Rights and Islam in a Multi-ethnic Society*. Paper presented at the workshop "Negotiating Development: Translocal Gendered Spaces in Muslim Societies," 13–15 of October 2005 in Bielefeld.

Sieveking, Nadine. 2005. *Negotiating Development in Senegal: Women Organisations, Issues and Strategies*. Paper presented at the workshop "Negotiating Development: Translocal Gendered Spaces in Muslim Societies," 13–15 of October 2005 in Bielefeld. http://www.uni-bielefeld.de/ tdrc/pdf/sieveking.pdf

———. 2006. "Subversive Körper. Sabar-Tanzen im Senegal und in Deutschland" in *Kulturelle Verwandlungen. Die Gestaltung Sozialer Welten in der Performanz* edited by Ursula Rao. Berlin: Peter Lang, pp. 107–132

Sisters in Islam 1993. *Memorandum on the Syariah Criminal Code (II) 1993 State of Kelantan*. sistersinislam.org.my/memorandums 25121993.htm

———. 2005. "Reforming Family Law in the Muslim World" in *Baraza! A Sisters in Islam Bulletin*, vol. 1, no. 1, pp. 3–6

Sow, Fatou. 1996. "Family and Law in Senegal: Continuity and Change" in *Dossier Special 1: Les frontières mouvantes du mariage et du divorce dans les communautés musulmanes*. London: Women Living Under Muslim Law (WLUML), pp. 142–157

———. 2003. "Fundamentalisms, Globalisation and Women's Human Rights in Senegal" in *Gender and Development*, vol. 11, no. 1, pp. 69–76

Spiegel, Anna. 2005a. *Women's Organisations and Their Agendas: Empirical Findings from Malaysia*. Paper presented at the workshop "Negotiating Development: Translocal Gendered Spaces in Muslim Societies," 13–15 of October 2005 in Bielefeld. http://www.uni-bielefeld.de/tdrc/pdf/spiegel_1.pdf

———. 2005b. *Women's Movement and Trans-local Networking in Malaysia*. Paper presented at the workshop "Negotiating Development: Translocal Gendered Spaces in Muslim Societies," 13–15 of October 2005 in Bielefeld. http://www.uni-bielefeld.de/tdrc/pdf/spiegel_2.pdf

———. rapporteur, 2005. *Public Spheres, Public Islam, and Modernities*. Report on Workshop 2002 with Armando Salvatore. Working Paper No. 347, Sociology of Development Research Centre, Faculty of Sociology, University of Bielefeld. http://www.uni-bielefeld.de/tdrc/publications/working_papers/Wp347.pdf

Spiegel, Anna, and Nadine Harig, rapporteurs, 2002. *Gender and Translocal Networking through Information Technology. Report on Workshop with Gillian Youngs*. Working Paper No. 342, Sociology of Development Research Centre, Faculty of Sociology, University of Bielefeld. http://www.uni-bielefeld.de/tdrc/publications/working_papers/wp342.pdf

Stauth, Georg. 1995. "Globalisierung, Modernität, nicht-westliche Zivilisationen" in *Kleine Staaten in grosser Gesellschaft* edited by Josef Langer and Wolfgang Pöllauer. Eisenstadt: Verlag für Soziologie und Humanethologie, pp. 89–107

———. 1998. "Islam and Modernity: The Long Shadow of Max Weber" in *Islam - Motor or Challenge of Modernity. Yearbook of the Sociology of Islam Vol. 1* edited by Georg Stauth. Hamburg: LIT, pp. 163–186

Stivens, Maila. 2003. "(Re)Framing Women's Rights Claims in Malaysia" in *Islam, Society and Politics* edited by Virginia Hooker and Norani Othman. Singapore: Institute of Southeast Asian Studies, pp. 126–146

Strauss, Anselm. 1987. *Qualitative Analysis for Social Scientists*. Cambridge: Cambridge University Press

Strauss, Anselm, and Juliet Corbin. 1998. *Basics of Qualitative Research: Techniques and Procedures for Developing Grounded Theory*. Thousand Oaks: Sage

Tan, Eugene K.B. 2001. "From Sojourners to Citizens: Managing the Ethnic Chinese Minority in Indonesia and Malaysia" in *Ethnic and Racial Studies*, vol. 24, no. 6, pp. 949–978

Taylor, Vivienne. 2000. *Marketisation of Governance: Critical Feminist Perspectives from the South. DAWN Development Alternatives with Women for a New Era*, Cape Town: SADEP, University of Cape Town

Tripp, Aili Mari. 2005. "Regional Networking as Transnational Feminism: African Expenences" in *Feminist Africa*, 4 http://www.feministafrica.org/2level.html

United Nations Research Institute for Social Development UNRISD. 2005. *Gender Equality. Striving for Justice in an Unequal World*. Geneva: www.UNRISD.Org

Villalón, Leonardo A. 1995. *Islamic Society and State Power in Senegal. Disciples and Citizens in Fatick*. Cambridge: Cambridge University Press

———. 1999. "Generational Changes, Political Stagnation, and the Evolving Dynamics of Religion and Politics in Senegal" in *Africa Today*, vol. 46, no. 3/4, pp. 129–147

Weiss, Meredith L., and Saliha Hassan. 2003a. "Introduction: From Moral Communities to NGOs" in *Social Movements in Malaysia. From Moral Communities to NGOs* edited by Meredith L. Weiss and Saliha Hassan. London: RoutledgeCurzon, pp. 1–16

———. 2003b. "Preface" in *Social Movements in Malaysia. From Moral Communities to NGOs* edited by Meredith L. Weiss and Saliha Hassan. London: RoutledgeCurzon, pp. vii–ix

Werner, Karin. 1997. *Between Westernization and the Veil: Contemporary Life Styles of Women in Cairo.* Bielefeld: transcript

Westerlund, David. 1997. "Reaction and Action: Accounting for the Rise of Islamism" in *African Islam and Islam in Africa. Encounters between Sufis and Islamists* edited by Eva E. Rosander and David Westerlund. London: Hurst, pp. 308–333

Whitehead, Tony Larry and Mary Ellen Conaway. 1986. *Self, Sex and Gender in Cross-Cultural Fieldwork.* Urbana: University of Illinois Press

Wichterich, Christa. 2000. "Strategische Verschwisterung, multiple Feminismen und die Glokalisierung der Frauenbewegungen" in *Frauenbewegungen weltweit. Aufbrüche, Kontinuitäten, Veränderungen* edited by Ilse Lenz, Michiko Mae and Karin Klose. Opladen: Leske + Budrich, pp. 257–280.

Willemse, Karin. 2005. "On Globalisation, Gender and the Nation-State: Muslim Masculinity and the Urban Middle Class Family in Islamist Sudan" in *The Gender Question in Globalization. Changing Perspectives and Practices* edited by Tine Davids and Francien van Driel. Aldershot: Ashgate, pp. 159–178

Wolf, Diane L., ed. 1996. *Feminist Dilemmas in Fieldwork.* Boulder, Colo.: Westview Press

Women's Aid Organisation. 2002. *WAO Statement 07 June 2002. Terrenganu Hudud Laws,* http://www.wao.org.my/news/20020601waohudud.htm

Women Watch. *Women Watch –Beijing+10 Global Forum,* http://www.un.org/ womenwatch/ followup/beijing10/#to

Wone, Katy C. 2002. *Idéologie socialiste et Féminisme d'Etat au Sénégal: De Senghor à Abdou Diouf.* Paper held at the plenary session on gender relations in Africa at the "10ème Assemblée Générale du CODESRIA du 8 au 12 décembre 2002, Kampala/Ouganda": http://www .codesria.org/Links/Home/Abstracts%20GA%201-5/gender_Wone.htm (download 24 Jan 2005

World Bank. 2001. *Engendering Development through Gender Equality in Rights, Resources, and Voice.* Washington: World Bank

World Bank. 2005. *Overview on Gender and Development in the Middle East and North Africa: Women and the Public Sphere.* Working Paper Report No. 34963, Washington: World Bank

Youngs, Gillian. 1999. "Virtual Voices: Real Lives" in *Women@Internet. Creating New Cultures in Cyberspace* edited by Wendy Hartcourt. London: Zed Books, pp. 55–68

Index

~

About the Contributors

Gudrun Lachenmann, Prof. Dr, studied sociology, political science, and economics at the University Konstanz, Germany. She received her Ph.D. in 1982 from the University of Konstanz and her habilitation in 1989 from Free University, Berlin. Formerly, she had a long-term assignment as a research fellow at the German Development Institute, Berlin, Africa Division, doing policy research, advice and training. Since 1992 she has been a professor at the Faculty of Sociology, Sociology of Development and Research Centre, Bielefeld University. In March 2006, she officially retired from her teaching position. Her current research interests are global and local networking for engendering development policy, civil society, transformation processes, women's and peasant movements in Africa, engendering embeddedness of economy, translocal spaces of migration, and methodology of multi-level field research and global ethnography. She has done extensive empirical research mainly in francophone West Africa (Senegal, Mali, Cameroon etc.). She is a member of the Section Sociology of Development and Social Anthropology of the German Association of Sociology (DGS), the International Sociological Association and the Society for International Development (SID), Berlin. On behalf of the European Association of Development Research Training Institutes (EADI) she was on the editorial board of the "European Journal of Development Research" and the second convenor of the Gender Working Group.

Petra Dannecker, Dr., was lecturer at the Faculty of Sociology at Bielefeld University, Germany from 1998 to 2007. After one year as research fellow at the German Development Institute, Bonn, she is now Professor of Global Studies and Development Sociology at the Faculty of Sociology, Project International Development, at Vienna University, Austria. She completed her M.A. in political science, sociology, and literature in 1993 at the University of Konstanz. She received her Ph.D., with distinction, in 1998 from the Faculty of Sociology, Bielefeld University. Her special fields of research and teaching are development theory and policy, gender studies, migration, industrialisation, and globalisation, as well as methodology and methods. She has done extensive fieldwork in Bangladesh and Malaysia and conducted workshops on methodologies and methods in Sudan and Sri Lanka. She is a member of the European Network of Bangladesh Studies; the German Society for Sociology; the NGO-Forum on Gender, Germany; and the European Association of Development Research and Training Institutes. She is also a member of the Scientific Board of the Journal Peripherie and editor of the Working Paper Series by the Sociology of Development Research Center, Bielefeld University.

Salma A. Nageeb, Dr., obtained her Ph.D. in sociology/social anthropology from Bielefeld University and her M.A. in developmental studies, gender, and development from the Institute of Social Studies in the Netherlands. Her research work focuses on Sudan and includes processes of Islamisation, social space, translocal construction of space, gender and Islam, gender peace and development, and qualitative research methodology. In 2004 she published a book titled *New Spaces and Old Frontiers: Women, Social Spaces and Islamisation in Sudan* (Lanham, MD: Lexington Books), in addition to being part of the project "Negotiating Development: Translocal Gendered Spaces in Muslim Societies." With a Lise-Meitner fellowship at the Transnationalisation and Development Research Centre at the Faculty of Sociology, Bielefeld University, Germany she continued her research work on the subject of "Gender and Peace Building: The Transformation of Islamists' Discourses and Practices in Sudan." She continues as a staff member at Ahfad University for women in Sudan.

Nadine Sieveking, Dr., obtained her Ph.D. in social anthropology from the Free University of Berlin in 2003. Her thesis on the transcultural experience of African dance in Germany was published in 2006 under the title "Abheben und Geerdet Sein. Afrikanisch Tanzen als transkultureller Erfahrungsraum," Münster: LIT (Series Performances: Intercultural Studies on

Ritual, Play and Theatre, Bd. 12). Her fields of research include performative trans-cultural practices, religious movements, Islamisation processes, female social spaces in West Africa, African diaspora, migration, and development. After being part of the project "Negotiating Development: Translocal Gendered Spaces in Muslim Societies," she did research on the transformation of female spaces in the context of newly emerging religious movements in Senegal as a fellow in the Lise-Meitner programme. She completed a study on the "Development Potential of African Migrants in Northrhine-Westphalia (Germany)" on behalf of the Ministry of Generations, Family, Women, and Integration of North-Rhine-Westphalia in 2007 and carried out a project on "Dynamics of Migration and Development Cooperation between Sub-Sahara Africa and Europe" on behalf of the Ministry for Economic Cooperation and Development (BMZ), on the basis of empirical research in Ghana and Mali in 2008. She continues research on gendered aspects of African migrants' engagement in development at the Transnationalisation and Development Research Centre at the Faculty of Sociology, Bielefeld University, Germany, where she is presently employed as a lecturer.

Anna Spiegel studied sociology, social anthropology, and gender studies at Bielefeld University, where she graduated with a diploma thesis on translocal life-worlds of Bolivian female migrants in Buenos Aires in the year 2003. In 2005 she published the results in a monograph titled "Alltagswelten in translokalen Räumen. Bolivianische Migrantinnen in Buenos Aires" (Frankfurt, London: IKO, Verlag für Interkulturelle Kommunikation). Within the project "Negotiating Development: Translocal Gendered Spaces in Muslim Societies" she extended her research on translocal social spaces to the field of women's organisations and the negotiation of women's rights in Malaysia. Recently, she concluded her doctoral studies in sociology at the International Graduate School at Bielefeld University with her dissertation, "Striving for social change in trans-local spaces. Female activism in Islamising Malaysia." Her fields of interest include globalisation, migration, women's movements, and processes of identity construction in Latin America and Southeast Asia. At present she is working at the International Office of Bielefeld University, where she coordinates programmes and services for transnationally mobile researchers.